AMERICAN ETHNIC AND CULTURAL STUDIES

John C. Walter and Johnnella E. Butler, Series Editors

AMERICAN ETHNIC AND CULTURAL STUDIES

The American Ethnic and Cultural Studies series presents critical interdisciplinary, cross-disciplinary, and comparative studies of cultural formations and expressions of racialized peoples of North America. Focusing on African Americans, American Indians, Asian Americans, Chicanos/as, and Latinos/as, and on comparative works among these groups and racialized Euro-Americans, the series also explores new and changing configurations of race and ethnicity as shaped by gender, class, and religion in global and domestic contexts. Informed by research in the humanities, arts, and social sciences; transnational and diasporic studies; film studies; legal studies; public policy, environmental, urban, and rural studies, books in the series will aim to stimulate innovative approaches in scholarship and pedagogy.

Color-line to Borderlands:
The Matrix of American Ethnic Studies
Edited by Johnnella E. Butler

Being Buddhist in a Christian World:
Gender and Community in a Korean American Temple
Sharon A. Suh

Complicating Constructions:
Race, Ethnicity, and Hybridity in American Texts
Edited by David S. Goldstein and Audrey B. Thacker

Beyond Literary Chinatown
Jeffrey F. L. Partridge

BEYOND LITERARY
CHINATOWN

JEFFREY F. L. PARTRIDGE

A McLellan Book

UNIVERSITY OF WASHINGTON PRESS *Seattle and London*

This book is published with the assistance of a grant from the
McLellan Endowed Series Fund, established through the generosity
of Martha McCleary McLellan and Mary McLellan Williams.

Copyright © 2007 by the University of Washington Press
Printed in the United States of America
Designed by Pamela Canell

12 11 10 09 08 07   5 4 3 2 1

University of Washington Press
PO Box 50096
Seattle, WA 98145–5096, USA
www.washington.edu/uwpress

Library of Congress Cataloging-in-Publication Data
Partridge, Jeffrey F. L.
Beyond literary Chinatown / Jeffrey F. L. Partridge.
p. cm.—(American ethnic and cultural studies)
"A McLellan Book."
Includes bibliographical references and index.
ISBN-13: 978-0-295-98706-4 (pbk. : acid-free paper)
ISBN-10: 0-295-98706-5 (pbk. : acid-free paper)
1. American literature—Chinese American authors—History
and criticism.   2. Chinese Americans in literature.   3. Ethnicity
in literature.   4. Multiculturalism in literature.   I. Title.
PS153.C45P37 2007   810.9'8951—dc22   2006036518

The paper used in this publication is acid-free and 90 percent
recycled from at least 50 percent post-consumer waste. It meets
the minimum requirements of American National Standard for
Information Sciences—Permanence of Paper for Printed Library
Materials, ANSI Z39.48–1984. ⊗◉

Cover illustration: Portion of mural at Chinatown gate in Boston,
"Chinese Folktales (Journey to the West)," painted in 1997 by the
City of Boston Mayor's Mural Crew. Jon Tran and Alyssa Tang,
lead artists. Photo © 1998 Marie Rose Wong.

Contents

Preface

Literary Chinatown is an imagined community, not in Benedict Anderson's sense, but in Edward Said's Orientalist sense: it is a community imagined by others—for their own purposes and their own pleasures. All ethnic American writers must write either with or against the grain of a ghettoizing principle, but for the Chinese American writer this ghetto has a distinctly exotic flavor that sells well if entertained and embellished, but sells poorly if contradicted. For the Chinese American writer who wishes to move beyond the horizon of literary Chinatown, the expectations of readers and publishers are a distinct hindrance.

Beyond Literary Chinatown is a reception study of Chinese American literature that seeks to engage a historically grounded close reading of contemporary Chinese American literature with current formations of race and ethnicity in America. In particular, the book examines the dynamic relationship between reader expectations of Chinese American literature and the challenges posed by recent Chinese American texts to the assumptions of readers, challenges that push our understanding of multicultural society to new horizons—what I am describing as the emergence of the polycultural.[1]

The horizon metaphor has been used by reception theorists since Hans Robert Jauss to explain the ways readers respond to texts. Readers approach a text with various expectations and assumptions, and as the story unfolds, the text will often challenge and modify those expectations. Readers therefore bring a "reading horizon" to a piece of fiction or a poem. But, as I argue in this book, it is also true that writers often take into account the horizons of readers—and especially so with ethnic literature, or what Gilles Deleuze and Félix Guattari would call a "minor literature." Writers, in this sense, *read* the reader's horizon. Evidence of the writer's expectations of the reader can be found in the text she or he produces. Thus, the multiple meanings of the horizon metaphor reflect the complex processes at play at the nexus of reader, author, and text.

I imagine three reading communities for this book: reception theorists, Asian Americanists, and scholars of race and ethnicity in America. Asian Americanists will find that my discussion of Chinese American literature and specific readings of texts continue the expansion of Asian American critical studies into an important critical phase marked by books such as *Narrating Nationalisms* by Jinqi Ling, *Edith and Winnifred Eaton* by Dominika Ferens, and *Form and Transformation in Asian American Literature* edited by Zhou Xiaojing and Samina Najmi. This critical phase, as articulated by Zhou in her introduction to *Form and Transformation*, seeks to "explore the impacts of historical forces and various cultural and literary traditions on Asian American writers' appropriations of, negotiations with, and transformations of established literary genres and traditions" (17). My critical readings of specific texts furthermore seek to lift Asian American literature out of the sociocultural realm, where the text is often treated as a "window" into "real" Asian American life, and place it in the aesthetic realm, where formal literary qualities are allowed to speak, and where Asian American writers converse with each other, with American literary tradition, and with their readers (Sue-Im Lee, "Introduction"). Students of reception studies will find an application of the basic premises of Hans Robert Jauss, Wolfgang Iser, and the early Stanley Fish sustained in a book-length study, as well as an extension, and revision, of Mario J. Valdés's "phenomenological hermeneutics" based on Paul Ricoeur's writing. Chinese American literature provides a fruitful case study for reception theory, but more important to my purposes, reception study provides a useful lens for comprehending the vast changes in Asian American literature in the short span of fifty years. Finally, but equal in importance, this book aims to engage with the ongoing dialogue among scholars of race and ethnicity in America, specifically regarding conversations on the issues of multiculture, polyculture, and the persistence of race.

I want to be upfront about several crucial issues. First, this is not a teleological project—one that situates the emergence of the polycultural and the postmodern sublime as a qualitative advancement in Asian American literature; in other words, one that pits the "enlightened" perspectives of writers like Gish Jen and Li-Young Lee against the "limited" and "naïve" perspectives of Pardee Lowe or Jade Snow Wong. I concur with Jinqi Ling's philosophy in *Narrating Nationalisms*, "The newness of recent Asian American literary articulations lies not in their inherent power of being contemporary nor in their actual severance from previous sources of resistance, but in their fuller expression, under more enabling (or seemingly more enabling) social conditions, of the possibilities of liberation problematically or incompletely envisioned by earlier Asian American realist and/or nationalist literary voices" (29). In this study, I wish to examine the changing context of textual production and reception as it intersects with developments in America's perception of race and ethnicity from the postwar period to the present.

Second, I do not see polyculturalism as an outright repudiation of multiculturalism, but as the next step after multiculturalism, a critique of its limitations, and a furtherance of its antiracist goals. Vijay Prashad, the theorist who has thus far articulated polyculturalism's agenda, argues vehemently and necessarily against multiculturalism's limitations. In Prashad's view, multiculturalism "tends toward a static view of history" ("Bruce Lee" 54) in a manner that "fetishizes" culture and demands an ethnic subject's allegiance to his or her essential and primordial cultural identity. Prashad is "deeply unhappy with the multicultural neoliberal condescension of our times— where diversity may be something of a fetish to flatten our complexities rather than to allow us space to breathe as political animals" ("Community Scholarship" 118). He urges scholars to "criticize the diversity model of multiculturalism and replace it with the antiracist one of polyculturalism" ("Bruce Lee" 82). Prashad quotes, with approval, Stanley Fish's 1997 critique of the movement as "boutique multiculturalism" and Slavoj Žižek's 1998 critique of multiculturalist diversity as "racism with a distance," and thus joins ranks with these and other scholars in a pointed critique of multiculturalism.[2]

What Prashad and others tend to lose sight of in their opposition to present articulations and manifestations of multiculturalism (from pop culture to academia) is a historical perspective on the multicultural movement and an appreciation for the sacrifices made by scholars, students, and activists in the name of antiracism and minority rights. Timothy B. Powell's critical assessment of Stanley Fish's, Slavoj Žižek's, and Susan Gubar's positions[3] seeks to recuperate this historical context, and he furthermore charges these scholars with uncritically conflating the politically engaged, antiracist multicultural movement with commercialized corporate expressions of multiculturalism and distortions of multiculturalism within academia. He writes, "I think that part of the problem is that, like Fish, many scholars have mistaken 'multiculturalism' as a singular entity (i.e., that 'strong multiculturalism' is really nothing more than 'boutique multiculturalism,' which is little more than Benetton billboards and ethnic food courts in suburban malls)" (175). Powell sees such critiques of multiculturalism as emanating not from genuine and historical engagement with the various tenets of multiculturalism or the movement's various phases and theorists, but from a postmodern "hermeneutics of suspicion" (155) that automatically reacts against any organizing principle or explanatory model as a Lyotardian "master narrative." Powell calls for critics to "accept the challenge of devising new theoretical paradigms flexible enough to encompass the ways in which these fiercely independent cultures continually come together and come apart in fractal patterns that cannot be fixed in a formulated phrase" (157, echoes of "Prufrock" unacknowledged).

My study of the changing reception of Chinese American literature is an attempt not only to describe changes in Asian American literature, but to describe the emergence of a "new theoretical paradigm" that I believe *is* "flexible enough to encompass" the historical valence of multiculturalism and the cross-fertilizing perspectives of postmodern hybridity theory while remaining cognizant of the persistence of racist and racialized thinking in contemporary American society. A tall order, I know. But I believe that the recent critiques of multiculturalism, however unhistorical and reductivist some may be, point out that multiculturalism as a term has been conflated, and not just in the popular imagination, with primordialism[4] and the fetishization of discrete cultures. Rather than counter this tendency with postmodern concepts like cultural hybridity and pastiche that, *as a replacement* for "multiculturalism," introduce problematic utopian ideals of color-blind societies and unraced subjects (E. San Juan Jr. calls it "the rebarbative postcolonial babble about contingency ruling over all" [371]), I believe we can combine the multicultural with the postmodern in a way that acknowledges the persistence of race. But to do so, we cannot continue to pour the new wine described here into the old wineskins of multiculturalism. In other words, it is not enough to simply explain the ability of multiculturalism to encompass cultural hybridity and racialization. I don't believe it can. The confusion over what multiculturalism stands for is not simply, as Powell would have it, an obfuscation of multiculturalism's laudable aims. It is this, but it is more. Multiculturalism, as critics such as San Juan Jr. have pointed out, is a "politics of difference" that fundamentally depends upon the maintenance of cultural boundaries.[5] Cultural hybridity, on the other hand, describes the porous and fluid nature of identity, and therefore seems inherently at odds with multiculturalism. This basic contradiction makes necessary the invention of new terminology. Polyculturalism, in my estimation, is a term that combines the power of postmodern identity critique with the strength of multiculturalism's political engagement.

In an insightful review of Prashad's groundbreaking book on polyculturalism, *Everybody Was Kung Fu Fighting: Afro-Asian Connections and the Myth of Cultural Purity*, Rosebud Elijah asks why "very few scholars and teachers in higher education have thoughtfully used" the emerging critiques of multiculturalism and U.S. racism to develop an "antiracist framework" such as Prashad's polyculturalism. His preliminary answer is that "we are unenthusiastically silent [about multiculturalism's inadequacies] because dismissing multiculturalism may mean unintentionally reinforcing colorblind and/or indigenous theories" (59). This is precisely the problem I have described above: multiculturalism is inadequate on its own because it promotes a view of cultures as monolithic and is, as Prashad frequently reminds us, inherently bound to the skin; postmodern hybridity theory is inadequate on its own because it leads us to another distorted and furthermore politically vacuous view, that race simply doesn't matter, that "we are all human after all" (Elijah 59). Rather, Prashad argues that the recognition of our multiple lineages and linkages are the basis for our combined efforts to acknowledge, resist, and dismantle racism. Prashad writes, "our cultures are linked in more ways than we could catalog, and it is from these linkages that we hope our politics will be energized" (*Everybody* 148). Where I differ with Prashad is in the relationship between polyculturalism and multiculturalism. While I agree that the polycultural is a radical break from multiculturalism, I would like to stress (with Elijah) that polyculturalism, a radical response to racism and multiculturalism's tendency to fetishize culture, evolved from and owes a great debt to multiculturalism, which is also a "response to racism . . . [that] has been useful in providing (limited) access and beginning a conversation about race in this society" (Elijah 59).

In sum, I see polyculturalism as a crucial rhetorical and theoretical maneuver that (1) recovers the political and antiracist impetus of the original multicultural movement from the grips of neoconservative backlash (Omi and Winant 12) and commercial and corporate culture, (2) recognizes the persistent influence of race and racialized thinking in American society (which cannot be elided by replacing the term "race" with "ethnicity" or "culture"), and (3) adopts the energies of postmodern identity theories such as cultural hybridity that destabilize and decenter the fetishizing gaze of popular multiculturalism.

For many readers, the difference between the terms "multiculturalism" and "polyculturalism" will be slight. There are clear commonalities between multiculturalism and polyculturalism; for instance, broadly understood, both take us beyond the Eurocentrism of the old "melting pot" model. However, I believe the "imagined worlds" of the writers I discuss in this study challenge readers to think about identity in ways that oppose popular notions of multiculturalism. In my analysis of the changing horizon of Chinese American literature, I want both to examine the artistic development of a nonessentializing and fluid view of identity that emerges in the face of American racism and racialization, and to acknowledge a shift from multicultural logic to polycultural logic in ways that illuminate the texts and our understanding of contemporary American literature and society.

Acknowledgments

I suppose Asian American literature would not have entered my radar screen if it weren't for English Language Institute and the opportunity it and many supporters gave me to teach in China in 1988 and 1989–90. I doubt that I would have thought beyond *The Joy Luck Club* and *The Woman Warrior* if I hadn't married an amazing woman from Singapore and left U.S. shores to live in that island republic for a decade. And I probably wouldn't have thought twice about the suggestion made by Ban Kah Choon, former Head of English at the National University of Singapore, that I do my Ph.D. dissertation on Asian American literature if it hadn't struck me that my two children were, technically speaking, "Asian Americans." Suddenly, Asian American literature was not just culturally interesting to me—it was deeply personal. As a literary scholar and social critic, I could have a hand, small though it may be, in shaping the world into which my children would grow. It's funny how, looking back, all that seemed haphazard and serendipitous at the time now takes on an aura of divine guidance.

John Whalen-Bridge has been my professional mentor and close friend through the writing of this book. This brilliant and generous friend has read draft after draft of my work, offering incisive critiques, challenging my assumptions, prodding me with more books, more ideas, more information—and more hope. John has taught me that literary scholarship is a community activity and he models that community beautifully.

Barnard Turner gave me the necessary tools and guidance to turn my rambling ideas into a cogent argument. Barnard's incredibly wide range of expertise inspired as much as it informed me—you'll see what I mean if you read his excellent book, *Cultural Tropes of the Contemporary American West*. Walter Lim read my work in its earliest form and shared his knowledge and insight.

I learned much about Asian American literature from Walter's lectures and our conversations when we co-taught Asian American Literature at the National University of Singapore (NUS). Other colleagues at NUS offered advice and feedback on my writing: Rajeev Patke, Robbie Goh, Chitra Sankaran, fellow "classmate" P. C. Khoo, and, then Dean of the University Scholars Programme, George P. Landow. Stephen Sumida also read my work and gave important feedback.

There are three Asian Americanists in particular who have always been there for me, to offer advice, to read my work, to write references, to be mentors in the field: I owe a great debt to Shirley Geok-lin Lim, Cheng-lok Chua, and Shawn Wong. Tina Klein influenced my thinking on transnational flows of culture and has been a friend and a great support. Gish Jen has been generous with her time, meeting with my students at the University of Connecticut and graciously agreeing to read to a packed house of professors at the 2005 American Literature Association conference. Thank you also to Kit Hume, David Leiwei Li, David Goldstein, and Ravi Shankar for advice, support, and insights along the way.

I have had the honor of teaching Asian American literature to intelligent and enthusiastic students at the National University of Singapore, Central Connecticut State University, and the University of Connecticut. Their thoughtful responses and lively discussions have impacted this book in ways that they will never know. I wish to acknowledge pioneer Asian Americanists whose works have influenced and inspired me, among whom Elaine Kim, King-kok Cheung, and Sau-ling Cynthia Wong stand out in particular. I clearly owe a debt to Vijay Prashad, too, whose writing on polyculture helped me to make sense of the world I was describing.

I wish to thank Jacquie Ettinger, my editor at University of Washington Press, for believing in my work and for guiding me expertly through the publication process. I am also grateful to Kathleen Pike Jones for her editorial work on the manuscript, Alice Herbig and her staff for their promotional effforts, and Pat Soden and the University of Washington Press faculty committee for supporting my efforts. The UW Press's anonymous readers graciously pointed out my blind spots and offered expert advice, which gave me the necessary vision to remake my material.

I thank my parents, Fred and Cheryl Partridge, for teaching me humane and ethical standards and standing by me always, and my children Lian and Hudson, who are a continual source of joy and inspiration.

Most of all, I wish to thank my wife, Joo Eng, for helping in so many ways, listening to my ideas, offering advice, and being my greatest support and best friend.

The author gratefully acknowledges permission to reprint the following:

Excerpts from Li-Young Lee, "The Cleaving" in *The City in Which I Love You*, Copyright © 1990 by Li-Young Lee, and "Eating Alone" and "Eating Together" in *Rose*, Copyright © 1986 by Li-Young Lee, reprinted with permission from BOA Editions, Ltd.

"Claiming Diaspora in Shirley Geok-lin Lim's *Joss and Gold*" originally published in *Asian Diasporas: Cultures, Identities, Representations* (Hong Kong: University of Hong Kong Press, 2004), 131–47. Reprinted by permission.

A portion of chapter 5 was originally published in a slightly different form under the title "Toward a More Worldly World Series: Reading Game Three of the 1998 American League Championships Against David Wong Louie's Short Story 'Warming Trends'" in *American Studies International* 38.2 (June 2000): 115–25. Reprinted by permission.

"The Politics of Ethnic Authorship: Li-Young Lee, Emerson, and Whitman at the Banquet Table" was originally published in *Studies in the Literary Imagination* 37:1 (Spring 2004): 101–26, Copyright Georgia State University. Reprinted by permission.

A portion of chapter 7, "Beyond Multicultural: Cultural Hybridity in the Novels of Gish Jen," was originally published in slightly different form under the title "America Is No America—Or Is It? Transcending Cultural Binaries in Gish Jen's *Typical American*" in *Complicities: Connections and Divisions: Perspectives on Literatures and Cultures of the Asia-Pacific Region* (Bern: Peter Lang, 2003), 85–95. Reprinted by permission. Another portion of chapter 7 and a brief segment from the Introduction were published as "Re-Viewing the Literary Chinatown: Hybridity in Gish Jen's *Mona in the Promised Land*" in *Complicating Constructions: Race, Ethnicity, and Hybridity in American Texts* (Seattle: University of Washington Press, 2007). Reprinted by permission.

BEYOND LITERARY CHINATOWN

Introduction

The reviews of *The Woman Warrior* upon its publication in 1976 prompted Maxine Hong Kingston to write the article "Cultural Misreadings" on the misunderstandings and "false" assumptions of critics. Kingston argued that "about two-thirds" of the reviews reinforced stereotypes of the "exotic, inscrutable, mysterious oriental" (55). One review claims that "the author becomes as inscrutable as the East always seems to the West," while another marvels at the book's "strange and brooding atmosphere" that is "inscrutably foreign, oriental" (56). Kingston responded vehemently to these assertions about her book: "How dare they make their ignorance our inscrutability!" she demanded (56). Kingston bristled furthermore at being forced into the cultural ambassador role. She was not read as an American writer, or simply as a writer, but always as a representative of the Chinese people. She asks, "Why must I 'represent' anyone besides myself? Why should I be denied an individual artistic vision?" (63).

I asked Kingston, in an interview in 2004, after the publication of *The Fifth Book of Peace* (2003) and *To Be the Poet* (2002), whether she still feels misunderstood.[1]

> No. I remember in that article I took a survey of the reviews and it was like two-thirds of them were reviewing a Chinese book. It almost was as if I were writing in Chinese. They would get the one Asian that was working for the newspaper to review my work, and it could be a sports writer. They would write about the traditions that I got wrong and so on. By the time *China Men* had come out, it was more the case that reviewers were understanding it. But there were still reviewers who would say "That's

not the way they do it in China." Or, in praise, "What an exotic work." But that has happened less and less through the years.

When I asked her what might account for this change in reception, she named education as the primary factor: "Ethnic Studies Departments, Asian American literature studies, the American Cultures requirements. Through education, there's been so much more understanding of people of color and our art."

Kingston concluded "Cultural Mis-readings" on a hopeful note. In a kind of prophecy of the future of Asian American writing and its reception, she wrote, "I'm certain that some day when a great body of Chinese American writing becomes published and known, then readers will no longer have to put such a burden on each book that comes out. Readers can see the variety of ways for Chinese Americans to be" (63). I asked Kingston whether this "prophecy," written in 1982, had finally come true by 2004. "Yes, I think it has," she replied. "Although with every new one that comes out, they'll go after that person again. And then the next one that comes out. . . . That person will carry the burden of being the representative Asian American and then another one comes out and the burden shifts to the next one, but, on the whole, there is such a diversity. I think that everybody breaks up the stereotype because we're all so different." Kingston affirms that the reception of Asian American literature has changed, but she clearly senses that the Asian American writer has not completely escaped the cultural ambassador role. There is much more diversity in Asian American literature today than there was in 1976, but, she suggests, each author still bears a burden of representation in ways that white authors do not.

Kingston's response—a subjective perception that will be tested more rigorously in the pages that follow—suggests what reception theorists would call a change in the horizon of expectations. Readers in 1976 expected Kingston to represent all Chinese people. Many expected her to confirm their ideas of the mysterious, inscrutable, exotic Asian. However, readers today (especially book reviewers and critics) are more familiar with Asian Americans and Asian American literature, and perhaps with the problems of "Orientalism," and they are therefore less likely to exoticize the book based on the author's ethnicity. Examining and characterizing this change in the horizon of expectation is part of the aim of this book, but it is not the ultimate goal. This book investigates the dynamics of reception as it is revealed in the works of various Chinese American writers in order to enlighten our understanding of reading horizons in general, and of contemporary conceptions of race and reading in America in particular.

Kingston highlights a rarely discussed aspect of a book's reception: the author's reception of the reader's reception. Besides a change in the horizon of expectations, her response suggests that an Asian American author may be deeply concerned with the impressions of readers—about her books, about her designs, and about her ethnic community and its history. This concern not only prompted Kingston to write "Cultural Mis-readings," but it is also traceable in her subsequent artistic works. For example, in *China Men*, she includes a brief history of the Chinese American experience in her narrative. In a 1980 interview with Timothy Pfaff of *The New York Times*, Kingston cites the "ignorance" of her "mainstream" audience as the impetus for this decision:

> The mainstream culture doesn't know the history of Chinese Americans, which has been written and written well. That ignorance makes a tension for me, and in the new book [*China Men*] I just couldn't take it anymore. So all of a sudden, right in the middle of the stories, plunk—there is an eight-page section of pure history. It starts with the Gold Rush and then goes right through the various exclusion acts, year by year. (Skenazy and Martin 15)

We do not in fact need this extra-textual evidence to explain the historical section in *China Men*. By providing cultural context and historical background within her narrative, Kingston shows her own horizon of expectation toward her audience.[2] Why else would she include the historical section if not to fill in gaps of knowledge in her perceived readers?

Kingston is not the only author whose response to the audience's horizon of expectation can be uncovered in her literary works. Close readings of Chinese American works reveal a fluid relationship between the reader's horizon of expectation and the author's anticipation of that horizon. For instance, when Auntie Lin says to her Mahjong partners in Amy Tan's *The Joy Luck Club*, "I was *chiszle*," she follows the Chinese phrase with an English translation, "mad to death" (34). Tan suggests that this is an example of the "special language" these Chinese immigrants speak, "half in broken English, half in their own Chinese dialect" (34). However, if all the women are Chinese speakers, and all of them are (including Jing-Mei, who understands more than she can speak) then why would the "half English" part of the sentence be a translation of the "half dialect" part? One explanation might be that they do not speak the same dialect. However, the phrase "chiszle" is Tan's own romanized version of the Mandarin phrase "qi si ren," as it would be rendered in *hanyu pinyin*. Mandarin, like English, is the bridge between Chinese dialects for many Chinese speakers, and so it would seem unlikely that Auntie Lin is translating her Mandarin words for the benefit of her listeners. It is far more likely that Tan includes the translation for the benefit of her readers. All ethnic writers face the problem of translating foreign words for their readers, and Tan's strategy is not unusual, though this particular instance is somewhat clumsy. She provides the translation because she believes her readers, not Jing-Mei or the other characters, are ignorant of the meaning. But why does she include the phrase at all? Why not render it in English if she has to translate the phrase in such an unnatural way? I would argue that Tan includes the Chinese phrase in the first place to lend the conversation authenticity for the reader, to simulate an authentic entry into a world that would otherwise be closed to the reader. We might even define it as an example of what Shirley Geok-lin Lim calls "easy exoticism" ("Reconstructing" 52). The text reveals Tan's own estimation of the reader's horizon in two respects: aesthetic needs or desires (i.e., the authentic and perhaps exotic experience), and information needs (i.e., the translation of a foreign phrase). A close examination of the text uncovers a wealth of information about the reader-writer relationship.

In brief, *Beyond Literary Chinatown* examines the dialectical process at the nexus of reader, author, and text. What are the predominant assumptions about Chinese Americans that readers bring to a Chinese American text? How can we define these assumptions, and how can we define these readers? How do texts challenge the reader's horizon of expectation? What strategies do authors employ? What are the results? Satisfying answers to these questions will account for the dynamic growth of Chinese American literature in recent years, and will allow a new view of the efficacy of multicultural trends that open the way for the polycultural, as explored briefly in the preface. The texts discussed in this book display their authors' deep concern with the possibilities of postmodern existence (cultural hybridity, diaspora, transnational flows, etc.) but also with the continued imposition of race as a defining characteristic in society and among readers. The challenges of recent Chinese American literary works, several of which are examined in this book, to our previously monocultural and currently multicultural views show a dynamic process of change in the reader's horizon of expectation.

As literary critics, however, talking about the expectations of readers makes us nervous—simply because this great mass of individuals that we lump together under the term "readers" seems to be an abstract concept. We have no trouble talking about these "readers" in the hallway after class, or after reading a review we disagree with, or after fielding questions at a literary reading. But formal discussion of reader expectations in scholarly books raises the question, "Who are these readers?" If we talk about "readers," we are forced to generalize—which seems an unscientific thing to do. If we get scientific and do objective, empirical tests, we feel we are not doing literary criticism—we have somehow bowed to the "uncreative" forces of the social sciences. A wealth of information is unfortunately lost to us when we assume that the interplay between reader responses and authorial designs is too nebulous to talk about seriously. This book takes as a given what we all know intuitively to be true: that such relationships between reader expectations and a writer's text do exist. Through a close reading of texts and observance of the way texts are promoted, this book shows that the interaction of reader-author-text can be talked about in ways that will enlighten our understanding of literature and society.

It would be naïve to assume, however, that the author-text-reader triad is hermetically sealed and self-contained. There are other factors that enter the arena, the most obvious being publicists, editors, critics, and academics. In my discussion of the literary Chinatown, I utilize these factors at various points to further illuminate the process I am describing. Promotional copy for books, for example, plays an important role because it is designed to capture the potential reader/consumer's interest and motivate him/her to buy the book. Rather than simply offering a glimpse into the actual book, however, these descriptions attempt to convince consumers that the given book is worth reading. The publicist foregrounds the particular aspects of the text that she/he believes will appeal to the reader, and in this way the words of the publicist, like the words of the text, anticipate the reader's horizon of expectation. Editors, likewise, listen to the voices of critics and examine the buying habits of readers to determine what kinds of texts their presses will publish and how to help their authors shape texts that will succeed in the market. Academics influence the author-text-reader dynamics not only by their critiques in scholarly journals, but also in their promotion of texts among students. This dynamic is complicated by the fact that many authors teach in universities, as creative writers or as academics that critique the very literature they help produce. In my study, David Wong Louie, Shawn Wong, and Shirley Geok-lin Lim all hold full-time academic positions, and Gish Jen teaches occasionally in university creative writing programs. Lim, in fact, is a formidable feminist and Asian American literary critic. Of the five writers covered in detail in this book, only Li-Young Lee chooses to remain outside academia, preferring instead to work a blue-collar job and publish poetry as a sideline.[3]

Often it is in the publicist's promotional copy that the projected audience of a book is most clearly defined. What separates a good marketing strategy from the rest is often its ability to anticipate, feed, and sometimes even produce taste. Identifying the consumer's tastes, or the possibility for certain tastes to develop, is critical to selling the product. Consider, for instance, the following advertisement for Patricia Chao's *Monkey King* as it appeared in HarperFlamingo's February 1998 book catalogue: "A critically acclaimed first novel that transports readers into the vibrant and sometimes harrowing world of a Chinese-American family as a young woman explores the past in order to come to terms with her hidden demons."

"Critical acclaim" comes first for obvious reasons: readers have a taste for novels that are already validated by those who are supposed to have good taste, i.e., professional critics. But the rest of the advertisement sells more than a good book: it sells an experience. The description promises the readers a journey into another "world." Readers will be transported into a new place, unfamiliar, dangerous, and restricted: "the vibrant and sometimes harrowing world of a Chinese-American family." The reader will witness the unleashing of the young woman's "hidden demons" by going back to their source: the Chinese American family's past. What the advertisement anticipates and feeds, therefore, is the reader's taste for ethnographic adventure— the opportunity to explore another world as an armchair social scientist, to move, that is, in the safety of virtuality from outside to inside.[4]

The HarperFlamingo copy is an example of the literary Chinatown phenomenon described in the first part of this book. Its fetishization of Chinese Americans as objects of exploration and ethnographic intrigue reifies notions of difference based on a special ethnic aura. Not only are the "demons" of Chinese American families unique to Chinese Americans, but they are expunged through the interrogation of family history and familial relations. Moreover, in describing the Chinese American family as "vibrant and sometimes harrowing," the summary draws on connections in the Euro-American imagination[5] between Chineseness and backwardness, exoticism, spiritualism, and superstition. The advertisement suggests, ultimately, that through the novel, non-Chinese Americans sit as privileged witnesses, or as consultant pathologists, to the resolving of internal and incestuous conflicts, not as participants.[6]

The assumptions and prejudices that make up the literary Chinatown have not gone uncontested. Asian American writers have written against this expectation by "claiming America" in their texts.[7] According to Sau-ling Cynthia Wong, claiming America refers to "establishing the Asian American presence in the context of the United States' national cultural legacy and contemporary cultural production" ("Denationalization" 16). This strategy has consistently placed the experiences of Asian Americans squarely on American soil, actively writing the histories of Asian immigrants back into the history books from which they were excluded.[8] Kingston says of *China Men*, "what I am doing in this new book is claiming America" (Skenazy and Martin 14). She goes on to explain,

> That seems to be the common strain that runs through all the characters. In story after story Chinese American people are claiming America, which goes all the way from one character saying that a Chinese explorer found this place before Leif Ericsson did to another one buying a house here. Buying a house is a way of saying that America—and not China—is his country. (Skenazy and Martin 14)

The tendency, especially for Euro-Americans, to view Chinese American literature as "their" experience or "their" community-building project, rather than integral to "our" American experience relates directly to the misconception that Asians are "unassimilable," or that their ability to fully assimilate is obstructed by the starkness of their difference. As Shirley Geok-lin Lim says, "the reified signifiers of Kipling's 'East is East and West is West, and never the twain shall meet,' are . . . still potent with divisive force" ("Introduction" xxii). At its foundation, this bias boils down to physical difference: a European immigrant, for example, might blend into American life within one generation, whereas fourth, fifth, and sixth generation Chinese Americans will continue to face the question, "Where are you from—originally?"[9] But this bias also relates to a problematic emanating from the European immigration model of assimilation that was adopted by social scientists in the early- and mid-twentieth century. The European immigration analogy, according to Michael Omi and Howard Winant, "suggested that racial minorities could be incorporated into American life in the same way that white ethnic groups had been" (12). This analogy fostered the expectation that non-European immigrant groups would assimilate into U.S. society following the four-fold cycle developed by Robert E. Park—contact, conflict, accommodation, and assimilation—that were based on his observations of European immigrants. In Omi and Winant's view, this analogy ignored "what was in many cases a qualitatively different historical experience—one which included slavery, colonization, racially based exclusion and, in the case of Native Americans, virtual extirpation. In addition, it has been argued, the paradigm tends to 'blame

the victims' for their plight and thus to deflect attention away from the ubiquity of racial meanings and dynamics" (21). Thus, rather than acknowledge
the racist barriers that excluded the Chinese from full assimilation, people
tended to view their failure as "the irrational products of individual patholo-
gies" (10).

In this way, the notion of the unassimilable Asian is the product of Euro-
American assumptions about Chinese immigrants and what they are
(in)capable of, or even what they desire—and this is where the literary
Chinatown, both as a metaphor and a reality, is grounded. For some people,
the prevalence of Chinatowns and sprawling Asian communities like
Monterey Park, California, supports their assumption that Chinese Americans
do not wish to belong to America. In the preface to Gwen Kinkead's 1992
ethnographic study of New York's Chinatown, tellingly subtitled *A Portrait
of a Closed Society*, the author concludes that "Americans" can learn much
from the "Chinese," but what the Chinese of Chinatown need to learn is that
"they can't have it both ways—they cannot charge mistreatment and racism
and, at the same time, refuse to talk to outsiders, or vote, or lend a cup of
sugar to their neighbor" (x). In what appears to be a balanced, democratic
approach to Chinese behavior in Chinatown—an approach that seems to say,
"we can learn from them, and they can learn from us"—Kinkead is in fact
making a contention about a general ideology of what it is to be "American":
that in order to get along in America, indeed to be "American," one must be
outgoing and "neighborly." She sets this notion of Americanness against
Chinese American behavior, suggesting that Chinese inwardness originates
from their preference to remain non-American. Although in her book
Kinkead does attempt to historicize her account of New York's Chinatown
with facts about the Chinese struggle for survival in an often inhospitable
environment, she not only repeats the long-held view of the insular and clannish Chinese as un-American, but she builds it up in a way that dramatizes
her own exploits.[10] In short, a view of Chinese Americans as "forever foreign"
(K. Scott Wong's phrase 4) remains central to Euro-American assumptions.

Literary Chinatown is situated in the crossover from the socio-historical
to the literary. The binary perceptions of outside/inside, ours/theirs,
American/Chinese color the ways non-Chinese Americans read Chinese
American literature. The tendency to see Chinese Americans as foreign and
clannish ghettoizes the literature of Chinese Americans—not simply by virtue of textual representations, but also by (and in response to and/or in anticipation of) the projections of reader prejudice upon the texts. In this way,
the assumptions and expectations regarding Chinese Americans are perva-

sive and powerful factors in the reception of Chinese American literature and this dynamic may also be essential to the reading of other "minor literatures" (Deleuze and Guattari's term).

By definition a horizon delineates the frontier, the edge of knowing. But as we draw near to that horizon, a new horizon unfolds and what was once unknown is now known. What we expected to find on that horizon may be quite different from the reality, and so we comprehend this data and anticipate the new horizon with modified expectations. In reception theory, the horizon is used often as a metaphor for the reading process. The theory asserts that readers approach texts with a set of expectations and these expectations are either confirmed, and reified, or challenged, and modified, as the world of the text unfolds. Philosophers such as Edmund Husserl, who coined the phrase *horizon of expectation*, Hans-Georg Gadamer and Paul Ricoeur, and reception theorists such as Wolfgang Iser and Hans Robert Jauss, use the horizon metaphor to explain the perceiver's interaction with the perceived—or, in the case of reception, the reader's interaction with the text—because it enables an understanding of the dynamic process of knowing. According to Ricoeur, "The meeting between text and reader is a meeting between the whole of the text's claims, the horizon which it opens onto, the possibilities which it displays, and another horizon, the reader's horizon of expectation" (*Reflection & Imagination* 492).

The reader's expectation of a Chinese American text will be colored by his or her impression of Chinese Americans. The world of the text presents its own horizon which, when "fused" with the reader's horizon, may result in a change of perception. Textual horizons may be constructed to match the expectations of readers, or they may be constructed to challenge the expectations of readers. Much, though not all, of the Chinese American literature written before the 1960s tended to match the expectations of readers in an attempt to gain acceptance in mainstream, white-centered America.[11] But many, though not all, texts written by Chinese American writers in the contemporary era seek to challenge our society's predominant views of Chinese ethnicity. These texts seek not to conform to the reader's expectations, but to transform them.

Reading horizons may sound credible in theory, but how can we make them tangible and verifiable? The "literary Chinatown" idea developed in Part One of this book is based on an American reading community united

by its Euro-American perspectives and its assumptions about Chinese Americans. I explain in chapter 1 that Euro-American, as I am using the term, refers to any reader—regardless of skin color, class, or ethnicity—who tends to see the United States as European at its core. As E. Robert Lee writes, "America, long, and almost by automatic custom, has been projected as a mainstream nothing if not overwhelmingly Eurocentric, Atlantic, east to west, and white-male in its unfolding" (1). Describing this horizon of expectation assumes that there *is* a Euro-American reading community and that we can speak concretely about that community. While reading communities as such are indeed an abstraction, it does not follow that they are no more than an abstraction or that there are no ways of describing them. After all, the publishing industry spends enormous amounts of money in marketing books based entirely on abstractions such as "markets," "audiences," "reading publics," and "consumer tastes." In fact, these reading communities can be described by examining the popularity of certain books with consumers (e.g., through best-seller lists), as well as through the comments of critics, publishers, and readers. According to Jauss, the horizon of an audience's expectations "can be objectified historically along the spectrum of the audience's reactions and criticism's judgment (spontaneous success, rejection or shock, scattered approval, gradual or belated understanding)" (*Toward an Aesthetics of Reception* 25). Put another way, as Gadamer explains, "all foregrounding [e.g., the best-seller list, the publisher's summary, the book review] also makes visible that from which something is foregrounded [i.e., the reader's horizon]" (305).[12]

In his articulation of this *Rezeptionsästhetik*, Jauss claims, "the way in which a literary work, at the historical moment of its appearance, satisfies, surpasses, disappoints, or refutes the expectations of its first audience obviously provides a criterion for the determination of aesthetic value" (*Toward an Aesthetics of Reception* 25). By applying this method to literature and critical response, we can not only articulate a description of a book based on an aesthetic value, but we can also establish a way of describing various audiences according to changes in a particular text's reception. For example, Elaine H. Kim's influential study *Asian American Literature: An Introduction to the Writings and Their Social Context* portrays the value of particular texts according to her particular aesthetic, which, as we will see below, she shares with a particular interpretive community. In her analysis of Lin Yutang's work, Kim quotes from books by Will Irwin (1913) and Jack London (1910) to indicate the kind of reception Lin's writing achieved:

[Lin] has been called a "critic of the Chinese and American ways of life," "critic of life and interpreter of ancient wisdom," "interpreter of the Chinese to the West," who writes in "certainly the very best [English] any Chinese has ever written," whose "balanced outlook is accompanied by a welcome sense of humor," and who is a "genial world citizen." (27–28)

Kim then uses this sample of quotations to construct the kind of attributes in Lin's works that were attractive to the Euro-American audience of his time:

Lin's enormous popularity in the West is attributable to three factors: he writes superficial, pithy pieces about China that are in perfect keeping with the American popular view; he is a bourgeois anti-Communist, the most popular political position for a Chinese in the United States; and he remains light, humorous, and not overly serious about himself or about China in his writings. (28)

Thus, according to Kim, Lin Yutang's writings were successful because they fulfilled his audiences Euro-American expectations of the Chinese and of themselves.

Furthermore, in her discussion of Lin's best-known publication, *My Country and My People* (1935), Kim reveals her own estimation of Lin's writing and marks her own distance from the audience for whom Lin wrote. In Kim's view, Lin's "description of the Chinese as backward, childlike, superstitious people, loveable but incapable of taking care of themselves, is in perfect keeping with the Western colonial view of them" (28). In acknowledging the negative stereotyping of the Chinese people in Lin's work, Kim aligns herself with a new and different audience, one which understands both the underlying objectives of Lin's writing and the fetishizing gaze of the audience defined by its "Western colonial view." While the original audience valued Lin's writings because they confirmed their prejudices toward the Chinese, this new audience devalues Lin's writings because they did not challenge the prejudices of his readers. In addition, we can locate the audience or interpretive community to which Kim belongs in the shared values and expectations of her contemporaries.[13]

This change in reception exemplifies the fact that, in Mario J. Valdés's words, the "identity [of a text] can never be completely fixed; it will change, for it is the response of the present and the future, and each [response of an interpretive community] makes and will continue to make the text relatively important or unimportant" (33). In other words, over the years a text will be regarded differently, and perhaps valued differently, because of changes in audience expectations and prejudice. These changes allow us to distinguish between Lin Yutang's Euro-American audience and the cultural critics of the multicultural era many years later who were Elaine Kim's contemporaries.

Jauss claims that the aesthetic distance between the audience's horizon and the text's horizon "determines the artistic character of a literary work, according to an aesthetics of reception: to the degree that this distance decreases, and no turn toward the horizon of yet-unknown experience is demanded of the receiving consciousness, the closer the work comes to the sphere of 'culinary' or entertainment art" (*Toward an Aesthetics of Reception* 25). In this sense, Kim's assessment of *My Country and My People*, with its reluctance to challenge the Euro-American horizon, defines it as "culinary or entertainment art." But to the interpretive community to which Kim belongs, the fact that Lin's text required "no turn toward the horizon of the yet-unknown" does not classify it as a "culinary" text, but as a "racist" one. In other words, an aesthetics of reception applied to ethnic literature may judge not only artistic value, as Jauss intends, but the value of ethnic representation. Thus horizonal distance may be a critical tool in "ethnopoetics."[14]

Finally, recent projects by critics such as Jinqi Ling, Dominika Ferens, and Christopher Douglas reveal the emergence of a new reading community, one that seeks to recover a sense of an author's embeddedness in a particular historical moment. Rather than unfairly and anachronistically demanding a heroic voice of protest from authors whose historical milieu was vastly different from ours, this reading community seeks to uncover subtle modes of resistance and habits of conformity within the context of the author's particular historical moment.

CHINESE AMERICAN LITERATURE

Asian American literature is a particularly dynamic body of literature, as the above discussion suggests, and a study of its reception may tell us much about the processes of its growth. Anyone with an eye to Asian American literature knows that great changes have taken place since the civil rights movement of the 1960s. In the 1970s, the first Asian American literature courses in universities began to appear; out-of-print works such as *Eat a Bowl of Tea*, *No-No Boy*, and *Yokohama, California* were discovered and republished; new works, most notably *The Woman Warrior* and *Aiiieeeee! An Anthology of Asian American Writers*, brought Asian American writers to the attention of a wider audience; numerous Asian American writers published noteworthy books (Janice Mirikitani, Joy Kogawa, Shawn Wong, Bharati Mukherjee, Frank Chin, and Laurence Yep, to name a few); and then Amy Tan's 1989 leap to fame with *The Joy Luck Club* essentially put Asian American writing on the popular map. A plethora of award-winning works by Asian Americans followed, including Pulitzer and National Book Award winners. In brief, Asian American publishing has moved swiftly from a trickle to a flood.

The popular success of Amy Tan's *The Joy Luck Club* marks a significant increase in interest among the general reading public and commercial publishers. No other Chinese American book has received the magnitude of sales and attention as *The Joy Luck Club*. (The possible exception is *The Woman Warrior*, which has found continuing interest in university curricula and academic publications.) In Sau-ling Cynthia Wong's words, "the sensational success of . . . *The Joy Luck Club* . . . is the stuff of publishing legend." Prior to the book's publication, Amy Tan was "entirely unknown to the literary world." Yet, as Wong explains, the advance praise, strong reviews, and other marketing efforts

> propelled *The Joy Luck Club* onto the *New York Times* best-seller list, where it stayed for nine months. The hardcover edition was reprinted twenty-seven times and sold 275,000 copies (J. Simpson, 66); frenzied bidding by corporate publishers pushed the price for paperback rights from a floor of $100,000 to an astonishing $1.2 million (Holt). *The Joy Luck Club* was a finalist for the National Book Award and the National Book Critics Award, and a recipient of the 1990 Bay Area Book Reviewers Award for fiction. (174)

As Janice Simpson reported in *Time* magazine in 1991, the success of *The Joy Luck Club* inspired publishers to seek "their own Amy Tan" (66). Within two years of *The Joy Luck Club*'s publication, major publishers produced novels by Chinese American writers such as Gish Jen (Houghton Mifflin), Gus Lee (Dutton), and David Wong Louie (Knopf), including Putnam's release of Amy Tan's second novel, *The Kitchen God's Wife*. Dutton paid first-time author Gus Lee a $100,000 advance and ordered a first printing of 75,000 copies—a clear indication of the publishing industry's high hopes for Chinese American fiction (Simpson 66). Merely a decade later, after the publication of numerous Chinese American works, immigrant writer Ha Jin's third book, *Waiting*, won both the National Book Award (1999) and the prestigious PEN/Faulkner award (2000), and his novel, *War Trash*, won the PEN/Faulkner award for 2004.

In the publishing sense, then, Chinese American literature has made enormous strides in recent years. The explosion of interest in Chinese American literature in the 1990s and into the twenty-first century seems to suggest a growing interest in the Chinese American experience among book consumers. In this book, however, I wish to interrogate this interest through a detailed analysis of the relationship between race and reading. I argue that the reasons people buy Chinese American works is closely related to how publishers "sell" them, and that this "selling," moreover, is tightly bound to Euro-American attitudes toward the Chinese American community. This book, therefore, examines the reception of Chinese American literature by exploring the various and complex relationships between Euro-American expectations and the socio-historical assumptions in America about the Chinese and their communities. The "rise" of Chinese American literature, I argue, may not be a "sign of arrival" for the Chinese American community if, like the Chinatowns of the American past, it continues to be perceived as a Chinese ghetto in an American city.

WRITING BACK

The reification of Chinese American stereotypes is nothing new to Asian American literature and is well documented in a variety of studies.[15] My approach departs from these studies, but also augments them, by focusing critical attention on the processes and dynamics of the *reception* of Chinese American literature and how that reception feeds back into the production of texts. My emphasis in Part One is not on the various misrepresentations of Chinese Americans in literature, but, as suggested in the brief discussion of the literary Chinatown above, on the *projections* of readers. Parts Two, Three, and Four of this book present readings of Chinese American texts that examine the response of authors to the literary Chinatown horizon of expectations. My premise is that the expectations of the reading public that I describe in Part One are intentionally contradicted by Chinese American writers in their works, and, by reading texts with a specific view to uncovering these tensions, we can learn much about the dynamic interplay between reader and author in contemporary ethnic literature.[16] The ultimate goal of this exercise is to surmise where these authors seem to be taking us—that is, what vision of American ethnicity is forming in contradistinction to the ghettoizing impulse of the previous horizon of expectation? What tensions develop in their writing between expressions of individual identity and resistance to persistent racist and racialized constructs? How do these authors' expressions of postmodern identity (with its emphasis on fluidity, multiplicity, and decenteredness) correspond with panethnic and antiracist agendas?

Part Two highlights the ways two authors, the poet Li-Young Lee and the novelist and Asian American scholar Shirley Geok-lin Lim, exceed the literary Chinatown borders by exceeding the marginality placed on them in American society and literary criticism. The chapter on Lee's "The Cleaving" shows how the poem redefines America as well as the important literary tradition borne in the writings of Ralph Waldo Emerson and Walt Whitman. "The Cleaving" aggressively transgresses the literary Chinatown barrier. Lee invokes what Sau-ling Cynthia Wong calls the "big eaters" trope in Asian American writing and combines it with a Whitmanesque celebration of humanity—for Lee, the specific humanity of the Asian immigrant community—that brings the poet into conversation with American poetic tradition. His Whitmanesque "singing," and his violent devouring of Emerson as a Chinese dish at the banquet table, dialogically asserts the Chinese American poet's position in the American literary tradition. The poetic urge at the heart of the poem—"I would devour this race to sing it"—embraces, by devouring, Asian immigrants and American poetics in a way that challenges the literary Chinatown horizon and revises "America."

Shirley Geok-lin Lim's writing is of particular interest to this study because of her status as a scholar of Asian American writing and culture. She displays her knowledge of reader expectations in the choices she makes in her fiction. In *Joss and Gold*, for instance, she sets the reader up for a typical immigration-to-America story, only to thwart the reader's expectations. The heroine, surprisingly, never leaves Southeast Asia, preferring to make a life for herself in Singapore. Lim pushes the limits of Asian American literature so that one wonders whether her novel can even be categorized as Asian American. By seeing the novel as Asian American, however, I argue that Lim writes against the expectations of readers, especially readers of Asian American literature, to reveal a vision for Asian American identity that is not bound to American nationalism.

Part Three pays close attention to the phenomenological interaction of reader and text in order to elucidate the dynamics of change—changes in reception and changes in readers. My aim in the analysis of Shawn Wong's and David Wong Louie's texts is to illuminate the text that is produced (as Ricoeur says) "in front of" itself in the act of reading, and to determine the types of transformations that may result in the reader's self-reflexive experience. Ricoeur claims that meaning is experienced through the dynamic interplay of the reader's world and the text's world—and hence the meaning is "projected" or "performed," not "uncovered" or "found." My reading of Louie's stories explores the role of the baseball motif in producing a racialized story "in front of" the text of "Warming Trends." While the text seems to signify a non-ethnic and non-racial meaning, the *experience* of reading baseball, both in American society and in other stories in *Pangs of Love*, helps to produce a racially charged meaning "in front of" the text. What I wish to question is the mutability of this effect. That is, because the phenomenological effect of the baseball motif depends entirely upon a culturally conditioned association between baseball and white America, we can anticipate a change in the experience of reading the story as the semiotic significance of baseball changes in that culture.

The dynamics of reading Shawn Wong's *American Knees* allows us to see how the "meaning in front of the text" becomes a medium of cultural transformation. While we might assume that all fiction reading is a "virtual" experience in another world, wherein the reader imagines himself or herself in the position of various characters, Ricoeur's description of the reading experience shows a far more complex process of dialectical interplay. By engaging with the "world" of Wong's text, "playful readers" (Ricoeur's term for readers who give themselves over to the textual world, who read as though "in play") experience a productive variation of the ego that allows them to reflect from this alternative position upon themselves. The reader's self-reflection provides the stimulus for new and different actions toward Chinese Americans in the real world.

Part Four seeks to illuminate the new horizon we find in reading recent Chinese American fiction, first in a close reading of Gish Jen's novels, and finally the conclusion brings focus to the worlds proposed by the five authors studied in this book. Through Gish Jen's novels, I explore the ways Jen disrupts the prejudices that help to define the literary Chinatown by re-defining ethnicity. In *Typical American*, the immigrant characters are defined, I argue, less by the clash of Asian and American cultures than by the processes of individual negotiation through various experiences and influences. The effects of this negotiation are marked in Jen's texts by cultural and linguistic hybridity, which seems to be pushed to the limit in Jen's second novel, *Mona in the Promised Land*. By bringing her Chinese American protagonist and other characters to self-realization through a multicultural, panethnic experiment known in the novel as "Camp Gugelstein," Jen valorizes choice, change, and hybridization as phenomena that are part of the American experience. In this way, Jen radically de-privatizes the Chinese American novel and significantly re-views all race and ethnicity in America as interdependent and dialogic—they are, as I argue in the conclusion, constructed as polycultural. In *The Love Wife*, Jen continues her challenge to America's view of itself. As with *Mona in the Promised Land*, this novel reveals that our racial and ethnic identities are not essential but are constructs. Jen's approach to Chinese American ethnicity uniquely challenges the expectations governed by the literary Chinatown. Her redefinition of Chinese American ethnicity contradicts the central elements of the ethnic-author function in the reception of Chinese American literature: namely, the assumption that Chinese ethnicity is homogeneous and static.

However, a postmodern view of identity might seem to elide issues of race and the persistence of racialized thinking in the United States. If we acknowledge that, as Omi and Winant put it, "race will *always* be at the center of the American experience" (6, italics in original), how can a fluid conception of individual identity coincide with the realities of racialization? In my discussion, I relate Jen's work to the ideas of Omi and Winant, in specific their distinction between micro-level social relations (where "race is a matter of individuality, or the formation of *identity*") and macro-level social relations (where "race is a matter of *collectivity*, of the formation of social structures: economic, political and cultural/ideological" [66–67]). My goal is to draw together the seemingly disparate discourses of multiculturalism, cultural hybridity, and racial formation into a symbiotic, dynamic, and ultimately productive relationship: a conglomerate of discourses that I believe can fruitfully be described as polycultural.

The novels discussed in this book vary widely in their plots, themes, and characterizations, but they have this in common: each anticipates the reader's horizon of expectation, about Chinese Americans, ethnic literature, and about American identity, and challenges that horizon with notions of American ethnicity that can be described as polycultural. Taken collectively, the modes of identity formation suggested by these works reveal that American ethnic identity—at least as it is imagined by these writers—is fluid and multifaceted and is not grounded in any particular cultural group. We see through these writers a gradual shift in perspective from multiculturalism to polyculturalism, which is the subject of the conclusion. According to Vijay Prashad, "polyculturalism, unlike multiculturalism, assumes that people live coherent lives that are made up of a host of lineages—the task of the historian [or literary critic] is not to carve out the lineages but to make sense of how people live culturally dynamic lives" (*Everybody* xi–xii). While Gish Jen's novels most directly introduce a polycultural view, all of the works discussed in this study, when taken together, evoke a culturally dynamic world in which individual choice and multiple lineages triumph over socially and historically ascribed identities. The challenge for me in the conclusion is to relate these postmodern expressions of identity formation with the ubiquitous and pervasive realities of "racial formation" (Omi and Winant). As suggested in the preface, I do not believe we should define the polycultural as diametrically opposed to the multicultural. I seek, in contrast to Prashad, to retain the strength of the multicultural antiracist legacy in my definition of the polycultural. For me, the polycultural comprises the political efficacy of strong multiculturalism, the historical valence of cultural hybridity, and the antiracist agenda that Prashad so eloquently and passionately articulates.

PART I

Literary Chinatown and the Reader's Horizon

To present contemporary Asian American literary production as if it were a simple relation to ethnic identity, decided only by the writer's descent status, is to occlude the material reality surrounding its production. Much of what is admitted as Asian American writing into the enlarged sensitized canon of contemporary American literature is a sensibility that has been constituted under the gaze of an Anglo literary community. The well-known Asian American works that are read as ethnic signifiers are exactly those that succeed first with European American readers. . . . [These works] should be read not simply as Asian American cultural production but also as an American production "authorized" by a mainstream non-Asian American readership mediating between that different ethnic identity and itself. These works already reflect non-Asian American values, and their narrative strategies, verbal resources, and postmodern stances say as much about mainstream American literary traditions and systems of values and interpretations as they do about Asian American identity. Admitted into the American canon, these texts become weighted as mainstream cultural products whose position in American culture is to act as signifier for a minority identity.

—SHIRLEY GEOK-LIN LIM, "Assaying the Gold"

1 *Literary Chinatown*

DYNAMICS OF RACE AND READING

The crucial point is that a mode of creating, marketing, and interpreting Asian American literature has emerged that lends itself to these prescribed formations and installs both a particular pedagogy for Asian Americans and a way of "reading" race in America.

—DAVID PALUMBO-LIU, *Asian/American: Historical Crossings of a Racial Frontier*

READING EURO-AMERICAN

The reception of Chinese American literature by a reading public defined in this chapter as Euro-American in outlook is linked to the ways readers perceive Chinese Americans. This reception is related both metaphorically *and* metonymically to the formation of the historic American Chinatowns. The relationship is on the one hand *metaphoric* because the dynamics that produce what I am calling the "literary China-town" are *like* those that produced the historic American Chinatowns. That is, what readers reading from a Euro-American perspective assume about, and expect of, Chinese American literature has to a large extent shaped it as a virtual version of the American Chinatown. The relationship is on the other hand *metonymic* in that the dynamics that produce the literary Chinatown are in fact *derived from* those that produced the historic Chinatowns. In this chapter, I trace the connections between these two processes—which I call the dynamics of race and reading—in order to describe the reception of Chinese American literature in contemporary America.

But first, what do I mean by "readers"? Who are they and how can we generalize about them? The notion of the reader in reception-oriented criticism has been conceptualized in a variety of ways, from *implied readers* (Wolfgang Iser) and *super readers* (Umberto Eco), to *professional readers* and *actual readers*. My approach in this book is to see readers in terms of *reading cultures* or *interpretive communities*. As Stanley Fish argues in "Interpreting the *Variorum*," the fact that readers both agree and disagree on the meaning of texts is evidence for the existence of interpretive communities (*Is There a Text in This Class?* 171). These communities exist on the basis that some readers share, with other readers, the same "strategies," as he calls them, for understanding texts. In Fish's view, readers comprise an interpretive community when they share interpretive strategies "for constituting [the] properties and assigning [the] intentions" of texts (171).

For example, an evangelical Christian shares with other evangelicals the view that the Bible is the inspired word of God, and that the goal of interpreting scriptures is to conform her or his life to its teachings. Thus, a Christian woman may struggle with a passage such as Ephesians 5:22 ("Wives submit to your husbands as to the Lord") because the term "submit" appears to contradict what she has learned in contemporary American culture about womanhood and the equality of the sexes. But, an evangelical woman is likely to agree with other evangelicals that the passage calls for a particular hierarchy in marriage, in which the husband is the leader (albeit a servant leader, modeled on the sacrificial Christ) and the wife comes under the husband's headship (Ephesians 5:23). She will interpret the text as an absolute truth for all cultures and all times. She may then interpret Paul's description of the marriage relationship as an analogy for, or pre-figuration of, the relationship of believing Christians to God. She will likely balance Ephesians 5:22 with Ephesians 5:25 ("Husbands, love your wives, just as Christ loved the church and gave himself up for her") and conclude, as the *New International Version Study Bible* does, that the husband's sacrifice is greater than the wife's: "To give oneself up to death for the beloved is a more extreme expression of devotion than the wife is called to make" (1798). Her interpretation conforms more or less to her interpretive community's interpretation because she shares with other evangelicals convictions about the "properties" and "intentions" of the biblical text—that it is inerrant, true, and "God breathed" (2 Timothy 3:16).

A woman who ascribes to a liberal view of theology, however, is likely to interpret Ephesians 5:22 as a statement about Middle Eastern culture of the first century A.D. that is not relevant to a twenty-first-century marriage partnership in American culture. She will consider the text as the product of one man (Paul) whose beliefs about women and men were determined by his culture and his times. She might not come to the conclusion that Paul's injunction to the husband suggests, as the *NIV Study Bible* has it, "mutual submission" in the marriage relationship (1798). For her, Paul's description of marriage is a flawed analogy for a believer's relationship with God that reinforces a view of God as paternalistic, even misogynistic. She struggles with the ideas, but her interpretation, because it is based on the assumption that the Bible is to some extent time-bound and subject to human bias and error, might reject the hierarchy suggested by the text.

While the example above explains Fish's claim that interpretive strategies are responsible for "constituting [the] properties and assigning [the] intentions" of texts, I do not believe, as Fish does, that interpretive strategies "determine the shape of what is read rather than, as is usually assumed, the other way around" (171). Such a deterministic approach ignores the power of texts to influence the beliefs and actions of readers and to surprise and delight readers in ways that they could never have imagined before opening the book. Rather, I believe reading literature is a dynamic and fluid activity that often comprises competing poles of influence: the agency of individual readers and the influence of interpretive communities; the transformational power of texts to transcend culture and the conforming power of culture to influence texts; and the agency of the individual writer over culture/tradition and the influence of culture/tradition on the individual writer. My readings of Chinese American texts in Parts Two through Four of this book reflect my belief in the dynamic interplay of reader, author, and text.

Fish's ideas about interpretive communities allow us to see that "properties" and "intentions" are not always organic to a text, but can be "assigned to" a text by a reader. Furthermore, the fact that readers share with others the same assumptions about particular texts is evidence that "interpretive communities" exist. In this chapter, I examine the ways in which Chinese American literature is sometimes influenced by the "properties" and "intentions" assigned to Chinese American texts and the Chinese American author by an interpretive community (and the publisher who anticipates the desires, beliefs, and tastes of that interpretive community) that is best described as Euro-American in outlook. The readers to whom I refer are those who are to various degrees conditioned by a Euro-American perspective. They tend to see America as an extension or development of European civilization, with various immigrant groups from around the world living within it (a view that could be held by a monoculturalist who defines "America" as white-European or by a multiculturalist who defines "America" as originally white-European but now culturally diverse). They may see the history of non-European immigrant groups as making important contributions to the building of America, but European history and the populating of the continent from the eastern seaboard remains for them the paramount American historical narrative. Furthermore, they tend to perceive white Americans of Western European ancestry to be the "mainstream" group of American society, not merely in numbers but, in the sense of defining "the norm." I am not judging the Euro-American interpretive community as "bad" or "good," neither do I expect them to be conservative rather than liberal, nor for that matter, white rather than black, Asian, or Latino/a.[1] The community of readers central to my analysis may be diverse in their backgrounds and their ethnicities, but they have this in common: they presuppose that "America" is a society rooted first and foremost in European history and tradition.

In the following section, I examine the discourse of a promotional summary and a review of a book on Chinatown in order to discover the kind of audience the writers envision. I hope, in this way, to describe some characteristics of what might be called Euro-American tastes and expectations as a means of exploring the connections between the historic and "literary" Chinatown.

SELLING THE DANGEROUS, MYSTERIOUS CHINATOWN

The HarperCollins' promotional copy of *Chinatown: A Portrait of a Closed Society* (1992) is a significant text in itself because of its position on the jacket of the book, a summary that is now used to describe the book on electronic cataloging systems in libraries and on cyber-bookstores like Amazon.com. The purpose of such a summary is to capture the interest of the potential reader and sell the book. To do this, the publisher highlights, and sometimes embellishes, various features of the book's content to stimulate reader interest. Thus, the image portrayed of Chinatown is not simply indicative of the book and the author's perspective, but of a major publisher's estimation of a reading community's taste. By exploring this text in its context as promotional material, we can isolate the features of Chinatown that the publisher deems "marketable" to potential book-buyers, and thereby describe the tastes and expectations of those readers. Below is the description in its entirety:

> Gwen Kinkead's fascinating book is an explanation of a mystery: Chinatown. In the first book in fifty years to break the code of silence about New York's *Chinatown*, Kinkead offers us an intimate portrait of an exciting community that is also one of the most insular and, until now, enigmatic in the Western Hemisphere, a vibrant, chaotic little piece of China

entirely segregated from the United States. Against all odds, Kinkead managed to get recent immigrants to Chinatown to speak to her—an astonishing feat for a *low faan* (a barbarian, white person) with a notepad. Her portraits of Chinatown's invisible people are intriguing. They work in its garment factories and restaurants, where child labor laws seem not to obtain; they do not speak English and have no desire or opportunity to learn the language; they rarely, if ever, venture outside Chinatown's boundaries and have no interest in the American world surrounding their enclave. Kinkead describes their family associations, the tongs, and the gangs they employ to extort and murder. She charts the growth of Chinese organized crime, now smuggling in half the heroin in the United States. She illuminates the Chinese work ethic, their attitude toward money, the extended-family obligations, their traditions of concubinage, the Chinese penchant for gambling, their newspapers—owned by Chinese in Asia who determine what is reported and how—the importance of food, Chinatown's millionaires, and more. A rich, eye-opening account of a little-known community, *Chinatown* is also a provocative reflection on assimilation and racism in this country.

The description of Chinatown in this text interweaves two broad themes: Chinatown as a mysterious and dangerous place, and Chinatown as a foreign and strange place. Chinatown is a "mystery," an "insular," "enigmatic," community of "tongs," "gangs," "heroin" smugglers, murderers, and extortionists who live under a "code of silence." The Chinese of Chinatown have their own way of life: their own "work ethic," their own "food," "newspapers," and laws (as suggested by the idea that "child labor" and "concubinage" are permissible in their community); and they have their own family relationships and habits (as in, for example, their "penchant for gambling"). They "rarely, if ever, venture outside"; and they look upon white people as "low faan," translated for us as "barbarians." All of these descriptions add up to an "exciting," "vibrant," "chaotic," "little piece of China" in the middle of an American city.

My concern here is not particularly with how accurate or inaccurate this picture of Chinatown may be, but with the way specific characteristics and problems associated with Chinatowns are portrayed to sell the book. Essentially, the book description produces an image of mystery and intrigue and invites the reader to join one brave white explorer in her dangerous ethnographic adventure into the interior of Chinatown. In the text, Gwen Kinkead is the champion of every sentence but one. She explains the mysteries, she "offers an intimate portrait," she "describes," she "charts," she "illuminates." "Against all odds," we are told, she "managed to get recent immigrants to speak." All this, the text proclaims, is an "astonishing feat." On the one hand, this kind of rhetoric in promotional copy is not surprising: the publisher is appealing to the reader's desire to get the inside story, to go where he or she could not go without a tour guide. However, the single-minded emphasis on Kinkead produces a story about the adventurer and the adventure, rather than about the community of people who live in Chinatown.[2] The copy follows the paradigm of white Orientalist rhetoric: the white adventurer from the civilized West explores the wild and chaotic pagan East in order to uncover its mysteries for her readers.

The fact that in this case there are no "wests" or "easts" in the geographical sense accentuates the cultural constructedness of Kinkead's adventure. The geographical territory is, as the description reminds us, "in the Western Hemisphere" and on American soil, yet it is constructed as foreign because of its cultural foreignness. The summary repeatedly calls attention to the territory of Chinatown, calling it "a little piece of China entirely segregated from the United States" and reminding the reader that the Chinatown "enclave" is "surround[ed]" by the American world. The insularity of its inhabitants is figured geographically as a border phenomenon: they are reluctant to "venture outside Chinatown's *boundaries*" (emphasis added). In this way, distinct "boundaries" are drawn between what is culturally American and Chinese in relation to the physical boundaries of Chinatown.

Moreover, we see from this description that Kinkead's "portraits of Chinatown's invisible people," the garment and restaurant workers and the child laborers, are presented not for the reader's concern or action, but for the reader's entertainment: they are "intriguing." Chinatown is given this mysterious and dangerous aura in order, it seems, to entice the reader into a titillating, voyeuristic quest. In short, the promotional copy divides *us* from *them* and offers to explore and explain *them* for *our* benefit and enjoyment.

Ultimately, the Chinatown produced in this summary cannot be equated with the actual Chinatown it claims to represent because its characteristics are selected and presented to match the book consumer's taste. This selective presentation of Chinatown endeavors not only to satisfy taste, but to *produce* taste. By presenting the cultural territory of Chinatown and its "fifty year . . . silence" as an enigma, readers are invited to desire answers, to know more, to encounter the secrets of the dangerous and sinister Chinatown.

The review of Kinkead's book by *Kirkus Reviews* lends more evidence to this reading of audience taste. The review is reproduced with the publisher's copy on Amazon.com, making it a promotional text even though its status as a "review" suggests that it is an evaluative text. In the *Kirkus Reviews*' description of Kinkead's book, the brave white adventurer motif is both repeated and enhanced. Furthermore, the dark underworld of Chinatown is mapped, not just physically, as in the previous text, but metaphorically. The review begins with this sentence: "Kinkead, a frequent *New Yorker* contributor, boldly knocks at the bamboo curtain shielding New York's Chinatown, until it lifts a bit—revealing a community so exotic as to be 'virtually a nation unto itself.' " As in the publisher's description, Chinatown is portrayed here as a foreign territory. Yet since the boundaries that divide the United States from this "little piece of China" are described as a "bamboo curtain," the text therefore imagines the dividing line between the two territories as a Chinese construction: "bamboo" providing the metonymical link to Chineseness. The image does not allow for a mutually constructed border, one in which white racism plays as distinct a role as Chinese xenophobia. Rather it is a unilateral construction and hence an emblem of Chinese insularity.

The exoticism of this image is compounded by the action connected with it. With the help of Kinkead, the curtain "lifts a bit—revealing an [exotic] community." The action of lifting the curtain signifies voyeurism. We readers stand on the outside of this enigmatic community and can now, thanks to Kinkead, peek behind the curtain. Like a lecher lifting a woman's skirt or a child lifting a rock to gaze at the teeming insects beneath, the reader is in the position of observer and Chinatown is the erotic or ugly object of the reader's gaze.

As with the publisher's copy, the review makes Kinkead the heroine of the story. The emphasis is not on the community of people, but on Kinkead's accomplishment. It is her knocking, her forthrightness, her hard work that allows us to peek behind the bamboo curtain. Added to Kinkead's persistence is a sense of her fearlessness and valor, as seen in the following excerpt:

> With the help of a Hong Kong-born translator, she slowly gains the confidence of waiters, shopkeepers, restaurateurs, healers, and so on, drawing on their stories, as well as on scholarly research, to piece together this personable look at "the largest Chinese community in the Western hemisphere." No mean feat, that: typical is the author's exploration of a dark alley leading to a decrepit tenement where she meets a withered ancient who says that Kinkead is the first white person he's spoken to in 60 years in Chinatown. What keeps 150,000 Chinese in this isolated, crowded, crumbling "slum"? Ironically, Kinkead finds, it's basically the urge to get out—

fulfilled through the single-minded accumulation of wealth. While Kinkead talks to men who work 80-hour weeks at menial jobs, live in dire poverty, and save a small fortune each year, her report makes it clear that the engine that drives Chinatown's economy is crime, festering in sweatshops and gambling halls, thriving on extortion and drug-dealing. Kinkead's too much of an outsider to penetrate the tongs and gangs that control Chinatown crime, but she offers comprehensive briefs on them, vivified by a tour of the mean streets with a veteran cop.

Kinkead is the image of bravery: she walks down the alleys, she meets the mysterious "ancients," she enters sweatshops, and rides the "mean streets" on night patrol with the police. It is important to recognize, however, that her bravery depends upon the characterization of the environment she explores. There is nothing valorous or even exciting about a reporter entering a warm, peaceful, hospitable community. Thus, the text plays on the image of the dark and dangerous underworld to enhance the danger, and hence the appeal, of the book. What lies beyond the bamboo curtain, then, is a world of dark alleys, decrepit tenements, gambling halls, sweatshops that are "festering" with illicit employment practices, streets that are teeming with drug-dealers, extortionists, and gangs. It is, both physically and morally, an "isolated, crowded, crumbling slum."

As the text states, "the engine that drives the Chinatown economy is crime." Yet this engine, the text implicitly reveals, is fueled by the "single-minded" devotion of the Chinese to making money. Thus, the vices and poverty of Chinatown are a self-created, self-perpetuating outgrowth of the Chinese mentality. What we see behind the curtain, or beneath the rock, is a morally degenerate race making a mess of their own community.

But why are we watching? What is the purpose of our gaze? These questions are answered in the final sentence of the review. The book, we are told in summary, is "an exotic and fascinating journey by a modern-day, urban Marco Polo." We gaze, therefore, because Chinatown is the Other: it is fascinating and exotic. Yet, more importantly, we gaze because Chinatown is the Beyond. It is foreign territory. It is a site so remote and inscrutable that, although it is urban and geographically American, it can only be accessed by the brave and bold journeys of a heroic adventurer.

The image of the dark, mysterious Chinatown produced in these two texts is the epitome of the Orientalist fantasy.[3] It presents an exoticized image of Chinatown, casting it as "the Far East" even though it stands geographically in America, and opening it up to the voyeuristic explorations of brave white people. We might expect such exoticizations of Chinatown to have disappeared in the more socially aware, multiculturally savvy 1990s, but, this is not the case. According to Edward Said, "Orientalism has less to do with the Orient than it does with 'our' world" (*Orientalism* 12). So it is with the dark, mysterious Chinatown. The two texts explored above allow us to see this self-reflective quality in the production of Chinatown because, as texts that promote and recommend a book, they necessarily anticipate the tastes of their readers. In both texts, it is evident that what sells is not the bridging of differences between the Chinatown community and the rest of the city, but the enhancing of those differences in order to territorialize, dramatize, and exoticize that community.[4] What sells, the texts assume, is the brave exploits of the book's author.

The questions I explore below center on the problematic suggested here of imaging and reception. Where does this image of Chinatown originate? Who produces it? Whose interests does it serve? What are its historical antecedents? Finally, and most importantly for this study, in what ways are these questions and their answers related to the production of, and reception of, Chinese American literature today?

THE PRODUCTION OF CHINATOWN

The reception of Chinese American literature can be described and understood in the historical context of the production of the American Chinatowns. In short, the ghettoization of Chinese American literature as a "literary Chinatown" is produced by the same dynamics that ghettoized the Chinese American community into literal Chinatowns. A brief history of the development of Chinatowns in America will help establish these connections.

What Ronald Takaki, in his acclaimed *Strangers from a Different Shore,* calls the "ethnic island" (230) of Chinatown has long been the icon of the Chinese American community in many large cities. At one end of the spectrum, Chinatowns have come to represent the expression of Chinese culture and the affirmation of Chinese "rootedness"; at the other, they have represented an emblem of backwardness and "dangerous" paganism. Whatever the portrayal, it is often assumed that Chinatowns are the creation of Chinese immigrants: an act of their will and an expression of their culture. What is often overlooked, however, is the role played by the "observers" in creating the conditions for such separate and disparate communities. According to K. Scott Wong, "portrayals of Chinatown [over the past century] had as much to do with Euro-American images of themselves as they did of the Chinese immigrant community" (4). The actual formation of Chinatowns was determined as much by these same Euro-American attitudes as it was by self-fashioned ideas of community.

The development of Chinatowns in the United States over the last century might appear to the casual observer to be a self-determining communal phenomenon. The clustering of Chinese immigrants in these "ethnic islands" reinforces a notion of essential cultural differences: that Chinese immigrants prefer their culture, their food, language, and social customs; and that Chinese immigrants desire not to assimilate, but to reproduce their culture on American soil. Such cloistering is perceived as an act of empowerment: rather than sprinkling themselves throughout the land, Chinese immigrants congregate in Chinatowns to increase their visibility and hence their representation in the American political and social imagination.

These perceptions ignore the historical reality of Chinatowns, revealing at best a half-truth. Takaki explains that by the 1940s, Chinatowns were indeed "home and community" (253) to Chinese immigrants; a place where grocery stores, clothing stores, and restaurants sold familiar goods, where temples, Chinese-language schools, and centers for family associations provided cultural coherence to a diasporic people (253). For many, Chinatowns were a "home away from home" that created the illusion of living in China (253–54). However, the formation of these cultural enclaves, as well as their continued development, had less to do with self-determined community than with exigency.

The establishment of the large, urban Chinatowns in the late-nineteenth century was the product of political and economic forces driven by racism.[5] The completion of the transcontinental railroad, the influx of white migrant farmers to the west, and the decline in the gold mining industry were three significant factors that "pushed [the Chinese] from the small towns . . . [and into] the metropolitan cities where employment was available in an ethnic-labor market" (Takaki 239). No longer useful to the project of western expansion, Chinese workers were left to find employment among their own people in a service industry of mainly laundries, grocery stores, and restaurants. A plethora of racist laws aimed to drive out the Chinese, most significantly, the Chinese Exclusion Act of 1882 and the National Origins Act of 1924 institutionalized the sentiment that the Chinese should leave the United States once their purpose had been served. Those who chose to stay met with strong resistance. Efforts to compete for white jobs or even to rent lodging in white neighborhoods were met with hostility and often violence (246). In short, "the Chinese had been driven out of the general labor market and forced to withdraw to those occupations 'where no bitter voice' would be raised against them" (240).

Although the development of the big urban Chinatowns was marred by overcrowding, insufficient sanitation, and squalor, the community soon found that their increased visibility in the large cities could reap economic empowerment, albeit at a price. "A ghetto, Chinatown confirmed views of the Chinese as unhealthy, unassimilable, and undesirable immigrants, yet this same negative imagery opened the way to the development of Chinatown as a tourist center—a 'quaint' and 'mysterious' section of the city, a 'foreign colony' in America" (Takaki 246). The tourism industry promoted China- towns as exotic and mysteriously dangerous places. Tourists were warned to stick together as they walked through bogus opium dens and witnessed dramatic antics like opium addicts fighting over slave girls. They learned of "dark underground tunnels filled with opium dens, gambling joints and brothels where slave girls were imprisoned" (249). In San Francisco alone, the tourist trade was generating $28 million dollars a year for the city by 1938, "of which nearly one fifth was spent in Chinatown" (248).

As with the economic, political, and social forces which led to the for- mation of Chinatowns, as well as with the imagery which advertised the exotic and mysterious in the establishment of the tourist trade, the representation of Chinatowns through much of the twentieth century was thus motivated by Euro-American attitudes toward the Chinese more than by Chinese Amer- ican definitions of their own community. K. Scott Wong argues that the rep- resentation of Chinatowns as "forever foreign to American sensibilities . . . perversely helped define what American communities 'ought' to be like: clean, without odor, safe, and Christian" (4). In other words, the representations of Chinatown were not motivated by a deepening interest in Chinese immi- grants and their welfare, but by a hegemonic aim to define and cement "cor- rect" notions of Americanness in a Euro-American model. Lisa Lowe connects these attitudes to the project of nation building, in which Asian Americans were "racialized" in the Euro-American imagination and rheto- ric in order to define the terms of citizenship: "the history of the nation's attempt to resolve the contradictions between its economic and political imperatives through laws that excluded Asians from citizenship—from 1790 until the 1940s—contributes to our general understanding of *race* as a con- tradictory site of struggle for cultural, economic, as well as political mem- bership in the United States" (*Immigrant Acts* ix). Thus, images of Chinatown and of Chinese Americans are not unilateral self-expressions of culture and identity, but are the result of a complex process of designation and response in a hegemonic, racist cultural situation.

Today, the image of Chinese America seems to be much different. Chinese Americans are no longer excluded from American citizenship, and indeed, they are positively regarded as citizens and contributors. Once confined to service industry employment in an ethnic market, Chinese Americans have propelled themselves into professional positions in American society (through hard work and the pursuit of education and, as some would argue, through the liberty afforded by American laws). Elaine H. Kim describes Asian Americans in the 1990s, of which Chinese Americans are of course a subset, as follows:

> Today, Asian American artists are making history with new novels, poetry, films and videos, sculpture, painting, installation, and performance art. We are already familiar with the Asian American female television news anchors. Now we are beginning to see more and more Asian American bylines at many daily newspapers across the country—not just in Honolulu and Los Angeles, but also in New York and Philadelphia. They write news stories of all kinds, as well as book and film reviews. One of President Clinton's speechwriters was a young Chinese American Yale graduate. Record numbers of Asian Americans are entering the professions, including law, public policy, and public administration. If present trends continue, the twenty-first century should be a century when Asian Americans will speak and write as well as listen and read, when they will be taken seriously as readers, viewers, voters and constituents. ("Gatekeepers" 205)

This vision of Asian Americans contrasts stunningly with the Chinatown experience of Chinese immigrants in the very recent past (though, as elaborated below, Kim sees negative implications in this new and "positive" image—as suggested by the title of her article, "Asian Americans: Decorative Gatekeepers?"). It would appear that, given this list of achievements, Chinese Americans have carved for themselves a definitive and significant space within the American landscape.

When we critically examine these images of achievement, we find what can aptly be called, to borrow the title of V. S. Naipaul's book, "the enigma of arrival."[6] In many cases, the high regard shown to Chinese Americans in American society is motivated by a Euro-American perspective that, as with the negative imaging of Chinatown in the past, seeks to contain and manage the foreign Other. This agenda of containment, whether consciously formulated or not, is manifested in various ways. One manifestation is the discourse of difference. For example, in response to positive descriptions of Chinatown, K. Scott Wong comments that "beneath this positive facade . . . Chinatown is still cast as foreign to America, where difference reigns and the people are bound by the confines of race and culture" (12). In other words, even what appears to be a celebration of cultural color and richness has its negative flipside. Difference, no matter how positively reported, is the *potential* building block of distance and containment: once the Other is named and categorized as different, it can then be rejected as not belonging, as, in this case, "un-American."[7] Conversely, as I elaborate in chapter 2, this "difference" can become the basis of a qualified "acceptance": in a society where ethnic difference is prized, it becomes a lucrative commodity. According to David Leiwei Li, "the apparent goodwill exhibited by commercial houses in publishing Asian American texts in recent years, and the occasional Asian media presence on network television must be read less as an indicator of cultural equalization than as a new realization of the ancient profit motive that undergirds capitalism" (*Imagining the Nation* 195).

Another manifestation of the agenda of containment is the characterization of the Chinese American community as the "model minority group." Following her list of Asian American achievements quoted earlier, Kim casts her eyes to the next century and cautions that "Asian Americans may find ourselves stuck in twenty-first-century versions of today's 'model minority' identity," what she calls a "gatekeeper function" in which Asian Americans become the token minority for those who lobby and argue against increasing opportunities for ethnic minorities and for the preservation of the *status quo* ("Gatekeepers" 206). K. Scott Wong echoes this warning in adding that the "'model minority' images of Chinatown were also part of a larger political agenda designed not to praise Chinese-Americans but to attack the African American underclass" (12). To those opposed or resistant to minority rights, evidence that one minority group is capable of succeeding in American society suggests that problems faced by other minority groups are due less to the attitudes of non-Asian Americans and the policies of the American government than they are due to deficiencies within those minority groups. Relating this to the case of literature, Frank Chin and his collaborators write in the introduction to *Aiiieeeee!* that "much of Asian

American literary history is a history of a small minority being cast into the role of the good guy in order to make another American minority look bad" (4).[8]

These warnings suggest that what seems to be acceptance, approval, and freedom for today's Chinese American should not be blindly and uncritically accepted as such. Even Kim's positive characterization of Asian Americans being "taken seriously as readers, viewers, voters and constituents" ("Gatekeepers" 205) can have its negative side. On the one hand, being "taken seriously" means (as I believe Kim intends it to mean) that American society recognizes Asian Americans as real people with genuine political clout. The caricatures and stereotypes of the forever-foreign Chinaman are finally beginning to disappear. On the other hand, there is something unreal and incomplete about a community that demands too much seriousness. It is, perhaps, in danger of encasing itself in yet another form of differential treatment based, for instance, on overcompensation, which is why humor in novels such as *American Knees* and *Mona in the Promised Land* can be seen as a strategic intervention. Once again, what seems to be achievement and arrival can all too easily become another form, or sign, of enslavement.

The prominence of Asia in the rise of the global economy in the last quarter of the twentieth century presents similar opportunities for Chinese Americans to rest uncritically on their laurels. Besides enjoying an increased involvement and influence in American life, Chinese Americans are at a historical juncture in their relation to the majority culture *vis-à-vis* their relation to a newly significant Asia (an especially precarious juncture since the late 1990s, considering the impact of Asia's financial crisis which began in 1997). In Sau-ling Cynthia Wong's analysis of this juncture, she cites among other phenomena the "growing permeability between 'Asian' and 'Asian American'" and a rising diasporic cosmopolitanism to explain the ways that today's Asian American population differs significantly from that of the recent past ("Denationalization" 5, 9). The economic and political forces that formed the Chinatowns of old put Chinese Americans in a position of subaltern dependence and desperation; fleeing political upheaval and economic deprivation in their homeland, they chose to live and work as immigrants in a hostile foreign environment. Today, however, the economic empowerment of many Asian countries, and the establishment of the Pacific Rim as a locus of trade and diplomacy that has begun to displace the Eurocentric focus of the American economy, has produced new attitudes among, and toward, Asian Americans. "Thus," writes Wong, "instead of being mere supplicants at the 'golden door', desperate to trade their sense of ethnic identity for a share of America's plenty, many of today's Asian immigrants regard the U.S. as simply one of many possible places to exercise their portable capital and portable skills" ("Denationalization" 5).

Elaine H. Kim's "gatekeeper function" applies not only to the maintenance of minority order in the United States, but also to the political, economic, and social maintenance of Asia. Asian Americans find themselves more and more useful as gatekeepers to an emerging Asia. "From this perspective," argues Sau-ling Cynthia Wong, "language and cultural maintenance [of Asian Americans] is chiefly a business asset, not a matter of community-building" ("Denationalization" 13). Today, therefore, Chinese Americans are no longer excluded from citizenship on racial and cultural grounds, but, because of the politics of an emerging global economy, they are embraced as a vital link between the United States and Asia. Likewise, Chinese American identity is no longer a matter of "ascription" in a Euro-American political agenda, but is now masked in the more positive construction of "achievement" (a difference in ethnic construction noted by Zygmunt Bauman [49]), which is, nevertheless, still a by-product of Euro-American perceptions, expectations, and motives.

Zygmunt Bauman's warning against the illusion of arrival is thus pertinent to the current development of the Chinese American community:

> True, communal self-determination may assist the initial stages of the long process of re-empowerment of human subjects—give the first push towards a fully fledged citizenship. But there is a dangerous and easily overlooked point where re-empowerment turns into a new dis-empowerment, and emancipation into a new oppression. (57)

In all appearances, Chinese Americans have finally achieved "fully fledged citizen[ship]" in American society. Yet there is a real sense, which many objectors to the "model minority" label have recognized, in which the seeming "re-empowerment" of the Chinese American community can all too easily turn into "a new dis-empowerment." There is a sense in which what seems to be "emancipation" threatens to become a "new oppression" (57).

LITERARY CHINATOWN

The enigma of arrival can be seen clearly in the reception of Chinese American literature, a literature which, by giving "voice" and "visibility" to the Chinese American community, can be seen as one of the key indicators of the empowerment of Chinese Americans. It is a well-known fact, for instance, that Maxine Hong Kingston's *The Woman Warrior* is "one of the most taught works on college campuses nationwide [in the United States]" (Yang et al. 29). "One chapter or another," writes Thomas J. Ferraro, "appears in all four of the major anthologies of U.S. literature published in the late 1980s and early 1990s. . . . [The book] has been treated to an early canonization" (218, 154). Surpassing *The Woman Warrior* in popularity is Amy Tan's best-seller *The Joy Luck Club*, which, according to a perhaps too exuberant estimation by the authors of *Eastern Standard Time*, is not only "the most commercially successful novel ever written by an Asian American writer, [but is] one of the most successful novels ever, regardless of author ethnicity" (Yang et al. 29). The film version of *Joy Luck* and David Henry Hwang's Broadway hit *M. Butterfly* have further increased the visibility of Chinese American artistic production. The "Preliminaries" to the Spring 1995 issue of *MELUS*, which was devoted entirely to Chinese American literature, describes the growth of this literature as follows:

> From the trickle of nineteenth century autobiography, travel writing and poetry, [Chinese American literature] has grown into *a formidable stream of distinguished works by writers recognized and celebrated throughout the country*. In the last twenty years, Frank Chin, Maxine Hong Kingston, David Henry Hwang, Amy Tan, Gus Lee, and Gish Jen have all *achieved levels of cultural visibility* that make them special; other Chinese-American writers, like John Yau, David Wong Louie, Marilyn Chin, Li-Young Lee and Shawn Wong, while not yet reaching so broad an audience, are as celebrated for their artistry. (1, emphasis added)

Like the burgeoning Chinatowns in the first half of the twentieth century, Chinese American writers have increased the visibility of their community. Yet, as Christine So has observed, some critics have "sounded a cautionary note to readers who readily assume that the recent proliferation of Asian American writings automatically stands as an act of resistance and an end to racism against Asian Americans" (141). The success of Asian American literature, in other words, can be seen as what Said, writing in a different context, calls "signs and symbols of freedom and status" that must not be taken as "the reality" ("Knowledge" 149).[9] The forces of racism and consumerism that led Chinatown into cultural prostitution threaten to undo the empowerment signified by Chinese American literature.[10]

A greater understanding of the meeting point between Chinese American literature and Euro-American expectations—that is, a greater understanding of its reception—is essential to assessing Chinese American literature at this point in its history. To avoid assumptions of "arrival," we must not look simply at the fact that Chinese American texts are being published (these are what Said calls the "signs" and "symbols" of arrival), but we must go beyond this question to ask what are the conditions of this acceptance and how are these texts viewed by readers? To establish more concretely the nature of the literary Chinatown, I will sketch out three of the literary Chinatown's manifestations: (1) the tendency to view all Chinese American works as a Chinese American cultural project produced solely *for* the Chinese American community, (2) the tendency to read inscrutability and exoticism into Chinese American literature, and (3) the tendency to conflate all Chinese American works into a homogeneous thematic preoccupation of nativism versus assimilation.

1. Cultural Companions: Misreading Pangs of Love

One manifestation of the literary Chinatown phenomenon is the tendency for readers to view Chinese American texts as Chinese American cultural projects. That is, the reader expects a Chinese American text to be about, or for, the Chinese American community and not necessarily about "America." To illustrate how this occurs, I will discuss the ways in which a review of David Wong Louie's book of short stories, *Pangs of Love*, confines the text to the literary Chinatown through assumptions of homogeneity of cultural vision among Chinese American writers and the marketability of Chinese American ethnicity among book-buyers. This review, produced by *Kirkus Reviews*, is now used in marketing Louie's book on Amazon.com and is quoted on the Plume paperback edition of *Pangs of Love*. It begins with the following sentence:

> A debut collection of 11 stories from Asian-American Louie, chronicling the displaced lives of Asian immigrants and of first-generation American-born children: mainly taut and energetic pieces, a worthy (if more prosaic) companion to recent similar chronicles by Amy Tan, Maxine Hong Kingston, and others.

The review first packages Louie's text into a niche genre: Asian American chronicle. The themes are neatly collapsed and labeled: immigrant experience. The writing is judged: "taut and energetic." Comparisons with the leading figures of the genre are made: "worthy companion to Amy Tan [and] Maxine Hong Kingston." That there are more than two Asian American writers in existence is acknowledged even if they are not named: "and others."

However, a close comparison between Louie's book itself and the above review proves baffling. Of the eleven stories, only one, "Displacement," is specifically about Chinese American immigrants adjusting to life in America, while two, "Pangs of Love" and "Inheritance," are about what some would consider "first-generation" children. This means a total of only three stories actually fit the description, "displaced lives of Asian immigrants and of first-generation American-born children." In four of the stories the ethnic identity of central characters is not specified. In the remaining stories, ethnicity is either decentralized, incidental, or approached in ways uncharacteristic of the type of literature to which the *Kirkus* review alludes: Asian American chronicle.

Far from being a "companion to Amy Tan, Maxine Hong Kingston, and others," Louie's book is clearly a *departure* from them. In fact, *Pangs of Love* does not tread old ground despite the obvious commercial success of works that do (one reason, perhaps, that *Pangs of Love*, at least at the time of this book, is out of print). Louie's book attempts to resist typical categorizations, however fair or unfair they may be, refusing to reify Asianness and thereby essentializing Asian Americans and placing them in a private corner of the American experience. Rather, the book creates a sense of hybridity in its presentation of Asian Americans and in the myriad ways in which Asian Americans—more specifically, Chinese Americans—engage in the totality of American life. In a description that contrasts sharply with the *Kirkus* review, David L. Eng describes Louie's book in the following terms:

> These short stories—set in cities, upscale suburbs, and the beaches of Long Island—depict an ostensibly desegregated and integrated Asian America through the proliferation and hybridity of their multiple locations. . . . Louie's male characters are not traditional Chinatown cooks, waiters, or laundrymen. They are no longer just the objects but also the subjects of capitalism, a professional class of commercial artists, café owners, corporate chemists, and designers of home video games—model minorities with economic mobility. (193–94)

Why, then, does the *Kirkus* review lump Louie's book together with other Asian American works of a quite different nature? And why does the review claim an overarching thematic unity based on three out of eleven stories?

To answer these questions, we turn to the seemingly innocent yet telling phrase, "Asian-American Louie." For it is here, in the notion of the author's identity (David Wong Louie's ethnicity) that the enigmatic categorization finds its most likely explanation. The author's ethnicity is the starting point for the selling and reception of the book, for, as will be established in chapter 2, the perceived ethnicity of the author is the lowest common denominator in the categorization of a literature as ethnic. From the author's ethnicity, expectations of ethnic literature, immigrant experience, identity shaping, and family narrative, among others, are foregrounded in the reader's consciousness. We could say, therefore, that the ethnic identity of the author semiotically codes the text from the outset, sealing it hermetically in terms of the perception of ethnicity in vogue at the time of reading.

A further dimension is added in the case of the above review, that, by its very nature *as* a book review, projects to an audience of book *consumers* and is therefore written to recommend (even, in its position as promotional material, to *sell*) the book. The reviewer clearly expects these readers to be familiar with *The Joy Luck Club* and *The Woman Warrior*, but not necessarily the "others." Thus, the categorization of Louie's book as belonging in essence to a genre of immigrant or ethnic-identity literature codifies for readers / consumers a specific type of reading experience with which they are familiar: literature about cross-cultural tension and interesting differences of perception, or, as Palumbo-Liu describes in a similar incident, "it has animated exactly the expected themes of subject-split, cultural alienation and confusion, and coming-to-terms that fits the stereotypical image of the model minority" (*Asian/American* 410). I would also argue that the review anticipates the reader's taste for mysterious and mystical elements in Asian American and other ethnic literature, such as spirits and ghosts and shamanism. The one difference identified by the reviewer which separates Louie's book from the others is its "prosaic" quality[11]; what seems to be on view here is the absence of mysticism and a kind of mystical mythology in Louie's book which color and, to borrow Shirley Geok-lin Lim's phrase, easily exoticize the experience of reading books like *The Woman Warrior* and *The Joy Luck Club*.

The rapid duplication of the style of Chinese American literature introduced by Kingston and Tan threatens to give Chinese American literature a privatized and comfortable quality. The type of Chinese American literature being published, or at least the way it is packaged, has tended to create the general perception that Chinese American literature is a specialized genre— usually about "mother-daughter" relationships—that is about and for the Chinese American community and those interested in "Asian things." I do not mean here that Chinese Americans are the intended audience of this literature or that non-Chinese Americans would not be interested in its themes. On the contrary, there has been a keen interest among readers in Chinese American literature since the mid- to late-1980s. What I mean is that readers perceive the aims of Chinese American literature as a community project: that is, in identifying, debating, and coming to terms with Chinese American identity, Chinese Americans are learning to "express" themselves and to "find" themselves. Non-Chinese Americans are therefore spectators. Palumbo-Liu argues in this regard that "the perpetuation in marketing of Asian American literature as the literature of an assimilated group now at peace after a 'phase' of adjustment is dangerous in its powerful closing-off of a multiplicity of real, lived, social contradictions and complexities that stand outside (or at least significantly complicate) the formula of the highly individuated 'identity crisis'" (*Asian/American* 410). Due to the oft-repeated themes of immigration and assimilation, Chinese American literature can fall into the category of family-assimilation saga, a kind of Chinese American *Bildungsroman*,[12] which suggests the recording of family history and with it the development of personal (most prominently, female) and communal identity.[13]

In short, it is the reader's perception (specifically here, the reviewer's perception) of Chinese American literature as a whole, not the content of Louie's debut book of stories, that the reviewer has in mind when claiming that the book is about "the displaced lives of Asian immigrants and of first-generation American-born children." By defining and packaging the book as immigrant "chronicle," the reviewer unwittingly projects the image of a non-threatening, comfortable reading experience. Thus, we can expect a book not about America, but about Asians. Ultimately, it is a comfortable book for white Americans to read because it is not about *us*; it is about *them*. As with the description of *Monkey King* discussed in the introduction, the reader is invited to view Chinese America from the position of an armchair sociologist.

Louie's book is thus emasculated, sapped of its provocative, dynamic vision of America, essentially because he is perceived as being ethnically Chinese and therefore engaged in an enterprise on par with, or easily categorized with, other Chinese American writers (who, by the way, are also *perceived*, perhaps unfairly, as cultural navel-gazers).[14] Moreover, the overarching message of the book is either missed or ignored because of the review's function in the marketplace. *Pangs of Love* is forced into a category of literature simply because that category *sells*.

What the reviewer sees in these stories is a reflection of the period in which the review was written. This is evident when we consider that the stories in *Pangs of Love* were written before Chinese American fiction began to sell well in the United States (that is, before the rise of the Chinese American novel signaled by the success of *Joy Luck* in 1989). As Louie revealed in an interview in *Time* magazine, it was the "rejection-slip" comments by editors in "the mid-70s" (or at least his perception of these rejections) that led him to de-emphasize ethnicity in many of his stories. Masking ethnicity in his work was therefore motivated by his (and his potential publishers') view of market tastes.[15] However, by the time *Pangs of Love* was published in 1991, market tastes had changed; indeed, "Displacement," his story about a Chinese immigrant couple adjusting to life in America, was published in *The Best American Short Stories 1989*, the year Amy Tan achieved international fame. The origin of this ethnic ambiguity is interesting from a reception perspective. It illustrates a dynamic interplay between the assumptions of authors about editors and of editors about readers that influence the ways stories are presented. In terms of the *Kirkus* review excerpt above, it reveals a profound irony: what Louie *wrote out* of his stories to make them more marketable has been *read back into* them for the same reason.

2. Reading the Inscrutable and Exotic

As with my discussion of the historic Chinatown, my analysis of the *Kirkus Reviews* treatment of *Pangs of Love* reveals that the image of Chinese American literature is not solely determined by the writers of Chinese American texts, since it is equally a product of reading markets (or, more precisely, the publishing industry's perception of reading markets). Nowhere is this more noticeable than in the reading market's conception of Chinese American literature as "inscrutable" and "exotic." Here the metaphor of the literary Chinatown melts into reality as the very imagery that painted the historic Chinatown (even as recently as HarperCollins' *Chinatown: A Portrait of a Closed Society* by Gwen Kinkead in 1992) as a dangerously mysterious and foreign terrain is transposed upon the literature of Chinese America.

My focus here is on the ways that readers *read* inscrutability and exoticism *into* texts. The images invoked by reviewers of Chinese American works often have more to say about readers and their attitudes than they do about the particular work under review. Response to *The Woman Warrior*, because of its significance in the emergence of contemporary Chinese American literature, provides an important and vivid example of this phenomenon. When Kingston's novel was published in 1975, it received mostly favorable reviews from the press, but at the same time, as explained in the opening pages of this book, was pegged as an example of the mysterious oriental mind. The following examples come from Kingston's article, "Cultural Mis-readings," which was introduced at the beginning of this book:

> Barbara Burdick in the *Peninsula Herald* [says]: "No other people have remained so mysterious to Westerners as the inscrutable Chinese. Even the word China brings to mind ancient rituals, exotic teas, superstitions, silks and fire-breathing dragons."

> Helen Davenport of the Chattanooga *News-Free Press* [contends]: "At her most obscure, though, as when telling about her dream of becoming a fabled 'woman warrior' the author becomes as inscrutable as the East always seems to the West. In fact, this book seems to reinforce the feeling that 'East is East and West is West and never the twain shall meet,' or at any rate it will probably take more than one generation away from China." (56)

This perceived inscrutability in *The Woman Warrior* led many (most poignantly, Frank Chin and the *Aiiieeeee!* editors, though their objection had more to do with the "feminizing" and "Christianizing" of Chinese Americans) to blame Kingston for continuing the Asian American literary tradition of "pander[ing] opportunistically to racist exoticism" (Ferraro 154). However, Kingston objected in her article to this perception of both her book and of herself: "what I did not foresee was the critics measuring the book and me against the stereotype of the exotic, inscrutable, mysterious oriental" ("Cultural Mis-readings" 55). "To say we are inscrutable, mysterious, exotic," she writes, "denies us our common humanness because it says that we are so different from a regular human being that we are by our nature intrinsically unknowable" (57). Kingston places the blame for casting an enigmatic aura over the book and exoticizing her in the process squarely on the reader. "The stereotyper aggressively defends ignorance" (57), she says.

Kingston's description exhibits the links between reader expectations and the images portrayed by the politically motivated, self-defining Euro-Americanism that sought to confine Chinese Americans to the historic Chinatown. Kingston writes,

> To call a people exotic freezes us into the position of being always alien—politically a most sensitive point with us because of the long history in America of the Chinese Exclusion Acts, the deportations, the law denying us citizenship when we have been part of America since its beginning. By giving the "oriental" (always Eastern, never *here*) inhuman, unexplain-

able qualities, the racist abrogates human qualities, and, carrying all this to extremes, finds it easier to lynch the Chinaman, bomb Japan, napalm Vietnam. ("Cultural Mis-readings" 57)

In other words, the exoticizing of the Chinese American serves a socio-political purpose. It is not an honest, accurate description of Chinese Americans. Rather, it is an act of distancing and containment. When readers exoticize Chinese Americans, they distance them from white America, making it easier to justify their exclusion from a Euro-American construction of "America."

The whole of Kingston's essay is a protest against the literary Chinatown. In her opinion, the inscrutable and exotic are myths that *The Woman Warrior* explodes. For example, Kingston explains that the "White Tigers" segment of the book is placed toward the beginning to emphasize that it is a "childish myth [in the] past" instead of the ultimate goal of a Chinese American. Moreover, it is "not a Chinese myth [at all] but one transformed by America" (57). But Kingston claims that the reason "Americans" privilege this segment, and even suggest that it should be the climax of the book, is that they "stubbornly . . . hang on to the oriental fantasy" (57). They refuse to see the book, and the author, as American, choosing instead to emphasize its foreignness to mainstream America.

Despite the seeming growth in sophistication among readers of ethnic literature in the more than twenty years since the publication of *The Woman Warrior*, the act of reading inscrutability and exoticism into it and other Chinese American texts still persists. Thomas J. Ferraro writes, "although critics sufficiently alert to Orientalism do not [in the 1990s] describe Kingston as exotic, a disconcerting tendency to impute mystery to *The Woman Warrior* has remained" (154). According to Ferraro, the "inscrutability" of *The Woman Warrior* is most often explained as a product of its form: "theoreticians speak of the doubleness of the memoir—a shuttling between two languages, two audiences, and two cultures—in such a way as to sustain the aura of impenetrability that surrounds the book" (154–55). However, he argues, "*The Woman Warrior* is neither as innovative in form nor as discomforting in its amalgamations as critics have assumed. . . . The way Kingston fuses fact and myth, her multiple voices, the insertion of oral traditions into written narrative— all date, at least, from the rise of modernism" (155).

If the mystique of *The Woman Warrior* is not attributed to its form or style, then what accounts for it? It could be, as some have asserted (Reed Way Dasenbrock and Michael J. Fischer, for example, both quoted in Ferraro [155]), that the seeming inscrutability of Kingston's book reflects the experience of ethnic difference in America, or the particular experience of grappling with an incoherent, fragmented oral tradition in Chinese American families. These views situate the mystique of the book in the Chinese American experience. I would like to suggest that it is not so much "the Chinese past" that tyrannizes Kingston's book as it is the American past—that is, the historic tendency of the Euro-American outlook to mysticize and exoticize the Chinese who immigrated to America.

3. The Nativist and Assimilationist Poles

In her oft-cited 1991 article published in *Diaspora* and entitled "Heterogeneity, Hybridity, Multiplicity: Marking Asian American Differences" (reprinted in *Immigrant Acts*), Lisa Lowe highlights an essentializing phenomenon in the reading of Chinese American texts similar to those explored above. Lowe identifies the common perception of Chinese American literature as a binary relationship between nativism and assimilationism which figures in literature "in the *topos* . . . of generational conflict" ("Heterogeneity" 34). At one pole is literature which valorizes nativism by characterizing Chinese American culture as essentially Chinese: the focus is on roots and the vision is one of stasis. Under this rubric, assimilation is the enemy of Chinese Americans, for the loss of what is Chinese is a capitulation to white imperialist forces and an erasure of self.[16] The resolution of generational conflicts in nativist literature thus emphasizes a renewal of Chinese sentiment. At the other pole is literature which valorizes assimilation by painting a modern picture of positive social transformation from the prison of, for example, patriarchal, pre-industrialized, or communist roots to the freedom of modern American democracy or Anglo-American feminism. The resolution of generational conflicts in assimilationist literature thus emphasizes the renewal offered by modern America. Readers tend to view all Chinese American literature as operating in this nativist/assimilationist binary.

Lowe offers readings of several Chinese American texts which suggest that while this *topos* of nativism versus assimilationism in generational conflicts features prominently in much Chinese American literature, the privileging of this motif by writers and critics alike masks the complex and importantly heterogeneous relationships within the Chinese American community and the wider Asian American community.[17] Lowe argues that

interpreting Asian American culture exclusively in terms of the master narratives of generational conflict and filial relation essentializes Asian

American culture, obscuring the particularities and incommensurabilities of class, gender, and national diversities among Asians; the reduction of ethnic cultural politics to struggles between first and second generations displaces (and privatizes) inter-community differences into a familial opposition. ("Heterogeneity" 26)

One example to support her thesis is Lowe's reading of *The Joy Luck Club*. Often read as the classic conflict between the nativism of the older Chinese generation and the assimilationism of the younger "Americanized" generation, Lowe suggests that a much broader and more complex vision is being portrayed. In her view, "*Joy Luck* multiplies the sites of cultural conflict, positing a number of struggles—familial and extrafamilial—as well as resolutions, without privileging the singularity or centrality of one" (35). Lowe notes that the tensions in the four mother-daughter relationships in the novel differ in their sources, expressions, and resolutions of conflict, and even extend beyond the mother-daughter relationship, thus refiguring generational conflict in a complex model and extending the interpretation of the struggle to "different conceptions of class and gender among Chinese-Americans" (37). An example of this is the scene in which Waverly Jong treats her mother to a visit to the beauty salon. While Waverly believes she is pampering her mother, the latter sees it as an insult, as though her daughter were ashamed of her. According to Lowe, "the scene not only marks the separation of mother and daughter by generation but, perhaps less obviously, their separation by class and cultural differences that lead to different interpretations of how female identity is signified" (37). What this analysis suggests is that *Joy Luck* does not have to be read as a simple generational conflict between the two poles of nativism and assimilationism with a unitary vision oriented toward one or the other.

What I find intriguing about Lowe's critique is what it implies, by extension, about the expectations of readers and the power of those expectations to influence the view of Chinese America in a text. In Fish's terminology, the nativist/assimilationist preoccupation is an *interpretive strategy* that is common to a particular *interpretive community*. As discussed earlier in this chapter, Fish's view is that our agreements and disagreements over the meaning of texts do not always hinge upon what the texts say but upon the interpretive communities to which we belong by virtue of the interpretive strategies we employ. In other words, Fish claims that what we "see" in a text is not inevitably the same as what is "there" in the text; and what is "there" in the text may simply be, and cannot be differentiated from, what we "see" in the text. Thus, the whole question of priority (which came first, the text or the interpretation?) is a bogus question to Fish because the two, text and interpretation, cannot be separated. In Fish's estimation, reading *is* interpretation. It is hopeless, if one accepts this view, to attempt to establish that a particular interpretation arises organically from the text. It cannot. What differentiates the various interpretations of a text, indeed what arguments over texts are all about, is not the text itself but the mode of interpretation, the way the reader reads, which is what Fish calls "interpretive strategies" (*Is There a Text in This Class?* 168). The act of reading can therefore be described as the application of these strategies. Whether the strategy privileges symbolic structure, thematic unity, super- and sub-structure, patterns of masculinity and paternalism, or, in our case, assimilationism versus nativism, readers will formulate an interpretation based on what their strategies are looking for.

As I explained previously, I do not agree with Fish's entire argument and its implications. However, I do agree that our expectations and prejudices are capable of coloring our reception of literature in the ways he describes, if not to the extent.[18] Thus, the tendency to reduce the complex and multiple variables in a Chinese American text to a singular, prefabricated formula, as with the aforementioned examples from *Pangs of Love*, *The Woman Warrior*, and *The Joy Luck Club*, may not be a function of the text, but a function of the reader—more precisely, of the interpretive strategies that readers employ. Thus, Lowe is suggesting that we apply a new and, in her opinion, more historically valid interpretive strategy. Furthermore, we should note that the privatizing of Chinese American themes and issues may have less to do with an author's communal or self-determining search for identity and empowerment and more to do with the beliefs and prejudice of readers. As Shirley Geok-lin Lim writes, Asian American literary works, especially those that win national literary prizes, "should be read not simply as Asian American cultural production but also as an American production 'authorized' by a mainstream non-Asian American readership mediating between that different ethnic identity and itself" (160). To bring down the walls of the literary Chinatown, we must understand the role played by authors, readers, and publishers in the construction of those walls.

2   What Is an Ethnic Author?

The function of an author is to characterize the existence, circulation, and operation of certain discourses within a society.

—MICHEL FOUCAULT, "What Is an Author?"

THE ETHNIC-AUTHOR FUNCTION

The development of Chinese American literature into a kind of literary Chinatown—a literature which, as I argued in chapter 1, is used by the publishing industry and driven by the consumer's appetite as was the Chinatown tourist industry—is fundamentally a function of the author's ethnicity. In other words, a reader's predominant strategy in approaching a Chinese American text, consciously or not, is to discover the themes of cross-cultural tension, identity-shaping, community building, or whatever expectation of ethnicity there may be, that set it apart as an exotic experience beyond the mainstream, and all this is predicated upon the reader's awareness of the author's ethnicity. According to Kandice Chuh, U.S. multiculturalism trains us to see ethnic literatures as "transparent, self-evident expressions," and she argues that "such a positioning obviously makes difficult an engagement with minoritized literatures as anything other than ('authentic') artifacts of an ethnography of the Other" (18). These ethnicity-based expectations not only color the reader's interpretation of the literature, but also account for the abundance of ethnographic-autobiographical narratives in Chinese American literature to date. According to Dominika Ferens,

The demand for ethnographic fiction has continued to draw Asian American writers to 'armchair ethnology.' Amy Tan, Gus Lee, Aimee E. Liu, D. H. Hwang, Belle Yang, and many others have produced fictional accounts of the long ago and far away or of contemporary Asian/Asian American communities with which they have had little contact. From the point of view of the mainstream press, the "factuality" of these fictional works is *authenticated by the author's ethnicity*. In recent decades, critics have pointed out that ethnography and ethnographic fiction have tended to represent non-Western people as dehistoricized and essentially other. Such representations are *easily commodified* because they appeal to larger audiences than does work that problematizes interratial relations. (*Edith and Winnifred Eaton* 14, emphasis added)

The aim of this chapter is to examine the role of the ethnic author in the reception and commodification of Chinese American literature and suggest some ways that this feeds into the production and marketing of Chinese American texts.

As the chapter title suggests, I will use the famous article "What Is an Author?" by Michel Foucault as my reference point in this discussion. Foucault sketches the various ways the "author-function," as he calls it, operates in discourse by delineating several essential characteristics (130):

1. "The 'author-function' is tied to the legal and institutional systems that circumscribe, determine, and articulate the realm of discourses" (130). A text with an author's name attached to it is an "object of appropriation . . . [a] form of property . . . a possession caught in a circuit of property values" (124). For example, in terms of such legalities as copyright, the "author" functions as a sign of property ownership.

2. The "author-function" "does not operate in a uniform manner in all discourses, at all times, and in any given culture" (130). In some cases, the "author" functions as a sign of authentication, in others an "index of truthfulness," in others a lexical marker for an idea, a theorem, a school of thought, and in still others it is entirely absent (126). The author-function is malleable.

3. The "author-function" "is not defined by the spontaneous attribution of a text to its creator, but through a series of precise and complex procedures" (130). Foucault explains that the reader constructs "the rational entity we call an author" through a series of "projections" upon the text: projections of the reader's own concerns, preoccupations, designations, identities, "comparisons," "traits," and so forth (127). Thus, the author becomes a part of the reader's psyche more than the distinctive (biographical/biological) human being who writes.

4. The "author-function" "does not refer, purely and simply, to an actual individual insofar as it simultaneously gives rise to a variety of egos and to a series of subjective positions that individuals of any class may come to occupy" (130). This function is best grasped as the writer's "second-self" (the "implied author" theorized in Wayne C. Booth's *The Rhetoric of Fiction*). Foucault shows that even an "author" of a mathematical treatise is not equal to the "writer" of that same work, but is rather the projection of various egos that pose as the writer (129–30).

Foucault's designations for the author-function are largely individual-oriented. They are either the projections of an individual writer (Point 4) or of an individual reader (Point 3); they are the modes of legal designation for an individual writer or publisher (Point 1); they are the signifier of a particular discourse propounded by an individual (Point 2). There is obviously space within these points where a reading of group or anonymous agency could be hazarded; for example, Point 2 allows for a community with no author-function; and Point 3 could lead to a collective emphasis depending on the reader's projections and preoccupations. However, Foucault's author-function characteristics seem to assume a world, a culture, a discursive community that values and expects individuality.

THE COMMUNAL FUNCTION

Foucault's analysis of the author-function therefore privileges a view of the author as an individual who speaks for and represents his or her own artistic self. Yet we see something quite different in the reception of Chinese American literature. As exemplified in chapter 1, readers tend to amalgamate Chinese American literature into a homogeneous field, sometimes despite clear textual evidence to the contrary. Chinese Americans, although the designation is now written without the hyphen, are still perceived as "hyphenated" people, living between the poles of nativism and assimilationism in an Old World/New World dichotomy. They are perceived by many still today as unassimilable, ultimately and inextricably rooted to the geo-political space of Asia. The literature they write, especially in its focus, real or perceived, on Asian American problems of assimilation, is construed as inward and private experiments in community building, despite the fact that so few are explicitly speaking for community.[1]

The perceived ethnicity of the author semiotically codes for the reader a group or community project, a function less obvious among writers from more "assimilable" ethnic groups. Gilles Deleuze and Félix Guattari discuss this phenomenon in *Kafka: Toward a Minor Literature*; they define "minor literature" as the literature of an ethnic group (in the case of Kafka, the Prague Jewish community) writing in the language of a mainstream literature (for Kafka, the major literature was in German). Deleuze and Guattari argue that a minor literature cannot escape its association with its ethnic group: in a minor literature, they write, "everything takes on a collective value" (17). In other words, a minor literature is *read* as having a collective value, or, as Richard Dyer claims in his study of whiteness: "non-raced people" can "speak for humanity" because we do not expect them to "represent the interests of a race," but "raced people . . . can only speak for their race" (2, 3). Deleuze and Guattari contend that the major reason for this collectivity is "the scarcity of talent," given the relatively small pool of writers which represent a minor literature. "Precisely because talent isn't abundant in a minor literature, there are no possibilities for an individuated enunciation that would belong to this or that 'master' and that could be separated from a collective enunciation" (17).[2] In contrast, the literary Chinatown phenomenon reveals that this "minor" status has less to do with a small talent pool than it does with the homogenizing expectations of readers and the market demands of the book industry. Brian Niiya, in a brief 1999 article on the early development of the Asian American autobiography, calls this the "collective self." According to Niiya, "the story of the Asian American autobiography is the story of the collective-self *imposed* on writers who never intended it. . . . [P]ublishers, through selection, appealing to the audience's taste, inadvertently but inevitably imposed a false 'collective self' on Asian Americans of that time" (430, 433, italics in original).

According to Deleuze and Guattari, what an author within a minor literature says "individually already constitutes a common action" (17); whereas, in a major literature "the individual concern (familial, marital, and so on) joins with other no less individual concerns, the social milieu serving as a mere environment or background" (17). Such expectations of communal representation and, as discussed below, "authentic" representation tend to foreground standards of verisimilitude. This was a central problem in the *Woman Warrior* controversy. Questions regarding the veracity of Kingston's portrayal of Chinese Americans were closely tied to her use of, and revision of, Chinese fable and folklore. Underlying these questions appears to be the readers' demand that representations of Chinese Americans be "realistic" and "authentic." As Kingston noted, readers tend to force the Chinese American author into a cultural-ambassador role. The *Woman Warrior* controversy also reveals that Asian American readers place a further burden on the Chinese American author. Like white readers, they may expect realistic and authentic portrayals of Chinese American life, but many Asian American readers also expect fictional portrayals to reflect positively on their community. Chinese American authors may face conflicting demands if they anticipate that what they deem the "realistic" account will not be considered a "positive" account by Asian American readers. According to Shirley Geok-lin Lim, "The expectation of positive portrayals of the Asian American community frequently is accompanied by an equally vehement demand that the text reflect an authentic picture of the Asian American community" ("Assaying the Gold" 151). These two demands cannot always be reconciled. Thus, unlike mainstream writers of the major literature, ethnic authors are likely to experience a conflict between authentic/positive representation of their ethnic community and genuine artistic freedom.

Kingston's objection to the assumption that she was representing all Chinese Americans in *The Woman Warrior*, especially by one reviewer who sees the book as atypical because his Chinese American wife does not identify with it, makes these comments,

> I have never before read a critic who took a look at a Jewish American spouse and said, 'There's something wrong with that Saul Bellow and Norman Mailer. They aren't at all like the one I'm married to.' Critics do not ask whether Vonnegut is typical of German Americans; they do not ask whether J. P. Donleavy is typical of Irish Americans. You would never know by reading the reviews of Francine du Plessix Gray's *Lovers and Tyrants* that it is by and about an immigrant from France. Books written by Americans of European ancestry are reviewed as American novels. ("Cultural Mis-readings" 63)

Gish Jen has objected to the cultural-ambassador role in similar terms: "What we don't want is to be lumped together, ghettoized. I hope that 25 years from now, we'll achieve the kind of standing that Jewish American writers have—that is, we'll just be judged as *writers*" (Feldman 27, italics in original). Chinese American writers are restricted to the spokesperson role because their Asianness is exoticized by readers in a way that many other minority writers, by virtue of their assimilability (of skin, of eyes, of name— that is, their racial markers) are not. Unlike works by white writers, where individuality is taken for granted by readers, or to put it differently, where readers are more willing to allow individuality, Chinese American works operate in the readers' consciousness as communal projects.

If the Chinese American author represents for the reader a collective ethnic enunciation, it is because the reader expects the Chinese American author to exert a high degree of authority *vis-à-vis* the author's ethnic authenticity. Liberal education and pop culture accentuate this expectation today in their celebration of ethnic diversity and multiculturalism. The assumption of authenticity relates to Foucault's second point about the varying functions of the author depending on the shifting nature of discourse. Based on a reading of religious authentication by Saint Jerome, Foucault suggests that not just Saint Jerome's model, but even modern criticism itself views the author "as a standard level of quality" (128). Foucault's use of the term "quality" refers to artistic or aesthetic quality, in that an author is recognized for producing works of artistic or aesthetic merit (or lack of merit), and through time that author's name comes to signify that quality. We can appropriate this idea to an ethnic literature like Chinese American literature, in which "standard level of quality" would refer not to artistic merit, but to *quality of representation*. That is, an author's name signifies the quality (read *authenticity* or *accuracy*) of his or her representation of the Chinese American community. Based on the perceived authenticity signaled by an ethnic author's name, readers endow that author not only with a right to speak of his or her ethnic community, but also with an assumed ability to represent that community accurately—and even an ethical mandate to do so. Again, as the controversy over Kingston's creative alterations to Chinese folklore in *The Woman Warrior* exemplifies, different reading communities may have idiosyncratic expectations of a Chinese American author's portrayal of Chinese American life. A reader unfamiliar with Chinese culture and history may simply expect authenticity from a Chinese American author, while an Asian American reader might demand it. Frank Chin's argument against Kingston's alterations reveals his own demand for positive portrayals of Chinese men and accurate portrayals of Chinese folklore, but it also reveals his anxiety about non-Asian readers. In Chin's view, Kingston and Amy Tan "fake" Chinese culture and folklore in their works because their white readership will not know the difference: "They're fake! They are constructed. I see all the references to European culture and European literature are correct—but every reference to Chinese culture, language, history is fake" (Morgan 54).

An interpretive community such as Asian American readers (or those with a high degree of learned knowledge of the Chinese American community and history) will likely make the representation of authentic Chinese American experience central to the enjoyment and judgment of a Chinese American literary work. Their enjoyment and estimation of the work will hinge upon how accurately they feel the work represents Chinese America and how successfully the work avoids stereotypes. For members of an interpretive community characterized by a Euro-American outlook with less knowledge of actual Chinese American life and history, authenticity will be assumed by virtue of the author's ontological experience as an ethnic Chinese American regardless of how distanced the writer may be from China or the Chinese American community. For this reason, the authenticity of a Chinese American writer's representation of China is rarely problematic among non-Chinese American critics, and the fact that many of these authors have never lived in, or possibly never even visited China is not an issue. Such readers perhaps assume that these authors have "experienced" China through their parents and elders or by virtue of some racial/biological essence.

For critics in Asia, authenticity is often more central to critical judgment than in the U.S. For example, when Amy Tan's novel, *The Hundred Secret Senses*, was reviewed in Singapore's *Straits Times*, book critic Koh Buck Song's main criticism revolved around the inauthentic flavor of the segments of the novel situated in China. According to him, only the segments of the novel set in America were convincing.[3] Koh begins his review,

> If the joss-smoke of mystique that surrounds things Chinese is ever to clear, Amy Tan's new novel will offer scant assistance. Given her stature now as almost a giant of Chinese-American literature, her third novel, *The Hundred Secret Senses*, will surely become much more than just a charming tale. It will be studied, by post-colonial literary scholars and others, for a cultural significance far beyond what the author could ever have intended. This novel, while it will probably be snapped up by Tan's many fans, will unfortunately do little to help dismantle Western stereotypes of China and the Chinese.

Koh reveals here not only a preoccupation with the quality of Tan's cultural representation, but a fear that this representation will wrongly influence Western readers and further distort their view "of China and the Chinese."

Especially for the non-Chinese American reader, the fundamental element in categorizing a work as Chinese American is the *perceived ethnic identity* of the author. A text about an ethnic group is deemed authentic if the author is perceived as authentically ethnic (whether through the ethnic sign of his/her name, photograph, biographical note, or by the "accuracy" of his/her representation). Two historical examples will illustrate this point: the case of Sui Sin Far and Onoto Watanna. Sui Sin Far's writing was highly popular in the early twentieth century, and today she is generally considered to be the first Chinese American writer. However, as the daughter of a Chinese immigrant woman and an English man, she and her thirteen siblings all bore the surname Eaton, and, "although biologically half Chinese . . . [she was] culturally English and Canadian" (Ling 307). Her name, Sui Sin Far, was a fiction, an instance of "creating one's self" as Amy Ling puts it. The purpose of this self-creation was undoubtedly to identify herself as ethnically Chinese, which, as Ling argues, helped her to forge solidarity with other Chinese Americans.[4] The invention of a Chinese name produced an aura of authenticity to validate the Chinese essence of her writing, themes, and information derived from travel writing rather than first-hand experience.[5]

It would be difficult to categorize Sui Sin Far as authentically Chinese if we see authenticity as located in the culture of the writer; rather, it is her racial categorization and her *perceived* ethnicity that validate for the reader an authentically Chinese voice. The act of self-creation in ethnicizing her name masks her hybrid, and hence, in her context, "diluted," identity, leading the reader to see her as wholly Chinese.

In Sui Sin Far's case, the act of self-creation through a pseudonym was less a case of deception than it was a case of emphasis; after all, she was ethnically half-Chinese. The name Sui Sin Far simply highlighted her Chineseness. The more complex situation is that of Sui Sin Far's sister, who went by the pen name, Onoto Watanna. According to Amy Ling,

> if we use an author's ethnic origin as an identifying criterion to classify her writing, then we may say, without qualms, that Chinese American fiction began with Sui Sin Far, but we may not say that Japanese American literature began with Onoto Watanna. In fact, we would have to say that [Watanna's novel] *Miss Nume of Japan* was the first Chinese American novel and that the twelve other "Japanese" novels of Onoto Watanna should be classified, despite their themes and settings, as Chinese American fiction. (306)[6]

Onoto Watanna's act of self-creation was an even greater fiction than her sister's. Yet Onoto Watanna, or rather, Winnifred Eaton, created works that were accepted during her lifetime as genuinely Japanese. Thus, what validated Onoto Watanna's works as Japanese writing for the audience of her time was not her actual ethnic identity, but her *perceived* ethnic identity conveyed by her pen name. In Ferens's words, Winnifred's "public persona was as much a figment of her imagination as it was a product of white mainstream readers' desire for the exotic, for a new yet intelligible aesthetic, and for an insight into Japan's leap from the 'feudal' era directly into modernity" ("Winnifred Eaton/Onoto Watanna" 31–32).[7]

As these examples illustrate, the ethnic sign in the author's name can work like a stamp of authentication in the reader's perception of the text. This "stamp" suggests to the reader that the ethnic work is accurate and representative. The importance of this stamp is made evident when counterfeits are discovered. For instance, there have been several controversies in Australia surrounding supposed aboriginal writers. In one particular case, a prestigious literary prize for a first publication by a female author was awarded to Wanda Koolmatrie, supposedly an aboriginal woman. A public uproar ensued, however, when it was discovered that Wanda Koolmatrie was the pseudonym for a Sydney taxi driver named Leon Carmen, who was neither female nor aboriginal (Gilman 23). This and other cases of ethnic impostors speak volumes about the values behind the reception of ethnic literature.[8] While the utilization of pseudonyms is deemed acceptable to modern audiences in some circumstances (in the case, for example, of female writers in nineteenth-century England adopting male pseudonyms to counter the sexist bias of their readership), public outcry today at white writers passing themselves off as ethnic writers reveals the significance of the authenticity of the writer's ethnicity to the reception of an ethnic text.

Thus, the enjoyment of an ethnic work, the estimation of its worth, indeed the very motivation for purchasing and reading it, are bound tightly to the perception of the author as an authentic representative of his or her ethnic community. The perceived ethnic authenticity of a Chinese American author, therefore, is a stamp of authentication on the Chinese American work. To the reader, it signifies the author's ability and right to speak for the Chinese American community and increases the socio-cultural value of the work and thus the literary value in a society that values multiculturalism.

THE SOCIO-CULTURAL FUNCTION

While some readers may think of authors as special "individual talents," as T. S. Eliot called them, or, as E. M. Forster imagined, as genius minds sitting in a room beyond the realm of temporality, Foucault sees authors as deeply embedded socio-historical figures. Again basing his observations on Saint Jerome, Foucault claims that the author is "a definite historical figure in which a series of events converge" (128). While a contemporary Chinese American author may not yet function in the reader's imagination as this kind of historical marker, I believe that for many readers the Chinese American author functions as a socio-cultural figure. As readers tend to see Chinese American authors as representatives of their ethnic group, so they rarely imagine the Chinese American author as standing distinct from his or her socio-historical milieu. Until recently, Chinese American authors have been valued largely for the information they supply about Chinese American community and history. According to King-Kok Cheung, "texts that contain implicit or explicit social commentary [for example, [Carlos] Bulosan's *America Is in the Heart*, Louis Chu's *Eat a Bowl of Tea*, and John Okada's *No-No Boy*] have long been staples in courses on Asian American literature. Many scholars and students have almost come to assume that Asian American writers furnish material that reflects ethnic experiences" (*An Interethnic Companion* 15). Cheung goes on to argue that postmodern and poststucturalist inquiry have destabilized this sociological approach to Asian American literature, but we might note that this rejection of "Asian American literature as mirroring society" (15) has taken hold largely in literary studies and not necessarily in the general readership. Unlike authors of European ancestry, Chinese American authors attract attention not just for literary merit, but also for the cultural information they supply readers.

The emphasis on the socio-cultural value of Chinese American fiction can also be attributed to the practices of Asian American literary scholarship. As Christopher Douglas argues, "ethnography continues to structure Asian American literature in its public reception, even in the academy" (102). Some of the most influential scholarship in the field of Asian American literature (e.g., Sauling Cynthia Wong's *Reading Asian American Literature*) has taken as its premise that Asian American literature and Asian American history and culture go hand-in-hand. The scholarly emphasis on historicity has been an important counterbalance to abounding misperceptions of Chinese and Chinese American culture and community. David Leiwei Li puts it in bold terms: "to be truly meaningful, any interpretation of Chinese American texts, I contend, ought to deal with the specificities of Chinese American history" ("The Production of Chinese American Tradition" 319).

Yet perhaps this scholarly emphasis on group and community history, though necessary to its own purposes, has further inscribed in Chinese

American authors a certain socio-cultural function, making the value of their artistic work dependant upon their ethnic identity and ethnic experience. Elaine Kim, for instance, locates the authenticity of Louis Chu's *Eat a Bowl of Tea* (as well as the inauthenticity of Lin Yutang's and Chin Yang Lee's writings[9]) in the author's ethnic experience (*Asian American Literature* 91–121). It is the author's experience as an ethnic Chinese American, or his or her position within the Chinese American community, that explains the quality of the textual representation. Kim explains that one factor which authenticates Chu's novel is the stylization of dialogue. Whereas authors like Lin and Chin and Euro-American writers like Mark Twain and Bret Harte stylize Chinese American dialogue in a pidgin form, often for comical effect, Chu translates the authentic Chinese speech into a grammatically correct and yet idiomatically distinctive English. Even if this argument appears to decentralize the author and explain the text's authenticity purely in textually stylistic terms, the centrality of the biographical author to Kim's argument is revealed when she suggests that Chu's appreciation for, and hence, experience with, the way the Chinese of Chinatown actually speak explains the authenticity of the dialogue. She writes, "the moving and vital quality of Chu's portrayal of Chinatown life can be attributed in part to his ability to appreciate the Chinese spoken around him" (*Asian American Literature* 119). Thus, it is the situation of the author in the historical experience of Chinatown that ultimately validates his fictional portrayal of Chinese Americans.

I am not against reading a text in the context of the author's real life, and I don't believe Kim's argument about the authenticity of *Eat a Bowl of Tea* is flawed. Providing the cultural context for any "minor literature" requires this kind of socio-historical emphasis. Asian American literary scholarship's emphasis on the author's socio-cultural function was necessitated by the mainstream culture's ignorance of Asian American culture. My point, however, is that the reader's belief in the Asian American author as a socio-cultural figure rather than an individual talent may be further entrenched by literary scholarship's emphasis on social, historical, and cultural readings.

THE COMMODITY FUNCTION

Since the 1980s, when the culture wars reached their zenith and multiculturalism began to flourish in schools, universities, and popular culture, one of the most significant functions of the ethnic author has been as a commodity in today's book market. This function is satirically presented in a passage of Gish Jen's *Mona in the Promised Land*. In the novel, Mona's sister

Callie is involved in a university project on racial stereotypes and perceptions with her African American friend Naomi, a project that turns into a prospective book deal. After meeting with the editor in New York, Callie informs Mona that the publisher was interested in the book but wanted Naomi to be the sole author. Their conversation highlights several functions of the ethnic author in the publishing market as Jen imagines them circa 1970:

> "We're not book material," Callie says [referring to Chinese Americans]. "After all, blacks are the majority minority. Also they've been slaves and everything."
> "Is that what the editor said?" [asks Mona].
> "She said I probably have a book in me too. People are interested in China, she said."
> "But you've never been to China."
> Callie shrugs. "She said I'm a natural ambassador."
> "I thought you wanted to be a doctor."
> "I think it would be cool to write a book." The next time she goes to New York, Callie says, she's going to wear a Chinese dress.
> "But you've never worn one in your life," Mona says.
> "I have a book in me," Callie sings in reply. (*Mona* 270)

Intertwined in this brief passage are many issues relevant to this discussion: Callie's assumed communal function because she is Chinese American (she is a "natural ambassador"); the management of her ethnicity in order to increase her authenticity (wearing a Chinese dress when it is not her normal practice to do so); the assumed authenticity of ethnic material by an ethnic author (Callie has never been to China, but the editor assumes she can write an authentic account of the culture). Yet, what is most clearly on view in this passage is the utilization of ethnicity as a commodity in the publishing industry. Callie may *have a book in her* because she has something interesting, something exotic that intrigues readers. She has China, and, as the editor says, "people are interested in China." Never mind that Callie has never set foot in China and is, in fact, learning Chinese for the first time at the university— the fact that she is ethnically Chinese American is enough to sell books. Ironically, the integrity of Mona and Naomi's proposed book on racial stereotypes is compromised by the publisher's blatant stereotyping of the authors and her intent to use their ethnicity to sell the book. As Callie's enthusiasm suggests, the lure of the book market tempts her to sell out.

In Foucault's first point about the legality of the author-function, he states that the author functions as an "object of appropriation . . . [a] form of property . . . a possession caught in a circuit of property values" (124). The "property" in the case of Chinese American literature is not simply the book copyright—it is the author's ethnicity and the potential of that ethnic identity to attract consumers. The examples of Sui Sin Far and Onoto Watanna discussed earlier are clear instances of the use of ethnicity as commodity; as Ferens puts it, Winnifred's "Japanese persona became inseparable from the commodities Eaton produced. It not only authorized her to produce ethnographic texts but also became a commodity in itself, subject to the rigors and constraints of the marketplace" ("Winnifred Eaton/ Onoto Watanna" 32). Elaine H. Kim further attests to the prevalence of this practice in the 1950s in the case of Jade Snow Wong. Kim claims that Wong sought acceptance in society outside the Chinese American community by defining herself through her books as "acceptably Chinese." Instead of distancing herself from her Chinese roots, Wong found herself "obliged to use [her] ethnicity as [her] 'point of distinction' in order to win even conditional membership in [white] society" (*Asian American Literature* 70). Kim shows here that publishers made use of the "insider" role of ethnic Chinese Americans like Jade Snow Wong to sell books when ethnographic writing on Chinese culture became popular.

In today's lucrative market for ethnic literature, the Chinese American author functions more than ever as a commodity in the publishing industry. This phenomenon is not of course solely restricted to Chinese American texts and to the American publishing industry. Indeed, in pondering the question of ethnicity as commodity, Sander L. Gilman cites the case of German Jewish writers in Germany: "In today's Germany Jewish writers are often self-identified as Jewish or are so defined by their publishers. This labeling often has nothing to do with religion; it may have everything to do with the marketability of certain forms of ethnicity" (23). Similarly, identifying Chinese American authors in such a way as to emphasize their ethnicity has more to do with the "marketability" of their ethnicity than it does with any overt relation between writers and the community they are perceived to represent.

The ethnicizing of texts through enhancing the author's ethnicity is evident in a variety of ways. The author's name, for instance, is one of the most important markers of ethnicity. In cases where an author puts his or her legal name on a book, it may not be fair to suggest that the name is being constructed or enhanced in order to market the book. However, especially among authors of mixed parentage or with female Chinese American writers who have adopted a Euro-American name by marriage, it is often the case that the author's ethnicity is accentuated by including the ethnic name as a middle name. This act of manipulating one's name to increase the perception of ethnicity is the counterpart to what Linda Hutcheon refers to as "crypto-ethnicity," that is, the hiding of one's ethnicity through a name change. As Hutcheon argues, the changing of one's name either to decrease or increase perceived ethnicity is much more than a nominal alteration; it is an act that can significantly alter a person's place in society. This was her experience when she adopted her husband's name, thus losing her Italian maiden name.

> When I went from being a Bartolotti to being a Hutcheon my social and cultural interactions within a predominantly Anglo-Saxon environment changed; my ethnic identity became encrypted, silenced, unless articulated by choice—a pointed lesson in the constructedness of concepts like ethnicity. (28)

Constructing a sense of the ethnic through manipulation of an author's name would affect more than "social and cultural interactions." In a period when ethnicity attracts the attention of the reading public, it would affect the commercial success of a book. The middle name "Hong" in Kingston's name, therefore, not only identifies her as ethnic (though we must recognize the role of feminism here as well), but it also affects the sale of her books. A book about a Chinese American character will appear more authentic, and trustworthy, if written by Maxine Hong Kingston than it would if written by Maxine Kingston, or by Ruthanne Lum McCunn rather than Ruthanne McCunn. I do not mean to suggest here that by including their maiden names, Kingston, McCunn, and their publishers are creating an *illusion* of ethnicity, but I simply mean to illustrate one way in which authorial names are foregrounded to emphasize ethnicity. When *The Woman Warrior* was first published, the biographical note under the author's photograph introduced her name as "Maxine Ting Ting Hong Kingston." As Kingston's fame has grown, this extended emphasis on her Chinese identity was no longer necessary.

Another way that an author's ethnicity is emphasized in the publishing industry is through the pictorial and biographical representation of the author. The way a Chinese American author is described or shown on the book cover does not always guarantee a more or less exoticized reception: Kingston, for example, marvels at the way she was perceived as exotic by reviewers despite the fact that she wore a sweatshirt for the jacket photo on *The Woman Warrior* in order, as she puts it, "to deny the exotic" ("Cultural Mis-readings" 55). The presentation of the author is, however, one part of the management of the ethnic commodity. For example, the photograph of Amy Tan on the Flamingo hardback edition of *The Hundred Secret Senses* (1995) shows her with a large metal pendant displayed on her chest with the character "Shou," or, "Longevity," engraved on it. On the back of the G. P. Putnam's Sons hardback of *The Kitchen God's Wife* (1991), she wears a similar pendant in the shape of an antique Chinese coin with three smaller coins attached. There is nothing inconsistent with Amy Tan's wearing Chinese jewelry, but the use of such "ethnic" emblems as Chinese dress and accessories on her novels clearly increases the perceived ethnicity of the author and hence of the work and stands as a clear example of "easy exoticism" (Lim, "Reconstructing" 52).

The photograph of Aimee E. Liu on the back of her debut novel *Face* (1994) is a more obvious use of ethnic visual imagery to highlight authorial ethnicity. In the photo, a Euro-American-looking Liu is made to pass as ethnically Chinese by wearing a Chinese embroidered blouse, shown from just below the shoulders. The authenticity of her ethnicity is highlighted in the first sentence of her bio: "Aimee E. Liu . . . like her heroine, has a half-Chinese father and an American mother." For the photograph on her second novel, *Cloud Mountain*, Liu wears a necklace with a large jade pendant that is also Chinese in style. In such instances where the author's ethnicity may be missed, these visual and textual reminders serve to emphasize ethnicity and the ethnic commodity.[10]

A third way in which ethnicity is emphasized by publishers in order to tap the ethnic literature market is through book design. It is common to find Chinese American books adorned with Chinese script, dragons, misty mountains, cranes, joss sticks, temples, Chinese architecture, or strings of Chinese New Year firecrackers. Chapter headings are often decorated with dragons, Chinese characters, Chinese "chops," or words displayed in fonts that suggest Chineseness. These are more than aesthetic decorations intended to beautify the book. These designs codify ethnicity and market the entire package—author's name, picture, biography, title, and design—as ethnic. These markers of "Oriental mystique" sometimes have less to do with the narrative and everything to do with commodifying the ethnic experience, as Cheryl Alexander Malcolm suggests in her article on whiteness in Gus Lee's *China Boy*:

> *China Boy* is packaged by its publishers (in its cover design and in its inclusion of the protagonist's family-tree, for example) to suggest that it will meet an American audience's expectations of Oriental exoticism. However, from the novel's first paragraphs, in which Kai Ting recalls being soundly beaten and called 'China Boy shitferbrains' by a black rival on the streets

of San Francisco, Lee's concerns are with violence, race, and gender in a specifically American context. (414)

In short, all these attempts to enhance ethnicity are designed to increase the authenticity of the author's ethnicity and, hence, to increase the ethnic authenticity of the work. As Paul Gilroy writes, "authenticity enhances the appeal of selected cultural items" (qtd. in Hutnyk 107). In the marketing of Chinese American literature, the authenticity of the author's ethnic identity is as much a commodity as the text he or she writes.

My discussion up to this point has emphasized the various ways in which the ethnic author signifies both for readers and the book market. Yet Foucault's claims about the author-function lead me to consider not simply the various meanings of the ethnic author, but also the ways in which these meanings come to delineate a specific type of literature. According to him, "the function of an author is to characterize the existence, circulation, and operation of certain discourses within a society" (124). This is true of the very term "author." As Foucault argues, contracts, insurance claims, letters, and posters may have "underwriters," "writers," or "signatories," but they do not have "authors." In other words, the word "author" signifies a specific type of discourse and excludes other types of discourses. Likewise, the "Chinese American author" stands for and characterizes a specific discourse—which is, as I argue below, largely influenced and manipulated by the publishing industry.

Asian American literature has seen much critical and popular success in the past two decades, but has it seen success always on its own terms? Many Asian American critics believe it has not. For instance, Shirley Geok-lin Lim argues, "much of what is admitted as Asian American writing into the enlarged sensitized canon of contemporary American literature is a sensibility that has been constituted under the gaze of an Anglo literary community. The well-known Asian American works that are read as ethnic signifiers are exactly those that succeed first with European American readers" ("Assaying the Gold" 160). King-Kok Cheung makes a similar claim and asks a number of pertinent questions about the limiting effects of "mainstream expectations" and "the publishing marketplace." She writes,

Although we must not detract from the achievement of writers who have received national acclaim, we need to question whether there is some unspoken formula for Asian American literary success that prevents those who deviate from it from being heard. Why, for instance, is there such a preponderance of autobiographical works by Asian Americans? Why is it that, unlike works by other peoples of color, Asian American works that are commercial triumphs seem to be those the least overtly concerned with racial politics? Why are the few Asian American writers who do rage about racism (Frank Chin, Lawson Inada, Janice Mirikitani) so neglected by a general readership? To what extent are Asian American writers complicit with Orientalism in order to meet mainstream expectations? I ask these questions not in any attempt to prescribe literary creativity, but to suggest that there are still invisible limits placed on Asian American writers. (*An Interethnic Companion* 17–18)

What Cheung and Lim suggest is that success in the literary marketplace may actually limit freedom of expression. The flip side of the argument, however, is that all writers are to some extent shackled by the expectations and tastes of readers and the exigencies of the publishing industry. All writers concerned with literary value struggle with the conflict between the demands of popular taste (that which sells books) and the integrity of their own artistic vision. Publishing is a business that, like all businesses, is concerned with the bottom line. An Asian American author can tailor his or her artistic creation to the demands of the public and publishing industry, or he or she can forego the lucrative possibilities of mainstream publishing and seek other avenues. Writers like Frank Chin who "rage against racism" ("Re-viewing" 17) find alternate routes outside the large commercial publishing houses for their works, such as Coffee House Press in Minneapolis or various university presses. Like Cheung, I am not interested in "prescribing literary creativity" (18) any more than I am interested in prescribing literary taste. Rather, I wish to examine the effects of the publishing industry's selectivity—that is, to describe the kind of discourse Asian American authors have come to represent for the mainstream reader as a result of the publishing industry's influence.

What Cheung calls the "invisible limits placed on Asian American writers" has foregrounded a particular type of Asian American writing that the Asian American author, and especially the Chinese American author, has come to signify. The function of the Chinese American author to "characterize the existence, circulation, and operation" (Foucault 124) of a particular type of discourse is the subject of the rest of this chapter. Yet, in saying that the Chinese American author characterizes a discourse, I am not suggesting that Chinese American literature is a singular, homogeneous entity.

I acknowledge that there are many dissenting views among authors and critics alike which result in various discursive strains. Moreover, we can legitimately speak of each author's individual discourse (the now famous divide between Frank Chin and Maxine Hong Kingston is a vivid example; but even between writers with a high mainstream visibility like Gish Jen and Amy Tan, there are significant differences and departures that distinguish their specific literary works). While a careful analysis of Chinese American texts reveals difference and heterogeneity in Chinese American writing, a study of the promotion of these texts reveals that the Chinese American author is often lumped with other Asian American writers in a homogenous discursive field.

One way to identify this discourse is to closely study the promotional materials of Chinese American novels. On the jacket flaps or the back cover, the novel is encapsulated in ways that not only summarize the text, but also, and more importantly for this discussion, anticipate the aesthetic tastes of the potential book-buyer. I am not concerned here with the actual discourse that an author constructs or participates in; rather, I focus on the publicist's characterization of the discourse the author is deemed to represent. The "existence, circulation, and operation" of such a discourse is introduced and maintained not by the authors themselves, but by the system that allows their works to be read: the publishing industry and the book-buying market.[11]

I will begin with extracts from the jackets of Amy Tan's four novels and will then extend my analysis to the publishers' descriptions of several recent Chinese American novels. I begin with Tan because of her status as the most popular and most widely read Chinese American writer. In this sense, she is essential to a discussion of the general public's perception of Chinese American literature. She is the only Chinese American writer many Euro-American readers are familiar with. Indeed, the name "Amy Tan" is often used by publishers as a kind of stamp of approval on other Asian American works— for example, her endorsement appears alone on the front covers of *China Boy* and *Honor and Duty* by Gus Lee and *Mona in the Promised Land* by Gish Jen. It would be reasonable to say, in fact, that for the general reading public, "Amy Tan" has become synonymous with "Chinese American literature."

Below are excerpts from the jacket copy of her first four novels, followed by an analysis of their discursive features.

I

In 1949 four *Chinese* women—drawn together by *the shadow of their past*— begin meeting in San Francisco to play mah jong, invest in stocks, eat dim sum, and "say" stories. They call their gathering the Joy Luck Club.

Nearly forty years later, one of the members has died, and her daughter has come to take her place, only to *learn of her mother's lifelong wish—*and the tragic way in which it has come true.

The revelation of this secret unleashes an urgent need among the women to *reach back and remember.* . . . (*The Joy Luck Club*, 1989, italics added)

2

Winnie and Helen have *kept each other's worst secrets* for more than fifty years. Now, because she believes she is dying, Helen wants to *expose everything.* And Winnie angrily determines that she must be the one to *tell her daughter, Pearl, about the past*—including *the terrible truth* even Helen does not know. Thus begins the *unfolding of secrets* that *takes mother and daughter back* to a small island outside Shanghai in the 1920s and throughout *China* during World War Two. . . .

Unaware that Pearl has *her own secret* to tell, *Winnie reveals* the hard-won knowledge she has never passed on to her daughter. . . . And in the end, she shows her daughter—and herself—why it is still possible *to change the past, to claim the future,* to go beyond the fate of the Kitchen God's Wife. (*The Kitchen God's Wife*, 1991, italics added)

3

Olivia Yee is only five years old when Kwan, her seventeen-year-old half-sister from *China,* comes to live with the family and turns her world upside down. She is bombarded day and night with *Kwan's stories from the world of Yin*—*romantic tales of ghosts* who were once bandit maidens, *strange accounts* of missionaries and mercenaries *from another world.* Olivia just wants to lead a normal American life. . . . Just when Olivia cannot bear it any more, the revelations of *a tragic, hundred-year-old family secret* give her the opportunity to *reconcile these ghosts from the past with the dreams of the future.* . . . (*The Hundred Secret Senses*, 1995, italics added)

4

LuLing Young is now in her eighties, and finally beginning to feel the effects of old age. *Trying to hold on to the evaporating past, she begins to write down all that she can remember of her life as a girl in China* . . . [Her daughter] Ruth decides to move in with her ailing mother, and while tending to her *discovers the pages LuLing wrote in Chinese, the story of her tumultuous life growing up in a remote mountain village* known as Immortal Heart. LuLing tells of the *secrets passed along by her mute nursemaid,* Precious Auntie . . . and of *the curse that LuLing believes she released* through betrayal. Like layers of sediment being removed, each page unfolds into an *even greater mystery*: who was Precious Auntie, whose suicide changed the path of LuLing's life? . . . Amy Tan gives us a mesmerizing story of a *mother and daughter discovering together that what they share* in their bones through history and heredity is priceless beyond measure. (*The Bonesetter's Daughter,* 2001, italics added)

These four novels by Tan have different plots and different characters. However, by comparing the basic elements of each jacket summary, we find that similar, if not identical, notions emerge in each. In *Joy Luck*, there are "Chinese women," "the shadow of their past," a mother's "lifelong wish" or "secret," and the attempt to "reach back and remember." In *Kitchen God*, there are Chinese women, "the past" full of "the terrible truth" and "secrets," and the attempt to "change the past [and] claim the future" through the revelation of secrets. In *Secret Senses*, there are Chinese women, "stories," "romantic tales," and "strange accounts . . . from another world [i.e., China]," and "the opportunity to reconcile these ghosts from the past with the dreams of the future" via the revelation of "a tragic, hundred-year-old secret." In *Bonesetter's Daughter*, there are "secrets," "mysteries," and "a curse." The mother and daughter "discover what they share . . . through history and heredity"—that is, the memory and the sharing of the Chinese past cement the bond between mother and daughter. The discourse advertised in these summaries centers, therefore, upon Chinese ethnicity, female relationships, the past/present relationship, and the revelation of secrets or terrible truths and tragedies, as summarized below:

Novel	Ethnicity	Relationships	Time	Enigma
Joy Luck Club	Chinese	Mother/ daughter	Into the past (urgent need to remember)	Wish/ secret
Kitchen God's Wife	Chinese	Mother/ daughter	Into the past (to claim the future)	Truth/ secrets
Secret Senses	Chinese	Half-sisters	From the past (to reconcile with the future)	Tragic family secret
Bonesetter's Daughter	Chinese	Mother/ daughter	Into the past (to find shared value)	Secrets/ curse

"The Chinese past" is full of intriguing secrets that would remain hidden from our eyes if it were not for the Chinese American author. Through the author, we are given a tour of family secrets. By association, however, these "family secrets" are also cultural, ethnic, or community secrets; each secret originates in China and requires the assistance of a guide who is both *in* the family and *in* the culture. Thus, the past described in the novel is a foreign territory to which the reader can gain access only with the help of the Chinese American author. In this way, the Chinese American author becomes the guide to the exotic.

When we consider the dynamics of marketing that is involved here, we can get a sense of the semiotic function of the Chinese American author. These summaries are more than a simple description of the contents of the book. By definition a summary cannot be equal to the object it describes; it must, rather, be a selection of ideas and statements about the object. Moreover, in a publisher's book description, this selection of ideas is guided by more than the aim of reporting "what the book is about." It is guided by marketing objectives: the book copy on the jacket is a key factor for consumers as they consider whether or not the book is worth buying. Thus, these summaries represent the concerted effort of the publisher to produce *attractive* book descriptions that will appeal to the tastes of prospective book buyers. They represent, in other words, what the publisher believes people want to know or what people wish to experience in a book by a Chinese American writer. As I claimed in chapter 1, they appeal to and generate taste.

Typically, a publisher's book description will introduce some enigma, a mystery hinted at but never revealed—just enough to whet the appetite of the potential book buyer. In all four summaries above, the same kind of enigma is suggested: the family secret hidden in the Chinese past. In the *Joy Luck* copy, "her mother's lifelong wish" is left undefined, beckoning the reader to come inside and find out what it is. In the *Kitchen God* summary, it is the "terrible truth . . . about the past" that leaves the potential buyer thirsting for more. In the *Secret Senses* summary, it is "a tragic, hundred-year-old family secret." In the *Bonesetter's Daughter* copy, it is the mother's "tumultuous" childhood, the "secrets" hidden there and the "curse" that seems to loom over her. The family secret, then, is the defining characteristic of Amy Tan's discourse as presented by the publisher. It defines her as a writer of Chinese family secrets and an intimate ethnic guide.

Not surprisingly, Amy Tan is not the only Chinese American writer whose discourse is defined as such by her publishers. I say this because the success of *Joy Luck* when it was published created a sudden "enthusiasm among publishers for Asian-American writing," as Janice Simpson put it her article in *Time* magazine (66). Publishers were, in editor Shannon Ravenel's words, "looking for his or her own Amy Tan" (qtd. in Simpson 66). Thus, we would expect to find similar descriptions of novels by other writers as publishers anticipate consumer tastes based on Tan's success, as the excerpts below reveal:

5

In this profoundly moving novel, Fae Myenne Ng *takes readers into the hidden heart of San Francisco's Chinatown*, to a *world of family secrets, hidden shames*, and the lost bones of a "paper father." (Fae Myenne Ng, *Bone*, 1993, italics added)

6

Maibelle Chung, daughter of an Amerasian photojournalist and his Caucasian wife, was raised in New York's Chinatown, where her red hair and green eyes marked her as an outcast. Now an adult, Maibelle is plagued by *nightmares that hint at family secrets and hidden shames dating back to her childhood and, beyond, to the China her father left behind*. (Aimee E. Liu, *Face*, 1994, italics added)

7

A spellbinding first novel that portrays four generations of the Wong family, *Disappearing Moon Café* is by turns as magical as myth and as dramatic as Chinese opera. Kae Ying Woo is the present-day narrator who *attempts to piece together the tangled and hidden history of the Wongs*. . . . Much of the story *centers around Chinatown in Vancouver*. . . . (Sky Lee, *Disappearing Moon Café*, 1991, italics added)

8

Monkey King tells the story of twenty-eight-year-old Sally Wang, a young Chinese-American woman whose mental breakdown and sojourn in a hospital set her firmly *on the path of memory*. Her recovery takes place against a *rich tapestry of culture* and personality that *unfolds before our eyes under the Monkey King's ghostly shadow*. For Sally has been living with *a terrible family secret*, one that has shattered her life. How she *pulls together her Chinese and American identities* into a cohesive self and rejoins the land of the living is recounted with a wry and *refreshing honesty*. (Patricia Chao, *Monkey King*, 1997, italics added)

Lan Samantha Chang's first collection . . . introduces a stunning new voice in Chinese [sic.] fiction. Suffused with quiet beauty, these stories tell of *displaced lives and exiled imaginations*. First generation Chinese-American immigrants hope and dream in a strange land. Their children are *haunted by tradition* despite themselves, and *weave their parents' histories into their modern lives*. (Lan Samantha Chang, *Hunger*, 1998, italics added)

As with the summaries of Amy Tan's novels, the five descriptions above highlight the same kind of enigma to evoke the reader's curiosity. The *Bone* and *Face* summaries employ identical phrases, "family secrets and hidden shames," while the *Monkey King* copy refers to a "terrible family secret" and the *Disappearing Moon Café* copy to "the tangled and hidden history of the Wongs." In the *Hunger* description, we learn that Chinese American children "are haunted by tradition." In each of these statements, the enigma is identified as unobservable to an outsider. The word "secret" obviously connotes this concealment, as does "hidden" and "family." Moreover, emotive words like "shames," "terrible," "haunted," and "tangled" suggest that the matters revealed in these books are both dark and intensely personal.

These mysteries at the heart of each summary promise to unlock more than the mystery of the family. In the *Bone* summary, it is not simply the family secrets and shames that will be revealed in the novel, but the "hidden heart of San Francisco's Chinatown"; the reference to the "hidden history of the Wongs" in the *Disappearing Moon Café* copy similarly connects the family enigma with the larger Chinese community of "Chinatown in Vancouver." The secrets revealed in *Face* originate, we are told, in "the China her father left behind." In the description of *Monkey King*, the "terrible family secret" connects to the "rich tapestry of culture" in which this "Chinese-American woman" lives. In *Hunger*, what haunts the lives of young Chinese Americans are the traditions and histories that connect to China through their parents. In each of these summaries, therefore, we see a link between the secrets and hidden shames of the family and those of the Chinese community. The descriptions seem to suggest that by uncovering the mystery of one family, we will also uncover the mystery of the Chinese people. Moreover, that which is *secret, hidden, terrible, haunted,* and *tangled* in the *family* becomes indistinguishable and inseparable from that which is *secret, hidden, terrible, haunted,* and *tangled* in Chinese *culture*. Both are mysteries we could not solve in normal circumstances.

In these summaries, we are not on our own in the face of these foreign territories—we are offered a guide. Unlike the summaries of Amy Tan's novels that *imply* the author's role as inside guide, some of these summaries make that role explicit. For instance, in *Bone*, the author "takes the reader into the hidden heart of . . . Chinatown." To get to the mystery in *Face*, we need the "nightmares" of Maibelle Chung and her determination to discover their origin, as we need Kae Ying Woo in *Disappearing Moon Café* to "piece together" the mystery of the Wongs. The journey into the mystery of *Monkey King* is guided by the "recovery" of Sally Wang from her mental breakdown; and here it is the "rich tapestry of culture" and the menacing "ghostly shadow" of the Monkey King to which Sally Wang guides us. Indeed, the phrase "unfolds before our eyes" emphasizes our own passivity and spectator status and hence our need for a guide.

By placing all nine of these book summaries together and identifying the "selling point" that each emphasizes, we perceive a unified discourse arising from otherwise distinct novels. What emerges is a kind of ethnographic autobiography: the revelation of personal and community mysteries as a Chinese American leads the reader into the Chinese past. In this discourse, the past is the key to the present: the Chinese past is reconciled, through "memory" or through "telling," with the American present in order to "pull together" the two cultures that presumably war in the breast of all Chinese Americans.

David Palumbo-Liu calls the literature described here "model minority discourse," which, he argues, limits Asian American writing to an "arena of disease and cure" (*Asian/American* 401). The *Monkey King* summary, in particular, instantiates Palumbo-Liu's point about "model minority discourse and the course of healing." The copy suggests that the protagonist's problem of "split self" comes not from an abusive father (as the actual novel has it) but from the split between her "Chinese self" and her "American self." As the summary puts it, "How she pulls together her Chinese and American identities into a cohesive self and rejoins the land of the living is recounted with a wry and refreshing honesty." Describing a similar instance, Palumbo-Liu remarks, "here we mark the collusion between the rhetoric of healing and the discourse of advertising that is applied to the marketing of Asian American literature that at once exploits its 'exotic' potential and conflates that exoticism into a universalized narrative of 'immigration' . . . in order to elide problematic historical specificities" (411). This "universalized narrative of 'immigration'" allows the advertisement for the book to be simultaneously political and safe. Model minority discourse, Palumbo-Liu argues, needs to be political in order to "satisfy the conditions of minority literature," but the political issues are not threatening to the white, middle-class reader because they are proscribed to the personalized space of the Asian American author/protagonist as "the 'ethnic split,' the 'crisis of identity,' and other elements of ethnic malaise" (401).

The model minority discourse delineated by these book summaries not only promises a touristic view of model minority healing, but it also promises the continued wellness of the white reader. For example, the publisher of *The Monkey King* suggests that the narrator's achievement of "a cohesive self" allows her to "rejoin the land of the living." The ethnic subject's goal here is the healing of the split self, signified by cultural coherence. Significantly, the reader, as armchair ethnographer and pathologist, is reminded that he or she exists in the "land of the living," which is marked by cultural belonging and cultural coherence. In an essay on reading ethnography in Chinese American fiction, Christopher Douglas claims that reading Chinese American fiction "ethnographically . . . produc[es] the coherence of the white reader" (119). The white reader, he argues, finds in the "cultural confusion" and the "crisis of identity" of the Chinese author/protagonist the foil to his or her own coherent self. The sense of dislocation and schizophrenia in the Chinese American reinforces the white reader's sense of belonging, wholeness, and racial health. According to Douglas, "the ethnographic legacy in contemporary minority writing continues to produce the ambivalent effect of inscribing minorities into the national fabric but simultaneously rendering their cultural citizenship status questionable. Through this uncertainty, white cultural citizenship is rejuvenated and made coherent again" (119).

The central point I wish to make is that this discourse is characterized by the Chinese American author because only she, or he, can lead the reader through the gate into that world— or at least this is what the publishers want readers to believe (or to continue believing). The Chinese American author offers us a vantage point that we could otherwise not achieve. This tour guide function rests upon the other functions analyzed in this chapter. Notions of the ethnic author's authenticity and historical status are integral to the kind of discourse characterized by the Chinese American author. In order to be the gatekeeper or the tour guide that leads us into the "hidden," "tangled," and "terrible" secrets of her or his culture, the author must be perceived as authentic. In order to go into the past to make sense of the present, the Chinese American author must be a part of that past and an emblem of that history. Enhancing the ethnicity of the author through various commercial means not only commodifies the ethnic object, but it validates and enhances the discourse that author comes to represent.

"The name of the author," writes Foucault, "remains at the contours of texts—separating one from the other, defining their form, and characterizing their mode of existence. It points to the existence of certain groups of discourse and refers to the status of this discourse within a society and culture" (123). In the case of the ethnic author, the name of the author becomes a site charged with assumptions, expectations, and contestations that intensify its importance and delineate its discourse. What the name of the ethnic author defines and characterizes is a specific "minor literature," in Deleuze and Guattari's sense, and its relation to the major literature, culture, and society. However, as Foucault's description clearly indicates, these distinctions drawn between one and another discourse and the status of each are not delineated solely by writers or texts, but by those who publish, receive, and perceive. The ethnic author does not necessarily produce a minor literature, but is assigned that role by the reader and the publishing industry; the ethnic author speaks from the margins because he or she is perceived to be in those margins.

In my analysis of the ethnic-author function in the reception of Chinese American texts, I have attempted to establish the specific ways that the ethnically Chinese author characterizes "the existence, circulation, and operation" of Chinese American literature. I have described four functions unique to Chinese American literature based on Foucault's essay, in that the ethnic author in Chinese American literature *amplifies* (1) the reader's expectations of communal representation; (2) the reader's belief in, or demand for, culturally authentic representations; (3) the reader's awareness of, or demand for, a correlation between the author and his/her ethnic culture; and (4) the reader's desire for an authentic tour guide into the culture. While this list is by no means exhaustive, I believe these four characteristics of the ethnic-author function are central to the reception of Chinese American literature. This understanding of the Euro-American horizon will, I believe, make possible a discussion of its expansion in the rest of this book.

PART II

Exceeding the Margins

If the process of understanding literary texts is not to give way to a free-floating production of differences . . . responsive self-understanding enabled by the other of the text and the life-world self-understanding arising from the statements and counterstatements of the other must be anchored in a prior understanding of the already said, misunderstood, and previously valid.

—HANS ROBERT JAUSS, *Question and Answer:*
Forms of Dialogic Understanding

The tendency to situate too strictly the minor only at the margins of the dominant downplays the uneven, complex and multiple imbrications of Asians in America.

—DAVID PALUMBO-LIU, *Asian/American:*
Historical Crossings of a Racial Frontier

3 The Politics of Ethnic Authorship

LI-YOUNG LEE, EMERSON, AND WHITMAN

AT THE BANQUET TABLE

The relationship between Asian American literature and mainstream
America has frequently been identified in terms of Asian American
literature's resistance or subordination to mainstream America's domination. . . . This critical approach overlooks the ways in which Asian American authors have resisted, subverted, and reshaped hegemonic European
American literary genres, as well as the ways in which such interventions
demonstrate a much more dynamic and complex relationship between
Asian American and traditional European American literature.

—ZHOU XIAOJING, *Form and Transformation*
in Asian American Literature

Another way to look at the commodity function of the ethnic author
discussed in chapter 2 is to recognize that in today's book market
marginality sells. Where once the marginal was a barrier to publication, it now appears to be an entryway. The fascination with marginality, however, is not just the preoccupation of mainstream readers, but also
of contemporary critical theory. As David Palumbo-Liu has noted, "we find
a valorization of ethnic individuals now empowered by the very 'fact' of being
'minor.' This can lead to a situation in which minority individuals become
the repositories of a reified 'difference'" (415). In this chapter, I seek to examine our fixation with marginality and offer a reading of Chinese American
poet Li-Young Lee that will destabilize our notion of the ethnic writer's marginal status.

The dynamics of Lee's poem "The Cleaving" reveal a blind spot in contemporary critical theory's discussion of the ethnic author. In valorizing the

so-called marginal element in ways that reproduce it as "central" to our cultural concerns, contemporary criticism, in spite of itself, insists upon the segregation of the "ethnic writer" from the "mainstream." As such, we are in danger of patronizingly valuing ethnic writing as a "dynamic" and "colorful" literature of outsiders that brings new "life" to America's tired literary traditions. By insisting on marginality for ethnic authors, we also ignore the dynamic relationship that exists between these writers and the various traditions of American literature to which they, like any other American author, belong. Li-Young Lee's dinner/communion with Emerson and Whitman in "The Cleaving" illustrates what is at stake when we approach a given writer as either "Asian American" or "American." The poem shrewdly questions the *either/or* between these authorial identities.

"ROMANCING THE MARGINS"[1]

We often use the word "marginal" as if it did not undergo its own shifts in meaning, but the shifting relevance of "the marginal" in relation to the larger body of contemporary American literature highlights one of the most remarkable paradoxes of ethnic authorship over the past half-century. A broad view of Asian American literary production and consumption over the past fifty years suggests that ethnic writing is no longer marginal, or, to see it another way, that marginality is no longer a negative marker to mainstream literary tastes. Asian American writers such as Diana Chang, Toshio Mori, Carlos Bulosan, John Okada, and Louis Chu published before the 1960s, but their works fell quickly into obscurity. Even in the wake of the civil rights movement, authors and publishers saw Asian American writing as a risk. One famous example is Knopf's decision to market *The Woman Warrior* as nonfiction in 1975, perhaps emphasizing its tour guide status to Chinese culture (which sold well at that time) rather than letting it stand on its strengths as a novel. Also in the 1970s, David Wong Louie removed the Chinese names from his stories in order to improve their marketability, a decision he made in response to rejections from editors who found his stories too Chinese[2] (Simpson 67). The marginal status of Asian Americans in the United States was at that time a purely negative factor for publishers. As a result, most of the Asian American literature published during this period served to satisfy the curiosity of white American readers, and it reinforced the illusion of white superiority, white "coherence," and white "cultural citizenship" (Douglas 119) in these readers by presenting Asians as non-threatening and inferior. The Asian American writer was then the tour guide to the literary Chinatown.

Elaine H. Kim, writing in 1982, argues that "until recently, published Asian American writers presented the Asian American experience lightly and euphemistically, even humorously, without significant expression of concern about the manifestations of social injustice" (*Asian American Literature* 59). In Kim's view, "publishers and a predominantly white readership" tolerated expressions of "Asian cultures and values, and Asian American values and life styles" when the ethnic writer wrote with racial "self-contempt and self-negation" rather than when the ethnic writer wrote to criticize "problems in American society" (59). In other words, Asian American works before the 1970s were consumed as light appetizers for the American body, which was understood at that time as white/non-marginal, and Asian American writers were not yet invited to the banquet table.

Since the 1970s, the status of the ethnic author within the literature of the United States has undergone a profound change. This change was the effect both of ethnic literary activism and shifts in mainstream literary tastes. A recap of the reception of Asian American literature presented briefly in the introduction will illustrate the magnitude of this change. *Aiiieeeee! An Anthology of Asian American Writers* (1974) and *The Woman Warrior* (1975) set the table for the publication of more Asian American works, and for the invitation of earlier "lost" works to the banquet (e.g., Chu's *Eat a Bowl of Tea* and Okada's *No-No Boy*). By the end of the 1980s, Amy Tan reached star status with *The Joy Luck Club* and a variety of other Asian American writers were picked up by the larger publishing houses. A story by David Wong Louie about an immigrant couple from China, "Displacement," finally saw the light of day and was published in *The Best American Short Stories 1989*. In the 1990s, Jhumpa Lahiri won the Pulitzer Prize for her short story collection, *Interpreter of Maladies*, and Ha Jin's work has been lauded with a National Book Award and two PEN/Faulkner Prizes. Asian American writers such as Li-Young Lee are also included in major anthologies such as the *Norton Anthology of American Literature*, which perhaps suggests that Asian American works are valued more for their literary quality than they were in the past.

There are many possible explanations for the ethnic author's change in status—we might cite the emergence of a more multicultural education system and curriculum, multiculturalism's success in the "culture war" over the canon, larger economic and cultural processes called "globalization," and other factors. But I believe we should also recognize the persistence of racialized thinking in American society as a significant factor. America's appetite for Asian American writing is growing, but to what extent is this interest still tied to a tourist mentality designed to make white, middle-class readers feel superior and coherent? According to E. San Juan Jr., "if the margin has moved to the center, or has been accommodated to the core by a strategy of co-optation and displacement, racism is preserved and strengthened in its polit-ical-economic functionality and ideological effects" (111). As my discussion of the ethnic-author function and the literary Chinatown suggests, we should be skeptical of the popularity of ethnic literature among the general readership. In the following discussion, however, I shift my attention to the status of ethnic writing in critical discourse, where, as Shirley Geok-lin Lim et al. put it, "Asian American literature can no longer be viewed as merely a minor ethnic province of a domestic American canon" (*Studies* x).

The rise of the ethnic author, insofar as it represents an "assimilation" of the ethnic author into the larger body of American literature, also implies a consequent shift in the status of "marginality" within American literature. Paradoxically, contemporary literary criticism's emphasis on the marginal has made the marginal central. One prominent example of the critical cel-ebration of marginality is found in Deleuze and Guattari's 1986 book, *Kafka: Toward a Minor Literature*.[3] Deleuze and Guattari argue in their book that the writer in the ethnic (and hence linguistic and literary) margins of society occu-pies the necessary position to rejuvenate the stagnant literary language of the "established" or "major" literature (18). They argue that marginality "allows the writer all the more the possibility to express another possible community and to forge the means for another consciousness and another sensibility" (17). Deleuze and Guattari are not writing about Asian American writers today; however, their analysis of the ethnic writer is meant to be transportable—Deleuze and Guattari suggest as much when they write that the revolutionary quality of Prague German for Kafka "can be compared in another context to what blacks in America today are able to do with the English language" (17). If we apply this argument to contemporary American litera-ture, as Deleuze and Guattari suggest we should, we elevate the ethnic author's position and celebrate the heroism of marginalized voices in their struggle against the hegemony of "mainstream" literature, but we also fetishize eth-nic marginality, making literary rejuvenation dependent upon ethnic difference and the maintenance of the ethnic author's outsider status.

Deleuze and Guattari's model of literary rejuvenation depends upon the literary segregation of "major" and "minor" literatures that reifies difference. In their view, a "minor" literature infiltrates the language and challenges the perspectives of a "major" or "established" literature and thereby revitalizes the major literature. The minor literature "deterritorializes" the major lit-erature, disrupting its hegemonic order and "reterritorializing" it in a new "sense"—thus changing the map or the landscape of the established literature (21). However, the validity of their theory rests upon the outsider status of the ethnic writer and thereby ignores the influence of the established literature and its various traditions upon that writer. A writer like Kafka may write "like a dog digging a hole" or "a rat digging its burrow" (18) in German literature, but one is left to conclude that German literature does not dig a hole in Kafka. In their emphasis on the ways minoritiness gets into a national literature, Deleuze and Guattari reify the relationship of ethnic authorship to an established, national literature as a one-way street. Romancing the margins therefore tends to neglect the dynamic relationship between an ethnic author and an established national literature, and thus treats the ethnic author as special or extraordinary.

Ethnic authors may draw from cultural codes "alien" to the codes of the established literature, but they likewise draw from the traditions, literary influences, and established codes of the major literature within which they are writing. To put it in Harold Bloom's terms, ethnic authors suffer from the same anxieties of influence as non-ethnic writers. Like other writers, they worry that a hole is being dug in them. In Asian American literature alone, there are many examples of the "ethnic" author's interaction with authors from "established" literatures: Walt Whitman in Maxine Hong Kingston's *Tripmaster Monkey* (the protagonist is Wittman Ah Sing), John Cheever in Chang-rae Lee's *A Gesture Life*, Sherwood Anderson in Toshio Mori's *Yokohama, California*, Sylvia Plath in Patricia Chao's *Monkey King*, the Bible in Joy Kogawa's *Obasan* and in Li-Young Lee's poetry and memoir, W. B. Yeats and Greek mythology in Robert Ji-Song Ku's short story "Leda," Auden, Donne, Keats, Houseman, and many other British poets in Shirley Geok-lin Lim's *Joss and Gold*, and F. Scott Fitzgerald in Gish Jen's *Typical American* and the first segment of Russell Leong's long poem *The Country of Dreams and Dust*. By insisting only on the marginality of ethnic writers, by continually marking them as outsiders to the "mainstream," we are in danger of missing their participation in the various traditions of "established" literature.

To return to Li-Young Lee's banquet table, a consideration of "ethnic eating" in his poetry, and particularly in "The Cleaving," will show that the ethnic author is simultaneously the diner and the dinner. Through a reading of "ethnic eating" in Li-Young Lee's poetry, we will see that the Asian American writer in contemporary American literature participates in, and inherits, American literature, and is not simply a marginalized, heroic voice challenging the status quo. Asian American writers in today's American literature are dynamically engaged with that literature and with its various and disparate traditions. A discussion of cultural eating in Li-Young Lee's poetry allows us to isolate both the "deterritorializing" function of an ethnic author's writing (as theorized by Deleuze and Guattari) as well as to appreciate that author's fluid engagement with literary forebears in the established literature.

DEVOURING RACISM

In "The Cleaving," Li-Young Lee announces his desire to devour Ralph Waldo Emerson like a steamed fish in a Chinese meal. The reader forgives this breach of table etiquette because, as Lee informs us, Emerson said the whole Chinese race was ugly. He deserves to be eaten. But Lee's poem is more sophisticated and more philosophical than this tit-for-tat scenario suggests. In "The Cleaving," eating is *assault*, but it is also *digestion* and *assimilation*. Lee brings the butcher's shop close to the banquet table by deliberately playing on the two senses of the verb "cleave" to suggest both chopping up and clinging to, and thus the poem vacillates between the act of rejection and the process of assimilation. Eating in this poem may begin with the butcher's chopping block, but it is ultimately about communion.

In other poems by Li-Young Lee, eating is a cultural activity that enacts familial and ethnic community. The Chinese meal of rice and steamed fish in "Eating Together" is a metaphor that combines generational continuity with a sense of familial belonging after the death of the poet's father, and this metaphor is juxtaposed with the loneliness of the meal described in "Eating Alone." These poems from *Rose*, Lee's first book of poetry, contextualize eating as a familial activity fraught with personal (though not just private) significance. In a much longer poem, "The Cleaving," from *The City in Which I Love You*, eating becomes both a sign of cultural communion with other Chinese immigrants (i.e., the larger cultural community) as well as an aggressive weapon against racism in American society and American literature. The poet "transforms words into things capable of competing with food" (Deleuze and Guattari, *Kafka* 20) when, in order to speak as a poet for his community, he "eats" that community, and he "eats" Ralph Waldo Emerson and his insulting and reductive remark that the Chinese "managed to preserve to a hair . . . the ugliest features in the world."

"The Cleaving" forcefully asserts the place of the Chinese American poet in American literary tradition by simultaneously attacking and embracing that tradition through the Asian American literary trope of what Sau-ling Cynthia Wong calls "the big eating hero."[4] Regardless of cultural contexts, eating is an image of both domination and acquiescence. As Wong reminds us, "ingestion is the physical act that mediates between self and non-self, native essence and foreign matter, the inside and the outside" (26). Deleuze and Guattari similarly argue that eating, like speaking, is a fundamental act of deterritorialization of the Other that ultimately reterritorializes the space of the Other through the activity of "the mouth, the tongue, and the teeth" (19). The difference between writing and eating for Deleuze and Guattari is that writing reterritorializes language as something more "capable of competing with food" (20), whereas eating merely deterritorializes.

Eating allows the speaker in "The Cleaving" to mediate between his own voice and American literary tradition. The poet expresses the seemingly divergent actions of attacking and embracing through his use of the verb "cleave." The verb "to cleave" encompasses opposing possibilities: to "split" or "divide by force" (here a transitive verb), and to "adhere closely," "hold fast," or "cling" (here an intransitive verb). Lee writes that "change / resides in the embrace / of the effaced and the effacer, / in the covenant of the opened and the opener" (86). Like the sharp-edged cleaver wielded by the Chinese butcher, the poem "coaxes, cleaves, brings change" through violent images of eating and devouring, the teeth also functioning as a kind of cleaver.[5]

Writing within the Chinese tradition of the conquering hero, the poet in "The Cleaving" is the "big eater": like Brave Orchid in *The Woman Warrior* who vanquishes life-threatening ghosts through eating, the poet is driven by "necessity" to ingest all forms of nutrition no matter how unpalatable they may seem to the reader. The speaker ingests the brain of the duck and the head of the carp. He also expresses a desire to eat the butcher, the Chinese race, Ralph Waldo Emerson, and even death itself. As these descriptions attest, becoming a big eater is not simply a matter of eating what one must to survive, but actually learning to enjoy as delicacies the parts that others may simply discard as inedible. According to Sau-ling Cynthia Wong, big eaters in Asian American literature are defined by "an ability to eat unpromising substances and to extract sustenance, even a sort of willed enjoyment, from them; to put it symbolically, it is the ability to cope with the constraints and persecutions Asian Americans have had to endure as immigrants and racial minorities" (*Reading* 25).

The sixth stanza of the poem launches into a frenzy of big eating that speaks both of the poem's response to racism as well as its function as poetic utterance. The pace of the poem is driven by the quick transition from one food item (if we can call them that) to another: fish, butcher, bodies, features, hairs, Emerson, and the carp's / Emerson's head. Although the poet expresses his desire to eat in the conditional voice ("I would eat"), the steady repetition of the monosyllabic and aggressive "eat" hurls the reader from one image to another.

> What is it in me will not let
> the world be, would eat
> not just this fish,
> but the one who killed it,
> the butcher who cleaned it.
> I would eat the way he
> squats, the way he reaches into the plastic tubs
> and pulls out a fish, clubs it, takes it
> to the sink, guts it, drops it on the weighing pan.
> I would eat that thrash
> and plunge of the watery body
> in the water, that liquid violence
> between the man's hands,
> I would eat
> the gutless twitching on the scales,
> three pounds of dumb
> nerve and pulse, I would eat it all
> to utter it. (82–83)

This segment describes more than simply eating a fish: the fish is not sitting idly on a plate, cooked and ready for consumption. The fish is alive and vigorous, and it is that vigor, that "violence," that the speaker wishes to absorb: "I would eat that thrash/ and plunge, that liquid violence." There is something vital in the fish that the speaker seeks to obtain, much the way that traditional Chinese eating relates the properties of the eaten to the desired properties of the eater. This traditional concept brings Lee's poem into conversation with that tradition, but also, again, with other Asian American texts. In Lee's poem, however, the "thrash," "plunge," and "liquid violence" relate to vitality (and in the image of the "liquid violence/ between the man's hands" may also suggest sexual potency). But, it also relates to death: the fish after all is in its dying throes. As the stanza develops, the presence of death and the speaker's reaction to it become central.

The fish's "twitching" death under the club of the butcher drives the speaker into a consideration of other deaths. The speaker's attraction to the fish is burdened with meaning. Eating the struggles of the fish (the "thrash" and the "plunge") in its dying throes is like eating the struggles of the immigrant community. The death of the fish ("the deaths at the sinks") leads the speaker to consider other deaths around him: "the standing deaths at the counters" are the butchers and fishmongers of the Hon Kee Grocery; the deaths "in the aisles" are the customers; "the walking deaths in the streets" are connected to the "Chinatown deaths," that is, the streets of Chinatown surrounding the grocery; and "Chinatown deaths" are immigrant deaths ("far-from-home" and "in-a-strange-land"). Finally, these deaths of immigrants from Asia are "American deaths": they occur in America, but more importantly the line suggests that leaving one's country to live and die in America is an American experience. The next line confirms that these are Asian immigrants whom the speaker wishes to ingest: "I would devour *this race* to sing it" (emphasis added).

The struggles, the thrashing, and plunging of the immigrant Chinese is the result of anti-Chinese sentiment, as the next segment suggests:

> I would devour this race to sing it,
> this race that according to Emerson
> *managed to preserve to a hair*
> *for three or four thousand years*
> *the ugliest features in the world.*
> I would eat these features, eat
> the last three or four thousand years, every hair.
> And I would eat Emerson, his transparent soul, his
> soporific transcendence. (83, italics in original)

The quotation from Emerson's journals is the point where Lee most explicitly enters a conversation with American literary tradition. For now, however, I will discuss Lee's emphasis on the quotation's racism, thus bracketing for the moment the literary and poetic tradition Emerson represents as well as the context of Emerson's journal entry. The speaker's response to the racist remarks of Emerson is central to the entire poem. The poet contrasts his own poetic utterance, the speaker's ability to speak, with the muteness of the fish, which as we have seen above stands for the Chinese immigrant: "the gutless twitching on the scales,/ three pounds of *dumb*/ nerve and pulse, I would eat it all/ to utter it" (83, emphasis added). The response of the Chinese immigrant to racism has been a "dumb" (i.e., mute) struggle: the immigrant thrashes and plunges, but remains unable to articulate a response to the discursive power behind popular, literary, and institutional racism. The speaker responds with a discursive feast modeled after the big-eating heroes of Chinese legends: "I would eat this head, / glazed in pepper-speckled sauce."

The head of the fish comes to represent both the immigrant community (whose "features" and "hairs" the speaker says he would eat) as well as Emerson's racist comments, the "opaque" eyes of the fish head reminding us of the "transparent eyeball" of Emerson's philosophy.[6] Perhaps the idea of eating these negative comments would strike some American readers as an odd gesture. Swallowing hardship for some might be a courageous act that reveals one's mental toughness, but it also carries connotations of acquiescence, of giving in. Yet in Chinese American literary tradition swallowing hardship, or "eating bitter," is often represented as a heroic act. According to Wong,

> disagreeable food puts to the test one's capacity to consolidate one's self by appropriating resources from the external environment, to convert the seemingly useless into the useful, refuse into nutrition. Physical survival is incompatible with a finicky palate; psychological survival hinges on the wresting of meaning from arbitrary infliction of humiliation and pain; survival of family and the ethnic group not only presupposes individually successful eating but may demand unusually difficult "swallowing" to ensure a continued supply of nourishment for the next generation. (*Reading* 26)

The speaker in "The Cleaving" turns the "seemingly useless into the useful" when he eats Emerson's racist remarks. Rather than cringing and retreating from them, he "devours" them much the way that he devours the head of the fish ("with a stiff tongue lick out/ the cheek-meat"). The speaker openly relishes the fish head, describing his experience as "sensual." This ravishing enjoyment is an act of defiance in Mikhail Bakhtin's sense of the carnivalesque—an overturning of hegemonic and hierarchical order, a response to the age-old argument that Chinese eating habits mark them as barbaric and inhumane. As with his response to Emerson's racist statement, the speaker embraces the notion of the champion eater; he does not adopt white American eating habits, but makes pride in his own culture's customs his weapon. That the speaker's eating is more than an individual response is suggested by the manner in which he consumes the fish's cheeks: "the way I was taught, the way I've watched/ others before me do." The speaker eats in a cultural way. He has learned this eating from his community. Thus, while those who came before him may have been able to devour only a literal fish in this way, the speaker meshes "ethnic eating" with linguistic skill and poetic discourse to devour racist discourse.

In Lee's poetry, cultural eating is not always expressed in violent terms, despite the carnivalesque and grotesque imagery described above. In *Rose*, Lee exalts the communal and relational significance of eating in a Chinese family, a significance that he expands to the immigrant community in "The Cleaving." His poem "Eating Alone" describes his loneliness as he tends his garden and thinks of his recently deceased father. The loss of his father is so poignant to the poet's mind that he imagines his father waving to him in the garden, only to realize that it was "the shovel, leaning where I had/ left it" (33). The poem then concludes with a stanza describing a Chinese meal that he prepares and consumes alone:

> White rice steaming, almost done. Sweet green peas
> fried in onions. Shrimp braised in sesame
> oil and garlic. And my own loneliness.
> What more could I, a young man, want.

The sardonic tone of the final line is achieved through the juxtaposing of his father's absence from the garden and now, implicitly, his absence from the table. There is no joy in the "bare," "cold,/ brown and old" garden without his father's presence. The illusion of his presence merely increases the loneliness he describes at the table.

Another poem in *Rose*, "Eating Together," provides an intertextual juxtaposition with "Eating Alone." In "Eating Together," the father is still absent, but the community of family around their Chinese meal remembers the father as the conveyor of tradition, and, significantly, as no longer alone. In the community of family, the poet is not lonely, and neither is his father. The family continues the tradition of eating together. Moreover, the mother now takes the father's place, as signified by her eating the sweetest meat nestled in the head of the trout. In "The Cleaving," this same love of community through the communion of cultural eating is contrasted with the violent eating required in devouring racism. In his paean to the Chinese immigrant in stanza five, the poet says of his fellow Chinese immigrants,

> happy, talkative, voracious
> at day's end,
> eager to eat
> four kinds of meat
> prepared four different ways,
> numerous plates and bowls of rice and vegetables,

each made by distinct affections
and brought to table by many hands. (80–81)

The cultural eating of the family in "Eating Together" opens to the cultural eating of the immigrant community in "The Cleaving." Cultural eating is as much an image of revolt against racism as it is a statement of community and, as we will see below, of transcendence.

TRANSCENDENTAL EATING

"The Cleaving" is a poetic cleaver that carves a space in American literary tradition, with Emerson standing as the overt (albeit negative) marker for that tradition. In some sense it would be more accurate to say that the poem "hacks" a space: hacking describes the action of a cleaver, and perhaps it more clearly describes the speaker's voracious attack on Emerson. Yet, as discussed above, Lee makes deliberate use of the verb "cleave" to suggest both hacking and adhering, splitting and joining. This same process is inherent in the analogy of eating: we attack by cutting, biting, chewing, swallowing, and digesting, but through this attack, we also absorb the nutrients of what we eat; we reterritorialize them. What we eat, in this sense, becomes a part of us.

The opposite actions of devouring and nourishing, and of deterritorializing and reterritorializing, are thus necessary to the speaker's response to Emerson, which is implicitly linked to this line toward the conclusion of the poem: "Change/ resides in the embrace/ of the effaced and the effacer,/ in the covenant of the opened and the opener" (86). By linking these lines with the speaker's response to Emerson, I wish to suggest that the poem is not an outright rejection of Emerson and the philosophy of transcendentalism. While eating Emerson seems to overtly and violently disassociate the speaker from Emerson and his influence, as a "food" substance Emerson becomes a nutrient for the speaker's poetic utterance (though later I will question the poem's reconstruction of Emerson). The poem suggests therefore that positive "change," as with expanding the horizon of consciousness and the reader's horizon of expectation, requires an "embrace" and a "covenant" between the racialized self and the racist other. Thus, while it may appear that Lee has set Emerson up as a straw man, what he expresses in the poem belies a deep-seated indebtedness to Emerson.

The poem explicitly rejects Emerson's racist remarks and Emerson's philosophy of transcendentalism, making no distinction between the two.

However, I believe it is necessary to make the distinction. First, the poet rightly objects to Emerson's inflammatory attack on the Chinese. There can be no denying that the remarks are inappropriate and ignorant. But given a fuller picture of Emerson's life and of nineteenth-century thinking on race, we can at least contextualize them and perhaps better understand them. Emerson entered these comments on the Chinese in his private journal at the age of twenty during a period in which, as Robert D. Richardson Jr. describes it, he was in a "gloomy and petulant" mood (55). His information about the Chinese came from one secondary source, a book he had just read called *Journal of the Late Embassy to China*. Richardson describes Emerson's early journals as "mostly dross and largely unoriginal" (42). Emerson's own, often self-parodic, comments in the margins suggest that he saw some of his own jottings as crude. His early journals are also full of tastes, opinions, and statements that would be completely inverted later in life. Richardson notes that "among modern poets he idolized Byron and made fun of Wordsworth, tastes he would later reverse. His college writings, like his college life, were full of contradictions. His long poem 'Indian Superstition' was a Southey-inspired tirade against the Hindu religious tradition he would later come to admire" (16).

Emerson's comments on the Chinese race are indeed "petulant" and dismissive, but the fervor of his tirade against the Chinese whom he had never personally encountered might be regarded as "comic," as Richardson suggests (55). His exclamation "I hate Pekin!" (*Journal* 229) is overexuberant and ridiculous. Given the breadth and depth of Emerson's mature writing, it might well be unfair to boil him down to one racist comment recorded in a melancholy period of his youth. On the other hand, we might also note that this kind of racialized discourse was common in nineteenth-century thinking, as unacceptable as it may appear to us today, and that Emerson's mature writing reflects his culture's understanding of race and its relation to character. In his essay on race, published in *English Traits* in 1856, Emerson writes, "on the English face are combined decision and nerve, with the fair complexion, blue eyes, and open and florid aspect. Hence the love of truth, hence the sensibility, the fine perception, and poetic construction" (*Essays and Lectures* 802). The positive traits of English culture, Emerson believed, were literally written on the face of the Englishman. Emerson furthermore explained the success of English imperialism in racial terms: "It is race, is it not? that puts the hundred millions of India under the domination of a remote island in the north of Europe" (792).

Emerson's insistence that the English race owed its "success" to its hybridity connects these observations to the journal comments quoted in "The

Cleaving": "The best nations," wrote Emerson, "are those most widely related; and navigation, as effecting a world-wide mixture, is the most potent advancement of nations. . . . Everything English is a fusion of distant and antagonistic elements" (*Essays and Lectures* 793). True to his belief in "evolutionary humanism, based on the pre-Darwinian theory of the French naturalist, Lamarck" (Ericson xi), Emerson argued that the more advanced races were those that experienced the broadest range of contact with other races. His argument against the Chinese race twenty-seven years earlier was based on what he perceived to be its purity: that the Chinese race "managed to preserve" its features explains why he claimed in the same journal entry that the Chinese empire enjoyed "a Mummy's reputation" (*Journals* 378). (In "The Conservative," Emerson refers to the lack of regeneration through reform as "the Chinese stagnation of society" [185].) Emerson's argument reflects the general American and British sentiment against China's protectionist policies regarding trade, a sentiment that led to the Opium Wars of 1839–42 and 1856–58.

In "The Cleaving," Lee explicitly contradicts Emerson's journal comments by valorizing the immigrant race's fluidity and variety. The butcher, by the end of the poem, is described as having a "Shang dynasty face" (86), which, as Zhou Xiaojing suggests, is a response to Emerson's comment about the static nature of the Chinese for the past three to four thousand years (129).[7] This Shang dynasty face is, in the speaker's imagination, transformed into an "African face with slit eyes" (86) suggesting a hybrid blending of races. He furthermore transgresses gender boundaries with the phrase, "he is my sister" (86). The speaker's valorization of the immigrant race's hybridity and variety responds to Emerson's claim that the Chinese race has "managed to preserve" itself over the centuries, but it joins with Emerson in privileging the hybrid over the pure. In addition, the speaker reads the butcher's physical features in much the same way that Emerson read the English face. The butcher reminds the speaker of a northerner because of the "boniness" of his face, "clear from the high / warlike forehead / to the sheer edge of the jaw" (77–78). At the same time, the "moodiness" of his looks and the way "his face [is] poised" suggest to the speaker that he is a southerner (78). Unlike the Emerson of the 1824 journal entry, the speaker sees variety in the Chinese race, but because the distinctions are inscribed in the physical features of the butcher, they serve to re-inscribe Chinese racial biases regarding northern and southern Chinese in much the way Emerson re-inscribed racial biases in *English Traits*.

At a deeper and more positive level, "The Cleaving" enters into dialogue with the humanism and universalism of both Emerson and Whitman. Judith

Kitchen, in a review of Lee's poetry for *The Georgia Review*, claims that "The Cleaving" "eschews the need for transcendence" (263). She does not elaborate this point, so one is left to speculate that, for her, the poem's statements about Emerson and his "soporific transcendence" constitute a rejection of transcendentalism. But the question remains: What does Lee mean by calling Emerson's philosophy a "soporific transcendence?" I believe that the phrase is meant to convey the ethereal qualities often associated with transcendentalism. In other words, the speaker sees Emerson's transcendentalism as a mystical philosophy devoid of action and empirical validity. By "soporific," the speaker may be suggesting that Emerson's is a non-active philosophy, and hence marked by lethargy, or that belief in transcendentalism leads to a dulling of one's awareness. Thus, in comparison, the transcendence that describes the metaphysics of "The Cleaving" is expressed in physical and aggressive terms. We are "bodies eating bodies, heads eating heads," and "as we eat we're eaten" (85), summing up the interconnectedness of all beings, not in mystical but in physical terms.

However, the poem misconstrues Emerson if its complaint against his philosophy is based on a distinction between active transcendentalism (illustrated in the violent, aggressive transcendence of "The Cleaving") and inactive or purely mystical transcendentalism (supposedly illustrated by Emerson's writings). Although Emerson's philosophy owed much to mysticism, his was by no means a soporific transcendentalism. As Edward L. Ericson writes in his introduction to *Emerson on Transcendentalism*:

> Despite the mystical strain in Emerson's philosophy, or perhaps because of it, he recognized that the action gives birth to the thought, providing the American mind with its unmistakable signature: "The preamble of thought, the transition through which it passes from the unconscious to the conscious, is action. Only so much do I know, as I have lived." (ix)

Besides the basic relation between physical action and mystical thought, as described here, Emerson's philosophy cannot properly be construed as causing lethargy or leading to inaction. According to Ericson,

> while metaphysical idealism is often considered a conservative philosophy, allied to the status quo, in Emerson it attains an antiauthoritarian, evolutionary outlook. It affirms a spiritual conception of democracy in which each person writes within his or her own heart the living scripture of personal worth and self-reliance. (x)

One could argue that self-reliance and the kind of tenacious individualism that has come to be associated with America are the direct legacies of Emerson's thinking and writing on individual action.

We might see little difference between Emerson's transcendentalism and the interconnectedness of Lee's immigrants through eating if we consider the way Perry Miller once described Emerson's notion of interconnectedness:

> Emerson . . . assert[ed] that should he ever be bayoneted he would fall by his own hand disguised in another uniform, that because all men participate in the Over-Soul those who shoot and those who are shot prove to be identical, that *in the realm of the transcendental there is nothing to choose between eating and being eaten.* (13, emphasis added)

To say then that Lee "eschews the transcendental" because the speaker in his poem wants to eat Emerson and calls Emerson's philosophy "soporific" is to miss the essential point that Lee's poem becomes what it seems to eschew. As seen in the quotation from Perry Miller, a victim in Emerson's transcendentalism sees himself in his attacker, and one who eats is at one with what is eaten. This is precisely the kind of transcendence portrayed in "The Cleaving." In the poet's words, we are "bodies eating bodies, heads eating heads."

The transcendental relatedness of all beings is present in the poem from beginning to end through identification and resemblance. "The Cleaving" begins with the speaker's observations on the Chinese butcher in the Hon Kee Grocery, a man whose face resembles the speaker's face and whose actions resemble those of an old woman: "He gossips like my grandmother, this man / with my face" (77). The poem therefore begins with an act of identification, but also with a broadening of the scope of resemblance. Not only does the man look like the speaker and gossip like his grandmother, but we are told that his "sorrowful," "warlike," bony face resembles a nomad from the Gobi regions of northern China (77), yet in his "light-handed calligraphy" on receipts and his "moodiness," he resembles a "Southerner from a river-province" (78). Moreover, the speaker says, "he could be my grandfather; / come to America to get a Western education / in 1917" (78). Personal history and ethnic history are thus located in this one man, in whom the speaker also sees himself.

The Chinese immigrant community from which the speaker descends is the beginning point for the transcendental foundation of the poem. By the end, this identity opens up to all immigrants:

the sorrow of his Shang
dynasty face
African face with slit eyes. He is
my sister, this
beautiful Bedouin, this Shulamite,
keeper of Sabbaths, diviner
of holy texts, this dark
dancer, this Jew, this Asian, this one
with the Cambodian face, the Vietnamese face, this Chinese
I daily face,
this immigrant,
this man with my own face. (86–87)

The butcher therefore stands for the Other in whom the poet sees himself, and in their shared humanity, they are not only connected, they are the same. "Was it me in the other I loved/ when I loved another?" he asks (79). But the face he sees also extends through the Asian diaspora (Asian, Cambodian, Vietnamese, Chinese), through the Middle East (Bedouin, Shulamite, Jew), and even hybridizes race and gender ("African face with slit eyes. He is/ my sister"). The poem constructs the immigrant community as a united family that transcends borders and boundaries.

In her discussion of the poem's dialogue with Emerson, Zhou Xiaojing suggests that Lee broadens the topic broached by Emerson by bringing to it a marginalized immigrant perspective:

> Lee's response to Emerson's words brings his narrowly conceived gener-
> alization to dialogue with multiple and heterogenous specificity pre-
> sented in the poem. The validity of the assumed universal truth in Emerson's
> remarks, acquired through transcendental consciousness, is challenged
> within a wider cultural horizon and from a different point of view. ("Inher-
> itance" 127)

I concur that Lee's attack on Emerson opens the conversation to a larger context, one that includes those who have been relegated to the margins of American society by racialized and racist discourse. However, in claiming that Emerson's comments were "acquired through transcendental consciousness," Zhou seems to be submitting to the same reductionist view of Emerson that the poem does. Zhou claims that "Emerson's transcendental generalization about the whole people becomes dangerously limited" (127).

I agree that Emerson's generalization is dangerously "narrow"; however, what is transcendental about Emerson's generalization? In equating the young Emerson's racist comments with his entire philosophy, Zhou fails to recognize the ways in which Lee's poem, perhaps unwittingly, embraces Emerson's philosophy. Zhou rightly claims that "Lee's 'telling' of the Chinese-American immigrants' experiences in his poems involves the processes of self-exploration and self-invention" and that through his poetry Lee reveals that "Chinese-Americans can remake themselves in images of their own invention" (131). What she neglects to recognize is how Emersonian these claims are.

"A MANY-MEMBERED BODY OF LOVE": EATING THE BODY ELECTRIC

For all its violent eating and grotesque devouring, the metaphysics of "The Cleaving" is Emersonian. The poet furthermore communes with his American literary forebears through the celebratory mood of "The Cleaving," reminiscent of Walt Whitman and his brand of transcendentalism. Through "The Cleaving," Lee enters a dialogic relationship with Emersonian transcendentalism that is similar to the relationship between Whitman's poetry and Emerson's philosophy. According to Jerome Loving, one "of Whitman's achievements in his first edition of *Leaves of Grass* was to advance Emersonianism or transcendentalism by contradicting it" (452–53). While Whitman's poetry maintained a transcendentalist perspective that God is immanent in nature and in the human soul (as encapsulated, for Emerson, in the rather disembodied notion of the Over-soul), his poetry departed from Emerson's transcendentalism in its language and philosophy of the body. Rather than seeing the body as merely "an emblem of the Soul" or as a "world of senses" that must be transcended in order to become "whole again in the mind of God" (Loving 453), Whitman celebrated the body as soul. In the twenty-first stanza of "Song of Myself," Whitman writes, "I am the poet of the Body and I am the poet of the Soul" (207). Similarly, in the closing lines of "I Sing the Body Electric," the poet equates the body with the soul, thereby breaking down the distinction between the two: "O I say these are not the parts and poems of the body only, but of the soul,/ O I say now these are the soul!" (258). This poem in particular established Whitman as "the poet of the body" and distinguishes his transcendentalism from Emerson's. Like Li-Young Lee, Whitman continued Emerson by challenging Emerson in an Emersonian way.

In a strikingly similar fashion, "The Cleaving" glories in the Chinese immigrants' physical bodies. Their physical features and their diversity become the window to their collective soul. The speaker delights in the bodies he describes; he "longs" for these "bodies/ and scents of bodies" (80). Even in describing their inadequacies ("straight/ or humped, whole, manqué, quasi") and stereotypical differences from the white race ("jut jaw . . . wide nose . . . thick lips" [81]), the speaker insists that "each pleases." This pleasure is reminiscent of Whitman's paean to the human form in "I Sing the Body Electric," in which some stanzas read like an anatomy lesson in their detailed descriptions: "Head, neck, hair, ears, drop and tympan of the ears/ . . . The lung-sponges, the stomach-sac, the bowels sweet and clean,/ The brain in its folds inside the skull-frame" (257). As with Lee's "cleaving" paradox, Whitman mixes seemingly incommensurable vocabularies of poetry and dissection. Moreover, the poet's contemplation of "the brain in its folds inside the skull-frame" is echoed by Lee's meditation on the duck's brain, which the speaker picks out of "the skull-cradle" (80). Lee's poem expresses identity with the immigrant community in terms of their shared blood; despite physical differences, they are "brothers and sisters by blood" (81). In Whitman's poem, the speaker identifies with humanity, in one instance with that of a black slave being sold at auction:

> Within there runs blood,
> The same old blood
> the same red-running blood!
> There swells and jets a heart, there all passions, desires, reachings,
> aspirations. (256)

In much the same way that the speaker in "The Cleaving" identifies with his immigrant community, Whitman's speaker identifies himself with the bodies he describes in the very first line of "I Sing the Body Electric":

> I sing the body electric,
> The armies of those I love engirth me and I engirth them,
> They will not let me off till I go with them, respond to them,
> And discorrupt them, and charge them full with the charge of the
> soul. (250)

In these lines, the speaker reveals two concerns that become central to the poem: one is his sense of shared humanity ("the armies of those I love engirth me and I engirth them"); the other is his responsibility to his fellow human beings to "respond to them," to "discorrupt them," and to "charge them full with the charge of the soul." In this second purpose, the poet sees himself as speaking for the entire human race, and through this poetic utterance (this "singing") to free it from "false" notions of corruption. He is a poet/prophet who will return honor to the human body and the interconnectedness of humankind.

"The Cleaving" shares with Whitman's poem this expressed desire to unite, to inspire dignity, and to give utterance.

What is it in me would
devour the world to utter it? . . .
I would eat it all
to utter it . . .
I would devour this race to sing it. (82–83)

The ultimate goal of eating in Lee's poem is poetry. The bodies of his immigrant community as well as the racial slurs of the white majority are nutrients to the poet in the same way that fish, pig, and duck are nutrients to the physical body. He must internalize everything—good, bad, or neutral—in order to have poetic control of everything. His poem does not discard the immigrant community as a burden, neither does it retreat into Chinatown in the face of discrimination. Rather, his poem speaks in an American poetic voice through a motif that affirms the ethnic community.

We must recognize, however, that the line "I would devour this race to sing it" echoes, but distinctly alters, Whitman's declaration, "I sing the body electric." Whitman celebrates the physical body, glorying in its form, and its reproductive and hence life-affirming powers. Lee, on the other hand, celebrates the Chinese immigrant body by declaring his desire to devour it as though it were food. To grasp the subversive and transformative potential of Lee's language, we turn to Bakhtin. In Bakhtin's conception of literature, each utterance is a site of dialectical struggle. According to him, "within the arena of almost every utterance an intense interaction and struggle between one's own and another's word is being waged, a process in which they oppose or dialogically interanimate each other" (*Dialogic* 354). "I would devour this race to sing it" is an utterance that allows us to appreciate Bakhtin's point of view. Despite Bakhtin's insistence that poetry is inherently monological, I argue that this one line from "The Cleaving" is the site of several dialogues elaborated by the entire poem. "Devour," as we have seen, is highly charged with cultural significance. The word signifies not only the "big eating" heroism of Chinese folklore, but also the struggles and successes of Chinese immigrants in America to survive hardship and to swallow—in order to overcome—racist oppression.[8]

Moreover, the word "devour" brings to mind the carnivalesque eating central to Bakhtin's *Rabelais and His World*, which, as Zhou argues, helps to explain Lee's emphasis on grotesque eating imagery (e.g., "bodies eating bodies, heads eating heads") and grotesque physical features (e.g., the "jut-jaw" and the backs "humped, whole, manqué, quasi"). According to Zhou, Lee's "celebration and descriptions of all sorts of physical features, including those which verge 'on utter grotesquery,' can be understood as a subversive strategy like what Bakhtin calls . . . 'the carnival-grotesque' image" (126). For Bakhtin, carnival humor, carnival feasting, and images of the "grotesque body" function in literature to deconstruct and overturn the prevailing hierarchical power structure. Devouring the Chinese race, licking cheek-meat from the "armored jaw" of a carp, sucking down the brain of a duck—to a Euro-American audience, these are all forms of grotesque eating that oppose standard, "mainstream" American foodways and hence stand in opposition to mainstream culture.

What makes the line "I would devour this race to sing it" carnivalesque is the Whitmanesque, celebratory nature of that eating: devouring, the line suggests, is necessary to singing. This celebration of the grotesque, like the carnival spirit described by Bakhtin, seeks to "liberate from the prevailing point of view of the world, from conventions and established truths, from clichés, from all that is humdrum and universally accepted" (*Rabelais* 34). The poem does not retreat from stereotypes and racist remarks; nor does it pretend "assimilation" by adopting what might be called "normal" American behavior. Rather, the poem embraces its own culture and, in its participation with Whitman's celebratory singing and with Emerson's transcendental interrelatedness, endeavors to expand the reader's horizon. What Bakhtin writes of the carnival spirit in literature can be applied fully to "The Cleaving": "This carnival spirit offers the chance to have a new outlook on the world, to realize the relative nature of all that exists, and to enter a completely new order of things" (34). "The Cleaving" echoes a Whitmanesque love for humanity, but achieves this tone through the Asian American motif of big eating. In this way the poet "cleaves to that which cleaves me" (86), which, if taken as an expression of a minority poet and a minor literature in relation to the mainstream tradition, suggests that the boundaries drawn by those who would denounce his "ugly features" can be transgressed and the map of the territory redrawn. However, as I suggested in Part One, the politics of ethnic authorship do not begin and end with the poet's marginal status. Lee's poem both contests *and* participates in the literary vision represented by Emerson. In his strong association with both his own ethnic community *and* his literary forebears, Li-Young Lee complicates the relationship between "ethnic" and "mainstream" authorship.

4 Claiming Diaspora in Shirley Geok-lin Lim's Joss and Gold

In our desire to find definite breaks between the territorially bounded and the deterritorialized, the oppressive and the progressive, and the stable and the unstable, we sometimes overlook complicated accommodations, alliances, and creative tensions between . . . diaspora and nationalism.

—AIHWA ONG, *Flexible Citizenship: The Cultural Logics of Transnationality*

CLAIMING AMERICA AND CLAIMING DIASPORA

The "tensions between . . . diaspora and nationalism" described by sociologist Aihwa Ong have been strongly felt in Asian American literary scholarship in recent years. While writers and scholars alike have worked for years to establish the rightful place of Asian Americans in American history and culture (a strategy known as "claiming America"), many writers and scholars have more recently shifted from ethnic nationalism to ethnic diaspora and transnationalism as identity markers and modes of inquiry. As King-Kok Cheung observes, "both the altered demography in recent years and the prominence of some immigrant writers are beginning to unfix the border of Asian American literature" (*An Interethnic Companion* 7). Shirley Geok-lin Lim is arguably one of the most important of these immigrant writers. Lim, in fact, has been so successful at maintaining her image as a diasporic writer rather than an American writer, that some wish to see her as standing outside the realm of Asian American literature altogether. When I presented an earlier version of this chapter at a conference in Singapore, an Australian colleague questioned my approach to Lim's novel,

Joss and Gold, on the basis that my Asian American framework might be inappropriate for a "diasporic" author such as Lim. Reading Lim as diasporic rather than American is, in many respects, a more "natural" position. Though a citizen of the United States, Lim aligns herself closely in her creative and academic writing with a diasporic identity. Lim is a Malaysian-born academic and creative writer committed personally and professionally to retaining and fostering ties with Southeast Asia. Much of her poetry, her short stories, and her first novel were published jointly by Times Books International in Singapore and by U.S. publishers such as The Feminist Press in New York. She returns regularly to Malaysia and Singapore for readings and conferences, and she has visited for extended periods under fellowships to the Centre of Advanced Studies and the National Institute of Education in Singapore. From 1999–2002, she served as the chair of the English department at Hong Kong University before returning to her professorship at the University of California at Santa Barbara. She taught again in Hong Kong in 2005 and 2006.

My Australian colleague wanted to know why so much of the literature coming out of U.S. academia was preoccupied with notions of American identity. The question is astute, and gets right at the heart of an unresolved issue that has been debated in Asian American scholarship for the last ten to fifteen years—the rift between "claiming America" and what we might call "claiming diaspora." This chapter is concerned with the problem of an either/or confrontation between claiming America and claiming diaspora in discussions of contemporary Asian American literature, another instance of "exceeding the margins." Through a reading of Lim's novel, *Joss and Gold*, this chapter explores what is at stake when we read a diasporic writer as only diasporic, and suggests that it is possible to understand such a text as *both* diasporic *and* Asian American. For the aims of this book, it is important to see a novel such as Lim's as diasporic Asian American writing to illuminate another powerful way that Chinese American writers today are transcending the horizon of expectation that I described in Part One as a literary Chinatown.

Asian American scholars largely agree that "claiming America" has been a central tenet in Asian American cultural politics since the 1960s. The trope of "claiming America" developed out of the long-standing exclusion of Asian Americans from U.S. citizenship (as in the Chinese Exclusion Act of 1882, the ban on Japanese and Korean immigration in Teddy Roosevelt's "Gentleman's Agreement" of 1907, the "Asiatic Barred Zone Act" of 1917, the National Origins Act of 1924, and the Tydings-McDuffie Act of 1934 that recategorized Filipinos as aliens) or from the full rights of their citizenship (as in the Cooper's Act of 1902 prohibiting Filipinos from owning property, voting, and operating businesses, and in the internment of American citizens of Japanese ancestry under Executive Order 9066). These legalized exclusions inscribed institutionally the popular belief that America was a society of European immigrants in which Asians had no place—even though Asian immigrants were instrumental in the development of the United States from as far back as the Gold Rush and the construction of the Transcontinental Railroad in the nineteenth century.

Claiming America, according to Sau-ling Cynthia Wong, refers to the strategy of "establishing the Asian American presence in the context of the United States's national cultural legacy and contemporary cultural production" ("Denationalization" 6). Maxine Hong Kingston, who uses the phrase to describe her first two books, *The Woman Warrior* and *China Men*, calls claiming America "a response to the legislation and racism that says we of Chinese origin do not belong here in America" (Skenazy and Martin 25). In recent years, Asian American scholars have questioned the appropriateness of the claiming America model to the realities of the twenty-first century, and some have turned instead to the notion of diaspora as an organizing principle for Asian American cultural politics and cultural production. For Asian American critics such as Lisa Lowe and Shirley Geok-lin Lim, "diaspora" rather than "claiming America" more accurately represents the demographic exigencies of Asian Americans in the new millennium. Largely because of changes in immigration laws and to U.S. interventions in Asian conflicts, the Asian American population is larger and comprised of more recent immigrants than ever before; it is also more diverse in terms of ethnic group, national origin, class, education level, and so on. Because of rapid advances in communication, travel, and information technologies, the Asian American population is more fluid and more closely linked to communities in Asia than in the past when immigration from Asia to the United States was likely to be an irreversible enterprise.[1]

Lisa Lowe argues in her seminal 1991 article for a diasporic vision of Asian American identity. Echoing the rhetoric of Homi Bhabha, Mikhail Bakhtin, and Gilles Deleuze and Félix Guattari, Lowe writes, "we might conceive of the making and practice of Asian American culture as nomadic, unsettled, taking place in the travel between cultural sites and in the multivocality of heterogeneous and conflicting positions" (39). Lowe's argument seeks to undermine ethnic nationalism as an organizing structure in the concept of Asian American identity by claiming a "fluid" and diasporic perspective, a maneuver Sau-ling Cynthia Wong defined as "denationalization." Largely in response to Lowe's article, Wong argues in "Denationalization Reconsidered" that claiming America is still a valid and necessary strategy in Asian American cultural politics. In her view, ethnic nationalism is essential to effective political struggle in America because it fosters solidarity and unity of purpose: "if claiming America becomes a minor task for Asian American cultural criticism and espousal of denationalization becomes wholesale, certain segments of the Asian American population may be left without a viable discursive space . . . the loosely held and fluctuating collectivity called 'Asian Americans' will dissolve back into its descent-defined constituents as soon as one leaves American national borders behind" (16–17).

David Leiwei Li is similarly cautious about moving away from the ethnic nationalist conception of Asian American literature that the claiming America thesis represents. Like Wong, he cautions against a hasty and uncritical embrace of diaspora. In his reading of Amy Tan's *The Joy Luck Club*, for instance, Li criticizes the book's conclusion, which he describes as performing the "voluntary removal of Asians from the United States" (*Imaging the Nation* 116). In his view, the novel figures the wounds that typify the four mother-daughter diads as Chinese in origin, and then presents a literal return to China as the method to heal those wounds. Li admits the ethnic nationalist model has its limitations, but he shows that we should understand what may be lost when we suggest that such models are now passé:

> Although ethnic nationalist strategies are likely to ignore the dialogic voices within Asian America and are inadequate for dealing with a plurality of interests, their insights about the hierarchy of social division and the necessity for broad social transformation are perhaps too easily dismissed in contemporary revisionist critique. (192)

Those who advance this "revisionist critique" of the claiming America thesis seek to de-emphasize U.S. national identity in the construction of Asian American identity. "The concept of the Asian diaspora," according to Li, "was introduced [in Asian American Studies] to argue against a single national identity with one destiny in favor of a shared history that recognizes different origins and multiple transformations" (196). While the claim about a diasporic perspective in this statement appears identical to the aims of multiculturalism (i.e., a revision of the "melting pot" theory; an expansion of the tent stakes of "America" to allow and appreciate ethnic difference), proponents of the diasporic view distinguish between the two approaches on the grounds that multiculturalists still argue within a "single national identity" and a "shared destiny." Shirley Geok-lin Lim, a sharp critic of the claiming America stance, argues that many U.S. feminist and ethnic critics question the patriarchal, Eurocentric interpretations of texts, but they seldom interrogate the national-identity parameters in these interpretations. Instead, they attempt to enlarge that American identity, appropriating myths and characteristics that construct more permeable, flexible, and plurally enclosing borders. ("Immigration" 289)

Lim's critique of Maxine Hong Kingston reveals what she sees as a two-pronged problem with the claiming America model: namely, that claiming America often means "disclaiming" diaspora on the one hand, and remaining complicit with U.S. hegemonic nationalism on the other. In her 1992 essay on the novels of Timothy Mo, Lim sets up Kingston as the negative to Mo's positive embrace of diasporic roots. Kingston is, in Lim's view, a "diasporic writer" whose work is "overtly non-diasporic" because of "its insistence on a United States site." She argues that "United States identity in Kingston's writing is continuously claimed, while the political and state elements of a China identity are disclaimed" (*Writing Southeast/Asia* 92–93).

In "Immigration and Diaspora" (1997), the essay in which Lim most clearly defines her position on these issues, she again returns to a critique of Kingston's notion of claiming America. Lim writes, "Kingston repeatedly asserts that in her books she is claiming America for Chinese Americans, a proposition that can be restated to mean claiming Chinese Americans for America" (302). In asserting that her ethnic group belongs to America, Kingston may be contesting the prescribed borders of the nation, but she is also complicit with the broad concept of U.S. nationalism. She is, Lim suggests, appropriated by "the" nationalist cause.[2]

Lim's argument about the power of U.S. nationalism to appropriate immigrant and minority literature to its own ends illuminates a problematic within popular and academic conceptions of multiculturalism. At the same time, Lim's argument fails to portray "U.S. nationalism" as anything but monolithic, static, and perennially evil. What is missing in the debate outlined above, and particularly in Lim's critique of Kingston, is an attempt to define nationalism as "nationalisms"—to understand the nationalist sentiments as heterogeneous and fluid.[3] While Lim may have in mind ultra-right forms of U.S. nationalism that could be described as fundamentalist, essentialist, or white supremacist, Sau-ling Cynthia Wong may have in mind a nationalism based on a sense of shared space within prescribed national borders and political realities that must be faced collectively. In my understanding of Lim's work, I believe she is deeply opposed to the former, but sympathetic to the latter.

Moreover, in positing such a staunch anti-nationalist stance, Lim leans toward an outright rejection of American identity and embraces instead a universal, exilic, or transnational aesthetic. It may be true that she privileges texts that do not treat Asia as "void," or as Other to U.S. identity, but it seems to me that Lim is not advocating the embrace of a global fantasy. She seems skeptical of writers who posit themselves as cosmopolitan nomads in a borderless world, calling them "elites" ("Immigration" 290). She is also critical of the tendency for U.S. academic and cultural critics to view diasporic writings as "falling outside U.S. canonical work" (290). Lim holds to a tenuous middle position between birthplace and the "intaking state" (296), as expressed in the following statement: "The discourse of diaspora is that of disarticulation of identity from natal and national resources and includes the exilic imagination but is not restricted to it" (297). She asserts the need to view American race relations from an international position (291), a position that belies a deep concern for the United States.[4]

Congruent with her theoretical stance, Lim's novel, *Joss and Gold*, can be read as an internationalization of Asian American literature.[5] The novel can be seen as a fictional participant in the conversation about what Aihwa Ong calls "the creative tensions between . . . nationalism and diaspora" (16). By exploring issues of language, literature, identity, race, and gender in a largely Malaysian/Singaporean context with intersections with the United States, the novel presents American identity as an important, but peripheral, concern to the Southeast Asian characters of the novel. America's marginality in the text (even though one third of the book is set in the U.S.) furthermore raises important questions regarding approaches to, and categorization of, the novel. Is it justifiable to read the novel as an Asian American text? Does reading it as such automatically appropriate, or recuperate, the book and its author under a U.S. nationalist "agenda"? On the other hand, is it justifiable to read the book as only diasporic? In removing the novel from an Asian American context, do we miss the opportunity to understand U.S. nationalism and Asian American literature in new ways? Is it possible to read *Joss and Gold* as an Asian American *diasporic* text?

U.S. IMMIGRATION PLOT DEFERRED

In its embrace of diaspora, *Joss and Gold* departs from the "claiming America" strategy within Asian American literature and discourse. One point of departure is the novel's refusal to fully plant its feet in the U.S. despite indications in its plot development that it will. The first few chapters of *Joss and Gold* raise the reader's expectations of a classic Asian American immigrant story only to thwart those expectations. Li An, the novel's Asian protagonist, is a Chinese Malaysian first-year English literature teacher at a university in Kuala Lumpur, who is defined as "Western" in her habits, attitudes, and dress. Li An is represented as an independent woman despite her recent marriage to Henry, a Ph.D. student in Biology, who comes from a rich and traditional Chinese family. We learn on the first page of the novel, for instance, that "she had insisted on keeping her motorbike after they married" (7). The motorbike is a symbol of freedom and singlehood—not only is it a hold-over from Li An's life as a single person, but the very nature of a single-seat vehicle makes it an emblem of individuality. The fact that she "insisted" upon keeping the motorbike further reveals her attitude toward her new life as a woman married to a man from a traditional Chinese family with its hierarchy and patriarchal order. She is determined to retain her identity as an individual woman.

Thus, from the beginning, Li An stands in contrast to the book's portrayal of the Malaysian culture of 1968, and she seems to be a likely candidate for immigration to America. Her love of classical English literature, Leavisite literary critique, and the language of British poetry all seem to align her with England, but there are hints early on that Li An will gravitate toward America. Henry notes, for instance, that "she was like a Western girl—bold, loud, and unconcerned about her reputation" (15). It is little surprise, then, to find that Li An has been contemplating the idea of moving to America after graduation—though why she would choose the U.S. over the U.K. is not made clear in the novel. When Henry asks in exasperation, "America? Why America?" Li An responds, "Why not America? Isn't that where everything is happening? It's so boring here. Nothing ever changes. No one is doing anything, no one is writing poetry, no one is painting, no one is singing, no one is going anywhere. So why not go to America?" (15–16). In a classically Orientalist (or Occidentalist?) construction, Li An sees Asia as the unchanging, inert contrast to the vibrant, liberating energies of the West, with "the West" clearly defined as the United States of America. This East/West dichotomy is especially apparent in Li An's identification of the West as a place of liberation from the traditions of patriarchy. In Malaysia, she feels stifled by the assigned role for women and envious of Henry. At one point, Li An complains to Henry, "You know where you're going and where you belong. I wish I were a man and a scientist. Then there would be a place for me here" (17).

It would seem, then, that the entrance of Chester Brookfield, an American Peace Corps volunteer, sets the stage for Li An's Asian exodus. Despite her marriage to Henry, Li An grows close to Chester and eventually sleeps with him on the night of the Kuala Lumpur race riots. Yet Chester is not the Orientalist white knight saving the Asian woman from patriarchy. In the novel, he functions to stir up in Li An a sense of meaning and belonging for Malaysia, as is evident from the early days in their relationship when Henry and Li An invite Chester over for dinner. At the dinner, Chester mocks Li An's love for English literature and declares, "You've got your own culture. That's what you should be teaching" (42). Chester's pronouncement against the English literature that Li An so cherishes propels her to examine her own presuppositions about language, literature, and national identity.[6] More significantly, Chester's assumptions about Malaysian race politics challenge Li An's views of allegiance and belonging. Chester, under the influence of his Malay roommates, argues that "Malay is the only real culture in this country" (43). He raises the issue of the Chinese diaspora in terms that echo the sentiments of his Malay friends: "The Chinese aren't really Malaysian, are they? . . . They're here for the money. They speak Chinese and live among themselves. They could as easily be in Hong Kong or even in New York's Chinatown" (44). Henry's enraged reply gives Li An a feeling of solidarity with her husband. Holding Henry's hand, Li An expresses, for the first time in her life, a vision of a united and peaceful Malaysia:

> You sound just like the ultra-Malay politicians who want to kick the Chinese out of the country. My mother's family has been in this country for five or six generations, and some of the Malays are really immigrants who have just arrived from Indonesia in the last few years. You can't make any judgments based on who or what is "original." Sure, the Chinese traditions came from China, but Islam came from Saudi Arabia, didn't it? And no one says it's not original. Everything in Malaysia is chompor-chompor, mixed, rojak. A little Malay, a little Chinese, a little Indian, a little English. Malaysian means rojak, and if mixed right, it will be delicious . . . Chinese and Indian are also Malaysians here. What matters is what you know you are, inside. . . . Give us a few more years and we'll be a totally new nation. No more Malay, Chinese, Indian, but all one people. (44–45)

What is striking about Li An's speech is the way it connects with American racial and identity politics, and the way it confuses such politics. Chester's comment "you almost sound like an American" (45) verifies what was implicit in her speech: the position of the Chinese in Malaysia is similar to, and analogous to, the position of the Chinese in America. Li An's solution and her hopeful sentiment are marked by Chester as "American," but the politics are decidedly Malaysian and unconnected with the U.S.

The text undermines both the solution and the sentiment in Li An's speech in at least two significant ways. First, Li An's metaphors conflate two dominant racial theories prevalent in the United States, creating a contradiction that marks the impotency of the theories for Malaysian and for American racial politics. Her "rojak" metaphor is an Asian equivalent to the popular "salad" metaphor in the United States: the idea that the nation is a place where all races live harmoniously without losing their individual and cultural markers.[7] Oddly, Li An conflates this metaphor with the one it is meant to displace, that is, the "melting pot" metaphor. Her concept of "a new nation" signifies the disappearance of race as a marker of difference: "no more Malay, Chinese, Indian, but all one people" (45). Suddenly the rojak has become a melting pot, at which point Chester "beams" and exclaims that she "almost sound[s] like an American." While both Chester and Li An seem to have missed the leap in logic that Li An's speech performs, the text seems to suggest that the hopeful American solution to the dilemma, with its popular elision of race (or its submersion of race within terms such as "ethnic" and "culture"), is a similar quagmire of muddy reasoning. Second, the failure of the rojak metaphor is prefigured by the historic setting of the conversation: less than a year later, in May 1969, Malaysia is rocked by racial riots. These riots signify the failure of Chinese, Indian, and Malay Malaysians to see themselves as a united nation with equal share in the governance and direction of the nation.

If we are to read Li An's daughter Suyin as a symbolic reference to a differently configured future than that offered by Li An above, then the novel does suggest an alternate vision of race relations. Suyin was conceived, significantly, on the night of the riots as Li An and Chester found themselves stranded at his home after the police declared a city-wide curfew. This child of the race riots is therefore biracial, a fact so obviously written upon her face that Henry refuses to accept her and Li An home from the hospital after the child's birth and soon after files for divorce. Bearing the stigma of adultery and divorce in a traditional Asian community, Li An finds she must leave Malaysia in order to make a home for herself and her daughter. The obvious solution would be America. America usually stands in Asian immigrant novels as the site of freedom and tolerance. Moreover, Li An has a legitimate claim to citizenship because of Chester's legal and moral obligation to his child. Professor Kingston, the only person Chester confides in back in the United States, makes this assumption when he says, "she's putting the screws on you to get them into the United States" (184). Yet Li An never contacts Chester. She refuses to chase after him, preferring instead to migrate to Singapore to make it on her own.

What Lim offers the reader in the first part of her novel is an interruption of the hermeneutic circle—a disruption that must be adjusted when the whole of the novel is comprehended. Once readers learn that Li An is never going to leave Asia, they recognize that the compact inherent in the genre of the American immigrant novel has been broken. According to Hans-Georg Gadamer, "the anticipation of meaning in which the whole is envisaged becomes explicit understanding in that the parts, that are determined by the whole, themselves also determine this whole" (259). Hence, the parts that seemed to suggest a particular and recognizable whole (the "envisaged whole") must be re-interpreted once the envisaged whole has been disrupted, and this re-interpretation produces a new whole. My point is that Lim's novel disrupts both the plot expectations and the genre expectations that were signaled from the beginning. When viewed from within Asian American literary studies, this generic break challenges our notions of Asian American literature and deliberately positions the novel beyond the typical margins and in a transnational space.

SINGAPORE AS SUBSTITUTE, OR "A NEW WOMAN IN THE FRESH NEW ASIAN CITY"

In the novel, Singapore replaces America as the site of freedom and tolerance, and, as with many Asian immigrant novels, the "promised land" turns out to be less tolerant and free than expected. We are told, for instance, "even after moving to Singapore, where a woman could be husbandless, a child must have a father's name" (199). Suyin does face prejudice in school at being mixed,[8] but more so at being fatherless. (It is not until Henry decides to be her father that her schoolmates stop teasing her, after which "no one in Cho Kang called her 'Sin-ner'" [297].) But being without a husband has not limited Li An to a lesser share of the Singapore capitalist pie: as their Indian friend Paroo puts it, "She's happy, got money, got condo, got car, got big-time job" (195). Chester thinks of her as "a new woman in the fresh new Asian city" (280), a description that registers his admiration for her success as well as for the success of Singapore. Li An is an independent Asian woman with a tenacious will to provide for her daughter on her own terms. For her, there is no desperate desire to claim America, despite her legitimate right to make that claim. Singapore, a nation that is home to a large Chinese diasporic community, is the preferred site of migration.

The freedom and tolerance fostered in Singapore contrasts not only with Kuala Lumpur in the novel, but also with New York. Asian feminism, as exemplified in Li An, contrasts sharply with the feminism of Chester's wife, Meryl, in the New York section of the book. Meryl is portrayed as a woman who places her rights to a fulfilling career above the needs of her husband and the good of her marriage. She insists, for instance, that Chester go for a vasectomy since they have decided not to have children. When Chester asks her if they have really agreed not to have children, Meryl says,

> We've looked at our priorities over and over again. I'm coming up for the deputy commissioner's position next year, and if the federal grant comes through, I'll have my own project in the New York Parks to administer. Dan said I could be commissioner in a few years, the first woman commissioner in the history of the Parks Department. (121)

Clearly, perhaps too clearly, the priorities Meryl lists as "ours" are in fact her own. Her insistence on not having children, and her insistence that Chester be the one to undergo surgery, suggests that her brand of feminism is self-serving ambition by another name. Li An, on the other hand, is driven by necessity to succeed as a woman in a male-dominated society for the good of her child. She, furthermore, forms a nurturing home for Suyin by assembling a "family" of females—made up of herself, her good friend Ellen, and Suyin's grandmother.

Thus, to say that Singapore is the novel's substitute for America should not suggest that it is either a better or a worse substitute. For Singapore resembles, but does not replicate, America. In moving to Singapore rather than to the U.S., Li An trades in her idealism for pragmatism and her poetry for security. She literally throws away her poetry books—which early in the novel marked her for immigration to the United States. In Paroo's words, "No more poetry, no more literature. She's trying to make a buck." Singapore life, as constructed in the novel, is writing with the poetry sucked out of it. Li An's love of the English language and of British literature inspired her as a young student and teacher to deep feelings for renewal and change. But, in pragmatic Singapore, this kind of idealism becomes petty and useless. As her friend Abdullah says, "What is the purpose of all the literature they're still teaching in the university? Malay literature, Chinese literature, English literature— no practical use. Better to teach communications, public relations, like you are doing now" (208). BioSynergy's news bulletin, of which Li An is editor-in-chief, fits Abdullah's definition of useful literature. The weekly bulletin is not only a constantly updated information sheet on business activities, but it is a much used document in Singapore business society: "it was a hot document studied by investors, shareholders, and the Monetary Authority of Singapore for clues to the company's health and future" (206). In short, Li An's work feeds the capitalist machine rather than humanistic ideals.

The kind of language Li An must use in the newsletter comes to characterize her changed approach to life. In her youth she was outspoken, passionate, and almost wild in comparison to her classmates; as editor-in-chief of *BioSyn-Sign*, Li An is as level-headed and composed as her business writing. When Chester shows up in her office eleven years after his departure from Malaysia, Li An keeps her emotions in check by invoking a business-writing style in her speech: "Li An kept her voice low, feeling for the steadiness of business writing, the clear agenda of the memorandum" (244). The novel constructs business writing as writing without poetry; it is steady, emotionless, and secure. For Li An, the pragmatism of business life in Singapore and in the language of her weekly stock articles marks the hard fact of growing up to a life of single motherhood. She had learned "to embrace the empty depth in the glittering surface of things" (210).

The Singapore of *Joss and Gold* seems at first glance to be America without a spirit. The country embraces capitalism and the minimal freedoms required to make it run, but it shines on the surface like a façade or an empty shell. However, although pragmatic capitalism is signified through business language, there is a difference in this particular business language that reveals a uniquely Asian quality. As BioSynergy's executive chief explains to a British visitor, "It doesn't matter that BioSynergy is a wholly research-oriented company, staffed by some of the best-trained scientists that money and top facilities can attract. . . . We Singaporeans invest our Sing-dollars cautiously, and every good omen and sign is needed to keep us loyal to the company" (207). The novel suggests that in the West, the strength of the company is reflected in the quality of its business plan and in its performance, but in Singapore investors look also at omens and signs. Singaporeans, the novel suggests, do not make business decisions on strictly pragmatic evidence; they may, for example, buy more stock in the year of the rooster because it is considered an auspicious year, or take good care of their ancestors' ghosts to enhance "auspicious conditions" (207–8). In terms of language, there is a distinctively Asian poetic even in business writing. As one character puts it, "no Singaporean believes that there is such a thing as unintentionality in language, especially once your language becomes fixed in print!" (207).

While on the one hand the novel suggests that Li An loses her soul, or at least her poetry, in her business transaction with Singapore, it suggests on the other hand that the language she writes in pragmatic, business-minded Singapore is far more nuanced than an outsider might imagine. Li An succeeds at her job because of her unique understanding of both local culture and the potentials of language. Unlike her American-trained predecessor who was fired for printing a slightly critical article by a prestigious writer that sent the company stocks plummeting (he chose personality over language), Li An knows her audience is driven by what she calls "the Singapore reflex"—"an advanced version of the desire to be superior" (211). Although not labeled as such in the in the novel, this "reflex" is known in Singapore as "kiasuism"—*kiasu* being a *Hokkien* dialect word meaning "the fear of losing out." This concept, which is closely associated with the Asian concept of "face," is Li An's guiding principle as editor-in-chief: publish facts, but only those that present "the company in its most positive light" (211). In a rewrite of Christ's words about losing one's soul, Ellen says "even if you conquer the world and lose face, you lose everything" (211).

The novel does not present a strong case for cultural resistance to Western and global forces through the process of localization, but Li An's adaptation of business language to local customs can perhaps be understood in these terms. According to Rob Wilson, "in Asia/Pacific interzones of heightened globalization and localization, 'global cities' like Taipei, Hong Kong, and Singapore have sprung up—cities that unevenly fuse transnational technologies to local customs" ("Goodbye Paradise" 313). Aihwa Ong remarks, "despite the widespread dissemination of the trappings of globalization—world markets, mass media, rapid travel, and modern communications—cultural forms have not become homogenized across the world" but have in fact "increased cultural diversity because of the ways in which they . . . acquire new meanings in local reception" (10). Li An's job is to linguistically do just that: to create new meanings for local reception, to "fuse" BioSynergy's transnational technologies to local sensibilities. She coined the newssheet's title "BioSyn-Sign" in order to suggest to its local Asian (mainly Chinese) readers "a doubling of the values of shares" (209) due to the double sound in the title. The newssheet functions as a giver of signs that the executive chief likens to "fortune almanacs" that some Singaporeans use to interpret dreams and events as lucky horse racing picks and lotto numbers (206). Such local vitality existing within and transforming global capitalist structures instantiates Wilson and Dissanayake's claim that "within these spaces of uneven modernity, we are witnessing not so much the death and burial of 'local cultural originality,' as Fanon once feared within residually colonial structures of national modernity, as their rehabilitation, affirmation, and renewal in disjunctive phases and local reassertions" (3).

Li An's negotiation of the global and the local is not as clearly drawn in the novel as is her negotiation of the poetical and the pragmatic. The global/local element, however weak, does in fact provide a more complex view of Singapore. Singapore, from this view, is not a soulless America, but has a vitality and agency of its own. There is an indication in the final pages of the novel that Li An will regain her poetic sensibilities and her "soul" in Singapore, without needing to emigrate to the United States. In Singapore, Li An finally regains her feeling, her "inner-ear," for poetry and its "rhythms" (306).

CLAIMING DIASPORA

While Li An's individualism and her choice of Singapore as home are significant in the novel's challenge to the reader's horizon of expectation, it is Suyin who embodies the novel's vision of a new future. Symbolically conceived in racial chaos, Suyin is a hybrid of Asia and America living in a modern Asian city that is similarly a hybrid of Asian and Western cultures. Suyin, by the novel's conclusion, is given two fathers, one Asian and the other American. Henry comes into her life at the death of Suyin's grandmother as Henry becomes the executor of her will. Through their interaction over legal matters and Grandmother Yeh's funeral, Henry comes to finally accept Suyin as his daughter, now that he is remarried and has a child of his own: "Suyin was a backward family bond; but Henry, being now a good Chinese father, would not refuse that bond" (303). At the same time, Chester travels from America to seek his daughter. Li An allows Chester to take Suyin out while he is in Singapore and eventually Suyin grasps that Chester is her father. Chester's invitation for Suyin to come to America for a visit seems to stand as an open invitation for Suyin to move to America when and if she chooses to do so. Suyin, by the end of the novel, does not simply have an Asian mother, but she has an Asian father and an American father. Ellen, Li An's good friend who acts as Suyin's second parent, criticizes Li An for allowing the two men into Suyin's life: "You have her all confused. One father in Kuala Lumpur, one father in New York. It was better when she did not know about either of them" (304). But Li An comes to the conclusion that it is better for Suyin to have choices. In the end, the choice is Suyin's. She is, at novel's end, an eleven-year-old hybrid girl with a transnational identity.

Joss and Gold's diasporic and transnational vision valorizes choice and mobility. The happy note on which the novel ends is that Suyin, unlike her mother who never really belonged in the country of her birth, belongs to both Asia and America. With the help, moreover, of her mother's financial success and the inheritance she will receive from her grandmother's will, Suyin has the legal freedom and the economic ability to move between Asia and America, her two symbolic fathers.[9] America remains a possible choice for Suyin, not an identity—and the text in no way marks America as the obvious or even the better choice.

Read as an Asian American diasporic text, *Joss and Gold* interrogates U.S. identity and exceeds the prescribed margins of ethnic literature in at least several significant ways. First, the United States is displaced as an object of immigrant desire. The U.S. remains a possible choice for several characters in the novel, but it is not the "Gold Mountain" of Asian aspirations. *Joss and Gold*'s substitution of an Asian city-state for the United States as the preferred site of migration questions "orientalist geography" by refusing the East/West binary (Li, *Imagining the Nation* 196). The novel's redefinition of America as one of several possible choices rather than the unavoidable solution challenges the claiming America thesis with its assumptions of a shared national destiny and identity (*ibid.*). Second, the United States has not cornered the market on human rights, and specifically on female rights. The Asian female is independent and strong without the legitimization of U.S. democracy and U.S. feminism. If anything, the novel suggests that certain brands of U.S. feminism may be inferior to certain brands of Asian feminism. As discussed above, Meryl's U.S. feminism in contrast to Li An's is restrictive, self-indulgent, anti-community, and anti-family. Third, the United States's nationalism need not be the locus of identity for an Asian American text, even if we continue to call it an Asian American text. My claim is that *Joss and Gold* performs a critique of American nationalism and of ethnic nationalist rhetoric within Asian American literary studies when it is read not simply as a diasporic, cosmopolitan, or global text, but as an Asian American diasporic text. *Joss and Gold*'s transnational structure and challenge to the claiming America thesis (however we might judge the effectiveness or validity of that challenge) can be fruitfully read within Asian American literature's turn to diaspora. The questions raised about its categorization are precisely the kinds of questions a non-nationalist, diasporic text is meant to raise.

PART III

Change and the Phenomenology of Reading

In spoken discourse the dialogic situation provides the full realm of identity, but a written text is addressed to unknown readers and potentially to
countless readers in the future, all of whom have the capacity and the interest to read it. This universalization of the audience can lead to only one
conclusion, and that is that identity can never be completely fixed; it will
change, for it is the response of the present and the future, and each makes
and will continue to make the text relatively important or unimportant.

—MARIO J. VALDÉS, *Phenomenological Hermeneutics*
and the Study of Literature

Although we can sometimes retrospectively interpret Asian American
texts . . . as having the potential to change the reader's horizon of expectations, a work's contestatory features cannot be viewed in absolute
terms. . . . Instead, a work's multivalent features should be seen as a point
of entry into sustained investigations of the cultural contexts of its emergence and reception—including the condition of the emergence of the
new interpretive positions—and of the interactive and mutually defining
relationship between its layered meaning and the reader's layered horizon
of expectations.

—JINQI LING, *Narrating Nationalisms:*
Ideology and Form in Asian American Literature

5 Changing Signifiers and Changing Horizons

BASEBALL IN THREE STORIES BY DAVID WONG LOUIE

A literary work is not an object that stands by itself and that offers the
same view to each reader in each period. It is not a monument that mono-
logically reveals its timeless essence. It is much more like an orchestration
that strikes ever new resonances among its readers and that frees the text
from the material of the words and brings it to a contemporary existence.

—HANS ROBERT JAUSS, *Toward an Aesthetic of Reception*

As I argued in the introduction, horizons of expectation are not static.
Inherent to the horizon metaphor is the idea that our consciousness (whether as individuals or as reading communities) can expand
to encompass new information and new perceptions. The literary text, as
the quotation above from Hans Robert Jauss and those heading Part Three
from Mario J. Valdés and Jinqi Ling suggest, is more than a document
embroiled in its own socio-historical milieu; the literary text is not simply
"fixed" in its meaning or identity—rather, it is a dynamic, dialogic "orchestration" that changes in significance throughout its own history. A literary
text, therefore, not only has a history of production, but also a history of
reception; these together give its textuality.

In this chapter, I identify specific ways in which the literary Chinatown
functions within a particular text and, particularly, how an author may invoke
elements of the literary Chinatown to manipulate the perception of the
reader. David Wong Louie plays upon the reader's expectations by invoking
the sport of baseball in three stories in *Pangs of Love*: "Warming Trends,"
"Birthday," and "Disturbing the Universe." I wish to show that baseball functions in each of these stories as a signifier of "white America." Louie may
not personally believe baseball to be an exclusively white American sport,

but he seems to expect the reader to interpret baseball as a mostly white, fully American activity that is foreign to, even opposed to, Chinese identity. However, when we compare this assumption about baseball at the time when Louie wrote these stories (the 1980s) with the realities of baseball in the twenty-first century, we will see that Louie's use of baseball relies upon a horizon of expectation that is currently undergoing a dramatic change. Black, Latino, and Asian players make Major League Baseball arguably the most diverse of all U.S. professional sports today, and hence one might expect a concomitant change in the reception of Louie's "baseball stories" among a twenty-first-century readership.

Finally, the fact that the success of Asian American sports figures influences public opinions on the "Americanness" of Asian Americans (consider, for example, the American public's fondness for figure skater Kristi Yamaguchi and tennis star Michael Chang) suggests that "Asian American" and "Chinese American" are themselves signifiers that undergo profound changes in the reader's perception from one generation to the next. "Chinese American" and "baseball" may have been mutually exclusive terms to readers in the 1980s, but readers in the twenty-first century are far more used to seeing Japanese, Korean, and Chinese names on the backs of jerseys in Major League Baseball today. To examine these changes and their effects on the reader's horizon of expectation, we turn to baseball in *Pangs of Love*.

"YANKS OR INJUNS?"

The world has changed since unemployed, Reagan-era Hank sat down in a David Wong Louie short story—beer, pretzels, cigarettes in hand—to watch the New York Yankees beat up the Cleveland Indians in Baseball's "Game of the Week." Just how much the world had changed was evident when I sat down in my living room in Singapore in 1998 to watch ESPN's live telecast of American League Championship Game Three between the same two teams, a telecast that was aired on cable television throughout Asia. Reagan was gone. Unemployment was lower in the U.S. than it had been in decades. And the Cleveland Indians were in the championships. For any baseball fan, that change alone is enough to disturb the universe. The ESPN color commentator put it succinctly: "Years ago Cleveland was the doormat of the American League. If you came in and didn't win at least two out of three, something was wrong." The former doormat, on the day of the telecast, was not only in the championship series, vying for a shot at the World Series, but it was demolishing the Yankees handily. The Indians' batters walloped four home runs, and their Dominican pitcher, Bartolo Colon, did not allow a single hit after the second inning.

What interests me about the resurrection of the long-dead Cleveland Indians, as well as several other differences between David Wong Louie's short story "Warming Trends" and ESPN's telecast in 1998, is what it says about perception and context both in terms of literature and Asian America. The Cleveland Indians are a symbol in Louie's story for the underprivileged, the economically disadvantaged, the racialized minority. Hank, an unemployed mortician, overweight and nicotine-addicted, aligns himself, "wrongly" it later turns out, with the Yankees. He enjoys their rout of the Indians so much that he continues watching enthusiastically even when the Indians are down 10-0 and their own fans turn against them. "Slaughters give me pleasure," Hank says to his daughter Natalia. "I like to see the Yanks punish the other team" (170). But Hank changes his tune when Natalia's punk-rocker boyfriend Bilbo finally answers his question: "Who do you like . . . Yanks or Injuns?" (174, 175). Bilbo answers, "I favor Third World nations . . . I'll take the side of the poor, oppressed, underdeveloped team." In keeping with his "mohawk" hairstyle, Bilbo sides with the Indians, and his words, to Hank's surprise, carry a powerful impact. In a moment, Hank shifts his allegiance from "the brutish Bronx Bombers" to "the pitiful Tribe" (174). It is an epiphany for Hank: "he realized his prospects for the future were no brighter than those of the Indians that afternoon. They were natural allies. It was so obvious. When you're poor, why love IBM?" (174).

Louie thus explicitly draws a metaphorical link between the two baseball teams and societal distinctions based on economic opportunity and productivity. What is less explicit, but nonetheless present, is the racial element, which can be uncovered by exploring what it is that allows Louie to use two real-life baseball teams as metaphors for social struggles. On the most fundamental level, of course, the team names carry the racial connotations. "Yankees" are white European settlers and "Indians" are Native Americans who were displaced by the whites. Thus, intrinsic to the team names is a historical "slaughter," a lop-sided, brutish, unfair battle that provides an easy allegory for Louie's tale of disenfranchisement. The connection between white brutality against Native Americans and the "brutish Bronx Bombers" slaughter of "the Tribe" codes Louie's text with a racial commentary.

It may be argued that the use of the name "Indians" by an American baseball team is itself an act of racism. Teams and schools are under increasing pressure to change names such as "Indians," "Warriors," "Braves," and "Redskins" from such activist organizations as the National Coalition on

Racism in Sports and Media. Critics are opposed not only to the names and mascots, but also to demeaning practices and cheers. For instance, despite more than a decade of such opposition, Atlanta Brave's fans could be seen in the 2005 playoffs shaking tomahawks to the beat of pom-pom drums to cheer on their team, a practice that critics argue revives racist imagery of "bloodthirsty savages" on the "warpath." However, as the ESPN announcer in the Indians/Yankees game revealed, the Cleveland Indians were named after a player by the name of Louis Sockalexis, the first Native American to play major league baseball. According to the club's official web site (www .indians.com), Sockalexis (1871–1913) was a popular player on the Cleveland club who was a Penobscot Indian from Old Town, Maine. After his retirement, a fan suggested in a 1914 newspaper contest that the team be called the Indians, "as a testimony to the game's first American Indian player." The history of the club's name, therefore, suggests that "Indians" was not chosen because of racism, but because of a fond regard for a member of the Native American community.

"Warming Trends," however, relies on more than a historical connection with the team names. Indeed, the allegory of racial and economic disparity works in the story because the Cleveland Indians were, from well before Reagan all the way to the mid-1990s, a pitiful excuse for a baseball team. I will contrast two statements, one from the story and one from the ESPN telecast, to illustrate this point. The announcer in Louie's story says, "They got great baseball tradition here in Cleveland; don't let one game fool ya; in '54 they brought home the pennant" (169). Hank's reaction to this statement is one of great amusement: he "chuckled so much the beer fizzled in his nose" (169). In light of the Indians's dismal showing for so many years, the announcer's statement comes across as a joke. Hank sees it as ironic and condescending, as would anyone who knows American Major League baseball. Even the other announcer cannot resist a rejoinder: "That was three decades ago almost, Joe; the only tradition here is losing" (169).

In the 1998 telecast of Game Three of the American League Championship, the ESPN announcer repeated the statement in Louie's story almost verbatim: "Cleveland has a great tradition of baseball going back one hundred years," he said. Although his statement matches that of the fictional announcer, the meaning is altered considerably by the context. There is nothing apologetic or ironic about Cleveland's baseball tradition when the Indians are playing in the league championships and slaughtering the opponent. In fact, the altered context re-writes the significance of the tradition: in the context of a long-standing slump, the Cleveland "tradition" is pitiful; in the context of the team's return to strength, it is a triumph of the human spirit, a testimony to the faithfulness of Cleveland's fans. In Louie's "Warming Trends," therefore, it is not simply the name "Indians" with its obvious reference to Native Americans that accounts for the story's racial tension, but the fact that at the time of the story's publication (i.e., 1986) the Cleveland Indians were regarded as underdogs. As will be discussed below, the empowerment of the Cleveland Indians in the late 1990s translates into a change in the reception of Louie's story, especially for those unfamiliar with, or too young to remember, the decades of Cleveland's dismal performance.

The essential point of my discussion is that Louie's metaphorical use of the Yankees and Indians relies not just on the allegory of names and the performance of the actual teams but, more fundamentally, on the general perception of baseball as America's game, or America's "pastime" (168). Hank makes this association explicit. For example, insisting that Natalia and Bilbo stay and watch the game, Hank says, "Be good Americans and come watch my Yanks beat up on the Indians" (172). However, when Hank and Bilbo finally ally themselves against the Yankees and Bilbo starts getting excited about an Indians comeback, Hank says, "That's the American spirit. No matter how you cut your hair, we're still a nation of sportsmen" (175). Clearly, at least for Hank, the "American spirit," or the identity of true Americans, is tied up with a love for the game of baseball.

This use of baseball to signify American identity is consistent with Louie's use of baseball in *Pangs of Love*. However, in other stories, we find that baseball not only represents "America," but it also represents "un-Chinese" behavior and even, in the case of one story, "whiteness." In order to establish this assertion and to contextualize Louie's use of baseball in this story, I now turn to these other stories before returning to "Warming Trends" and the ESPN telecast.

"BIRTHDAY": BASEBALL AND THE WHITE FANTASY

"Birthday," the first story in *Pangs of Love*, is not centered upon the motif of baseball; indeed, at first glance, baseball might seem trivial to the story. However, a close look reveals that baseball not only plays an important role here, but its role sheds light on Louie's use of the motif in other stories. In "Birthday," Wallace Wong, the protagonist and narrator, desires family life with Sylvie, a woman who is separated from her husband. The conflict of the story centers upon the affections of Wallace for Sylvie's child, Welby, through whom he attempts to penetrate the family and further alienate the estranged husband, Frank. Wallace lived with Sylvie and Welby for a while, but by court order the boy now lives with Frank. Sylvie has left Wallace, perhaps, as he fears, to return to Frank.

Wallace relates the story in the first person as he sits in Welby's room in Frank's house, where Wallace has ironically and comically barricaded himself to await the boy's return. Meanwhile, Frank "pounds away at [the door] with his fists" (3): "It's the boy's birthday, and back in the days when the world was cold and rainy and sane, back in the days when we still lived together, I had promised we'd go for an afternoon of baseball—sunshine, pop, hotdogs" (3). Baseball is the promise made to the boy, but here, it is also a kind of "promised land" for Wallace. Now he is physically and metaphorically trapped. He is locked inside a room in the boy's father's house unable to live the life he wants. Baseball is defined as "sunshine" and opposes the "cold and rainy" days that motivated the promise. Yet sunshine also opposes the "cold and rainy" mood of his present situation. Baseball is thus a promise of release and freedom from bondage; it is, as we will see below, "America." Moreover, baseball, with its associations to "pop" and "hotdogs" and other non-Chinese signs, signifies a "white" lifestyle for Wallace, as will also be shown in what follows.

Wallace's insistence on taking his ex-girlfriend's son to the baseball game is linked to his rejection of his Chineseness, expressed most glaringly in his refusal to procreate with a Chinese woman. His father implores him to marry "a girl [his] mother can talk to without having to use her hands" (6)—in other words, a Chinese woman, preferably someone intelligent like "Connie Chung" (6). "Just say yes," his father pleads, "and we'll go to China and find you a nice girl" (6). But Wallace has his mind set on marrying Sylvie and adopting Welby, which his father views as "adopting a used family" (6). Wallace associates Chinese women with materialism and cheapness: they can be lured by "Maybelline," "soft Italian shoes," and "bourgeois decadence" (7). They could, in a sense, be purchased. The rejection of Chinese women is explicitly linked to the propagation of his race. Recalling a radio documentary on the endangered California condor, Wallace imagines himself as a condor "at the dead end of evolution" (7):

> In my veins I felt the primordial soup bubbling, and my whole entropic bulk quaked as I gazed at the last females of my species. I know I was supposed to mate, but I wasn't sure how . . . I looked them over, the last three

in creation; she'd need to have good genes. Finally, after careful consideration, I chose—her, the bird with the blond tail feathers. (7)

The desire for Sylvie is therefore racially charged. His choice is a subconscious rejection of the non-white members of his "species." The suggestion that his choice is based on "good genes" further engrains racial difference as central to his desire for Sylvie. In continuing to refuse his parents' proposals for a Chinese match, Wallace rejects his own Chinese identity and attempts to live a white fantasy: to chase the bird with the "blond tail feathers" (7), to become white by co-opting a white family.

The desire to marry a white woman is a sexual expression of Wallace's ultimate desire to be white, a desire that Louie subtly codes as deep-seated and Oedipal. By holing himself up in the child's bedroom and refusing to open the door to the heavy fist of the father, Wallace's desire to be the white child of this woman is evident. Wallace is reduced to a child sitting in the boy's room on furniture much too small for his body, drawing pictures and symbols with crayons to communicate to the boy that he did not forget their baseball outing. Meanwhile, the annoyed father bangs loudly on the door and talks to him in tones suitable for use against a stubborn child: "his talk is nothing like his knock. His voice is gentle, soothing, contrite. I might even be tempted to say it's sweet" (3). In this comic situation, a clear Oedipal desire is revealed: Wallace becomes the errant child hiding from the father figure and desiring the mother figure. The racially charged subtext of the story further suggests that Asian Americans are similarly trapped within a white hegemonic order in the United States, a condition David L. Eng describes as "internal exile" (197). According to Eng, "'Birthday' suggests that internal exile may be the very normative psychic condition under which the Asian American male model minority continues to be racialized and excluded in the age of multiculturalism" (197).

While Wallace's father is concerned that he find a Chinese wife, his mother's concern centers on his eating habits: after Sylvie moved out, his mother wants to know if he is "eating rice again" (8). Here the linkage between Chinese food and Chinese identity, like that between a Chinese mate and Chinese identity, is made explicit. According to Sau-ling Cynthia Wong, whose discussion of alimentary images in Asian American literature was central to my discussion of "The Cleaving," "eating practices are shaped to an extraordinary extent by culture and can thus serve as elaborate mechanisms for encoding and expressing social relationships" (*Reading* 18). For Wallace's mother, eating rice signifies her son's relationship to the family and the culture. Her keen interest in Wallace's eating habits says less about her interest in her son's health than it does about her concern over the potential "loss" of his Chinese identity. The white woman may have moved out, but unless he is eating rice, he is still denying his Chineseness!

The alimentary code is a prominent feature in the story and indicates that Wallace's rejection of his Chinese identity goes beyond his choice of a mate, as implied by his choice of profession. Wallace owns and operates an "Italian-style café," a choice that he clearly sees as racially charged: "People didn't believe a Chinaman could produce a decent cappuccino. I could hardly blame them. I'd shy away, too, from moo shu pork from a Sicilian's pan" (7). Historically, the food industry was one of the few professions available to Chinese immigrants in America. It could be argued that Wallace's decision to enter this profession minus the Chinese cuisine indicates his unwillingness to "display [his Chineseness] for gain to the curious gaze of 'outsiders'" (Wong, *Reading* 56), thus resisting what Frank Chin calls "food pornography" (55). However, in considering the racially charged rejection of Chinese women in preference for a white family, we may conclude that Wallace's choice of profession is another instance of his desire to disown his Chinese identity. "Producing a decent cappuccino" signifies for Wallace a non-Chinese identity, an erasure of the image associated with the derogatory term "Chinaman."

This connection between food and identity illuminates the profound irony of the story's conclusion. At the height of humiliation in being thrown out of the house by Frank and by Sylvie, Wallace enters the kitchen of the white family and prepares the mousse for the boy's birthday cake—a cake that was made by the boy's father. Wallace's description of the procedure is replete with racial undertones. "I crack an egg and separate the yolk from the whites" (17) indicates Wallace's emphasis on differences between Chinese (signified by the yellow yolk) and whites (signified by the egg whites). "I add sugar to the yolks and beat them with a whisk. This feels good" (17). Sugar, which is white, dilutes and masks the yellowness of the yolks in the way that Wallace has tried to dilute and mask his Chinese identity. That Wallace takes pleasure in beating the yolks indicates his own fervor in attempting to disown his Chineseness. In contrast, his beating of the whites results in their holding "their peaks perfectly" (17); the whites, in other words, behave properly and are aesthetically pleasing. In the end, Wallace "fold[s] in the whipped whites" (17), which, ironically, is an act that Frank did not understand how to do (13). In other words, it appears that Wallace is better at being white than even Frank himself: he knows how to make a mousse and can handle the role of the (egg) whites expertly. The irony is complete when we consider that Wallace has made himself subservient to the white family by producing the mousse: he cannot enter the white family as a member and an equal; he can only serve them in the kitchen.

This analysis of the various racial codes in the story allows us now to unpack the meaning of baseball. Indeed, the centrality of race to the story's coding suggests that Wallace's definition of baseball as "sunshine, pop, [and] hot dogs" is more than a typical description of what happens at a baseball game. As discussed earlier, the "sunshine" contrasts with the incarceration Wallace experiences in his Chinese identity and his inability to get into a white family and thereby pass as white. The "pop" and "hot dogs" that connect metonymically with baseball because of their status as typical food and drink at baseball games also connect metonymically with "America." Hot dogs are American fare served at the typical summer barbeque and are a favorite among American children. While Coke and Pepsi are now globalized commodities, the designation "pop" is quintessentially American. "Pop" is shorthand in the Midwest for "soda pop," while on the west coast such beverages are usually referred to as "soft drinks." The word "pop" therefore signifies the Midwest, the "heartland" of America, and serves to define the Americanness of baseball.

Besides signifying what is American in "Birthday," baseball also serves to define what is not Chinese. This is revealed in Wallace's contemplation of his relationship with his father—a memory that his determination to connect with Welby triggers:

> I wish there was some way for me to know what [Welby is] up to, the way my father came home one day from Sears with a bat and ball and glove for me. There he was, son of China's great famines, who knew nothing of earned-run averages or the number of homers Mantle hit in '56, but somehow he anticipated my next step. (16)

The contrast between the father's Chinese identity and baseball could not be clearer. In Wallace's surprise at his father's purchase, we see his own perception of baseball as foreign to Chineseness. Wallace's father "knew nothing of" baseball history and trivia not simply because he had no interest in it, but because he was not American. This is clearly indicated by the phrase "son of China's great famines." In describing his father in this way, Louie leads us to see him as more than racially Chinese. "Son of" indicates that he is a product of China—that what makes him Chinese is more than race, but experience, conditioning, and history. He is more than a product of "China," he is a product of a specific Chinese history. This Chinese experience is marked here by the word "famine" and thus ties in with the alimentary coding discussed earlier. Indeed, in perfect keeping with Wong's central thesis in *Reading Asian American Literature*, the father's Chineseness is marked by "necessity," whereas the American experience (signified by the bat, ball, and glove, and by the reference to baseball trivia) is marked by "extravagance."

Furthermore, the bat and ball are signs for Wallace that his father "anticipated [his] next step." That is, he perceived what Wallace needed, revealing his own astute understanding of his son. But what is this "next step"? It could be a reference to Wallace's growing interest in baseball. However, the fact that his father "knew nothing of earned-run averages or the number of homers Mantle hit in '56" suggests that this is information Wallace already possessed when his father came home with the baseball equipment. Thus, it is more likely that the "next step" refers to Wallace's gravitation toward non-Chinese interests, a gravitation that would eventually lead to his desire to adopt a non-Chinese family and become white.

For Wallace, as he sits in Welby's room, the "next step" is taking the boy to a baseball game. Baseball is what is anticipated throughout the story. It is the bait that Wallace believes will win over Welby and bring back Sylvie. It is also the pinnacle of whiteness to which he aspires. But, like Vladimir and Estragon waiting for Godot, Wallace waits for a someone who never appears. In the end, Sylvie returns to Frank and Wallace realizes that his day at the ballpark with Welby is never going to happen. Baseball, like the whiteness it represents, is unattainable for Wallace. In the end we see that the image presented earlier in the story of big, white Frank looking up from the front path as Wallace gazes from Welby's window could not be more appropriate and foretelling: "He catches my eyes and gestures with his hand, like an umpire thumbing a guy out" (6). By the rules of the game, and by the rules of whiteness, Wallace is sent to the dugout with his head hanging low.

"DISTURBING THE UNIVERSE": THE BARBARIAN GAME

In "Disturbing the Universe," the status of baseball as an icon of Americanism is taken as the premise of the story and transformed in a way that parodies the mystique of China's and America's two great hallmarks: the Great Wall and the Great American pastime. In the initial stages of the story, however, baseball is not only absent, but it could hardly be expected to make an appearance (given the fact that the story is set in ancient China and the subject matter is too serious to include a preoccupation with games). First, we encounter the epigraph to the story:

> The journey to the horizon is long. But travellers to the horizon persevere for they believe such a place exists. Not just in illusion, but in the realm of hands.—Lei Zu Wei, the poet-historian, on the construction of the Great Wall of China (182)

The quote from a Chinese scholar on the construction of the Great Wall serves to locate the story within a discourse of China, and the gnomic quality of the language gives the story a kind of Chinese aura and perhaps even an "Oriental" mystique.

The long opening paragraph confirms this Orientalism by introducing the depravation and desperation of "the Emperor's conscripts" (183) working on the wall:

> It was a desperate hour. The sun sat in high sky. Water, as always, was scarce. The soldiers had cut our food with lime to deaden our appetites. Still we suffered hunger pains. The earth was dry. It was a fine dust that lined our lungs. Three more from our crew were found dead that morning. (182)

The story seems to be, at this point, an attempt to transport our imaginations back to the actual building of the Great Wall. The emphasis is clearly not on the remarkable achievements of the Chinese, as the Great Wall is often represented, but appears rather to condemn the cruelty of the Emperor and the imperial army. We are made to empathize with the workers' conditions: the lack of water, the lack of food, the cruelty of the soldiers, the dust, the desperation, the imminence of death. The sharp, terse sentences punctuate the desperation felt by the narrator and his co-laborers, as though he were gasping out their story in pain. In considering the epigraph here, it seems that the "journey to the horizon" refers to completing the wall, and that the focus of the story will be on the perseverance of the workers (i.e., the "travellers to the horizon [who] persevere").

By the end of the first paragraph, however, a mystery is introduced that suggests to the reader that this story is not simply about the hardships faced by the conscripts and the grueling perseverance demanded of them. The narrator explains:

But on that day in question other matters stole our attention. Early that morning we had witnessed a sea gull soaring overhead. Why had she flown so far from shore? We had witnessed a hare chasing a fox, trees bending against the wind. The signs were strong, calling for resolute minds and sharp instincts. (183)

The narrator's attention to portentous signs highlights the "Oriental" aura mentioned earlier. The reader may see these people as superstitious, or perhaps simply as attuned to nature, but the fact that they pay attention to signs of nature enhances their "Chineseness" for an interpretive community that already sees the Chinese as mystical "celestials." In addition, the reference to "that day in question" and the fact that mysterious signs do appear pique the reader's curiosity. The sea gull flying far from shore, the hare chasing the fox, and the trees bending against, rather than with, the wind are all unnatural phenomena, and thus the title of the story begins to come into focus: we anticipate that something significant is on the horizon, some event that will "disturb the universe."

The story is indeed about an event that disturbs the universe. However, the seriousness of the tone, the Oriental mystique, and the emphasis on the depravation of the conscripts invite us to expect a solemn and earnest event. Later, we realize that this has been Louie's elaborate set-up. The event that becomes the focal point of the story is not some historical occasion that frees the workers from their plight. Rather, the event is baseball—that is, the invention of baseball in ancient China.

Essentially, "Disturbing the Universe" produces a Chinese myth for the origin of baseball. The cruel Colonel emerges from his tent with the mysterious "commissioner" who has come from the south to visit the building site. Rather than raining down terror and hardship on the conscripts, the Colonel gathers the soldiers for a strange game played with "wooden clubs," "pig bladders," and a "peculiar orb" (189) and seems unconcerned that the workers stop their activities to gawk at this new attraction. The game of baseball, invented before their eyes as "the imperial game" (198), transforms the throng of exhausted workers into enthusiastic spectators, and hence the game of baseball offers itself as a kind of savior. But more than salvation from labor, baseball is presented as life itself. Rather than "home plate," "first," "second," and "third" bases, Louie's Chinese myth re-writes them as the elements "Earth," "Air," "Fire," and "Water" (190). Thus, the elements of life are re-fashioned as self-contained within the baseball diamond. As sports are to American culture, baseball at the Great Wall becomes life.

The signs that earlier foreshadowed a mysterious disruption of the universe are now confirmed as even greater unnatural phenomena occur. The Great Wall speaks out in protest, fearing anachronistically that the idleness of the workers will prevent the construction of "the only man-made object visible from the moon" (194). Even the celestial bodies protest, as the sun and moon stray from their paths and join as one orb (198). "Now you mortals have gone too far," says the Wall, "You have disturbed the way of the universe. The sun and moon are the only spheres for man to adore. But look how you worship that ridiculous sphere that strikes my flanks and threatens my completion" (194). It is significant that these protests are uttered by the Great Wall, the emblem of Chinese achievement that stands as a monument to Chinese ingenuity and determination (recalling the "perseverance" in the quotation by Lei Zu Wei). The Wall sets Chinese civilization apart from all others. For the Chinese to turn from the building of this icon to the worship of baseball is to go against the order of nature; indeed, it spells ruin for the entire race.

The disturbing of the universe is a double motif for Louie, in which both Chinese and American preoccupations with work and play, respectively, are unmasked and parodied. The sudden transformation of the Chinese from slaves and slave drivers (the equivalent of the modern day workaholic) to enthusiastic sports spectators challenges the "order of nature" in the sense that it parodies the Chinese overachiever stereotype. At the same time, this challenge makes fun of the stereotypical American preoccupation with sports and leisure. We see this, for example, in the transformation of the Colonel, whose slave driving, which once spelled doom for the men, is reversed in the end when he condemns a man "to death for the high crime of working during the imperial game" (198). Whereas idleness was once a capital crime, it is now a mandate. In short, the maniacal zealousness of the Colonel at both extremes mocks the work-mentality of the Chinese as well as the play-mentality of the Americans.

The invention of baseball in ancient China humorously challenges and displaces the Americanness of baseball. The game ends with the feared barbarians climbing over the unguarded wall and stealing the "orb" used as a baseball. The scene suggests that these "fabled barbarians, the demons from the North" (199), steal not only the orb but the game of baseball itself. Perhaps like gunpowder, baseball is yet another Chinese invention stolen and perfected by outsiders. This joke too acts as a double-edged sword. On the one hand, it is an elaborate rendition of the "invention" argument for the superiority of Chinese civilization: that the inventions of the ancient Chinese prove their superiority as a race. By placing the birth of baseball on the same soil as the birth of the Great Wall, Louie pokes fun at the invention argument. On the other hand, the story also pokes fun at America, since the story disturbs the American universe which orbits around its great pastime, baseball, and the historicity of which (its status as an American invention, an American tradition, and the American pastime) are all undermined by this myth and made to be un-American.

These jokes would be impossible were it not for baseball's status as the most American of sports. Situating the origin of baseball in China would not be comical if baseball were something we considered a "Chinese activity." Simply put, because baseball is American, it is a joke to call it Chinese. Moreover, the humor in making baseball yet another Chinese invention works because of the seriousness with which Americans take their national sport. The millions of dollars paid in player contracts and spent on tickets each year, not to mention the painstaking computation of statistics and the trade in baseball paraphernalia, are enough to indicate the general attitude in America toward the game. To then say that the sport is not American is to suggest the ludicrous.

The final scene of the story further speaks of baseball's function as a symbol of America. Through the narrator, we learn that the men on the Chinese side ponder the sadness of losing out to the barbarians who crept over the wall while they sat idly and watched the game. We are told that "some dreamed of being a barbarian. Some wrestled with their esteem for the soldier Reji" (200). Reji is the star Chinese batter, nicknamed "reji," or "hot chicken" in Mandarin, because of the way he digs at the soil with his feet before he bats. To get the joke of his name, the pronunciation needs to be Americanized and the reader needs to have some knowledge of major league baseball in the 1970s and 1980s. The shouts of "Reji, Reji, Reji" from the men on the wall would remind such a reader of the chants of the crowds whenever the home-run slugger Reggie Jackson stepped up to the plate: "Reggie, Reggie, Reggie," they shouted. The veneration of Reji is on the surface a reference to the irony felt by the narrator as they cheered lovingly for a man who just the day before was whipping their backs as they labored on the wall. But underneath, the veneration of Reji is disturbing, I believe, because he excelled at playing a "barbarian" game. Already, baseball has slipped from the Chinese and become an American symbol.

To an even greater extent than "Birthday," Louie allows the status of baseball as the American game to function as a marker of Americanness in "Disturbing the Universe." To displace that status, the story jokingly suggests, is to displace the order of nature and the history of civilization.

While "Warming Trends" may not go to the extent of ordering existence on the status of baseball, it is no less dependent on the perception of baseball as American. Indeed, the Americanness of baseball is one of several features responsible for the story's ability to produce a kind of ethnic ambiguity— what might be described as either a defamiliarization of Chinese American ethnicity, or simply an undermining of the reader's expectations of ethnicity. This ethnic ambiguity is, I believe, a significant aspect in the experience of reading the story.[1] How a reader answers the question of Hank's ethnicity can profoundly change one's perception of the story. If Hank is read as a white American, then his allegiance to the Yankees is tantamount to white racism and his switch to the Indians is a moment of transformation where he recognizes his own natural alliance with the underprivileged classes, because of his unemployed and unhealthy status. Race and ethnicity, in this reading, are implied, but they are not significant factors. However, if Hank is read as a Chinese American, then his support of the Yankees is, among other possibilities, ironic. Throughout his life he has identified himself with the dominant class, but now that his monetary means of class membership is erased, his Chinese features do not allow him to remain in the same status. Although these are just two possible ways of reading the story, I believe they show that how we perceive Hank's ethnicity can significantly influence our reading of the story.

Louie creates this ethnic tension by balancing the scale with evidence on both sides. In my own experience of reading "Warming Trends" several years after its publication, I was distinctly aware that Hank's ethnicity was left undefined. From my reading of the stories in *Pangs of Love* up to this story, I had noticed that not all of Louie's stories appeared to be "ethnic," in the sense that some stories were not about Asian American characters and therefore did not seem overtly "Chinese American." In particular, the two stories prior to "Warming Trends," "The Movers" and "One Man's Hysteria—Real and Imagined—in the Twentieth Century," encouraged me not to expect each story to center on ethnicity, which was not the case for me in reading the first two stories, "Birthday" and "Displacement."

In the first paragraph of "Warming Trends," we are told that Hank is unemployed, and in a humorous fantasy he sees "Connie Chung and camera crew on his front stoop, waiting to solicit from him, the personification of the eighteen-percent jobless rate, his feelings about inflation, the deficit, or some other fad" (160). The mention of Connie Chung might suggest that

Hank is Asian American—after all, at that time she was one of the most prominent and well-known Asian American personalities in America. In the fourth paragraph, there is what seems to be a similar clue to Hank's ethnicity: "If not for his family," we are told, "he'd be eating egg foo yung three times a day and napping after each dessert" (161). As with Connie Chung, egg foo yung may signify Hank's Chinese American ethnicity because of its association with Chinese Americans; Chinese American identity would surely not be suggested if Hank had a weakness for, say, pizza or hamburgers and dreamed of being interviewed by Walter Cronkite. On the other hand, egg foo yung is hardly an authentic Chinese dish. In fact, it is a staple item in Chinese restaurants that cater to non-Chinese tastes and therefore does not necessarily signify Hank's ethnicity one way or another. If Hank were to have a craving for a dish like *feng jiao* (chicken feet), that is, a food that is not commonly ordered by white people, his Chinese American ethnicity would be confirmed—indeed, we might even surmise he was a recent immigrant. Similarly, it is not necessarily the case that Connie Chung signifies Hank's ethnicity either. She may have come to his mind simply because he happens to watch the station on which she anchors the news, not because he identifies with her as a fellow Asian American.

However, because the author of the story is Chinese American, the reader is left to wonder whether these two references to Chinese America could really be coincidental. This was my experience in reading the story for the first time. Within the space of these four paragraphs, I began to see Hank as a Chinese American, but because of his love of egg foo yung, not an immigrant. Once I began to read Hank as a Chinese American, I saw more clues to support such a reading. For example, "he was preparing dinner and whistling the theme to 'Bonanza'" (175) would have no special significance if we read Hank as a white American. But as a Chinese American, the reference to Bonanza makes sense. Who, after all, prepares the meals in Bonanza? Hop Sing, the loyal, subservient, pigtailed cook for the Cartwright family.

Yet my impression of Hank's ethnicity was thrown into question as other clues to his ethnicity contradicted my notions of Chinese Americanness. Mostly, it was the characterization of Hank and his family that radically destabilized my initial perception. For example, Hank's relationship with his daughter suggests an informality not often associated with Chinese father-daughter relationships. When Elizabeth says that the shoes she bought would be perfect for the opera, Natalia "sneer[s]," "Opera, sure. . . . Right after Hank treats you to Burger King" (162). Similarly, in assuring Hank she is eating her food properly, she says, "with my mother out begging door to door and my father idle as a dog at the pound, it's my daughterly duty to maximize the nutritive value of each food dollar" (163). The sarcasm of her comments, the ridicule of her father, and the constant use of her parents' first names would surely be considered uncharacteristic in a "traditional" Chinese family. Of course, Hank does object at one point to being called "Hankie" (170), but it seems a feeble objection, and he never objects to being called Hank.

Besides parenting style, numerous examples of Hank's characterization suggest that he is not a Chinese American, or at least not according to some common stereotypes. For example, while indulging in beer and cigarettes is by no means uncharacteristic of Asians, it does seem uncharacteristic for an Asian to be drinking Lone Star beer and smoking Tareyton cigarettes, brands we might associate with working-class white Americans in that they are regional brands that are not prominent in the global marketplace (in contrast to, for example, Carlsberg and Marlboro). In fact, Marlboro is the brand smoked by Bilbo, the supporter of Third World nations (173, 174).

Of course, another prominent sign in the story that seems to code Hank and his family as non-Chinese is baseball. The motif of baseball anticipates the reader's expectations in several ways that should be clear by now. First, in considering the use of baseball in *Pangs of Love* (as discussed above in regard to "Birthday" and "Disturbing the Universe"), we can see that baseball is a symbol in Louie's writing for American identity (distinctly white American identity in the case of "Birthday") that contrasts with Chinese identity. Second, within "Warming Trends" itself, baseball is an overt sign of Americanness, as evidenced by Hank's belief in the sport's ability to mark one as American: "Be good Americans," he says to Natalia and Bilbo, "and come watch" (173).

What interests me here is not whether we can say definitively that Hank and his family are Chinese Americans, but the fact that wrestling with the question is such a rich and integral aspect of reading the story. In a phenomenological apprehension of the text, we experience more than Hank's struggles with unemployment, changes in his family, and the growing up of his daughter. On a different level, cast as Paul Ricoeur would say "in front of the text," is the experience of the reader's own expectations of ethnicity. It seems to me that the reader is made to ask: "Why can't they be Chinese Americans?" "Where does it say that Chinese Americans must act in ways consistent with 'traditional' Chinese culture?" More fundamentally, the reader must begin to recognize how significant performative criteria are to our expectations of ethnicity.

In summary, the ambiguity of ethnicity infuses this story with possibilities. This ambiguity, I assert, is made possible by the function of the author's ethnicity and the status of various signs, not the least of which is the motif of baseball. Yet the very fact that this particular reading experience rests upon mutable cultural signs reveals the inevitability of change. "Warming Trends," in other words, is not a fixed and stable entity because the status of these signs is not fixed and stable.

TOWARD A GLOBAL "WORLD SERIES"

An exploration of "Warming Trends" in relation to the changing significance of baseball reveals how changes in the perception of America and Chinese Americans can change the way Chinese American texts are received. Like the allegorical significance of the battle between the Yankees and the Indians, Louie's use of baseball as a signifier of Americanness is highly dependent on our perceptions of baseball. Likewise, it is dependent on our perceptions of Asian Americans. For baseball to work as a marker of Americanness, it cannot be seen as Asian. Once baseball is perceived as belonging equally to Asia and America, Louie's story cannot be read in the same way. I am not arguing here that Louie's story is somehow deficient or unnecessarily "time-bound." What I mean to suggest is that as the meaning of the terms "Asian American" or "Chinese American" changes for Americans, the reading and production of Chinese American literature will change. As a greater number of Asian Americans are seen in a wider spectrum of American life, and when Asian American heroes that both Asian American children and young people of all races can look up to and shout "Reji, Reji, Reji," then it is inevitable that perceptions of Asian American literature will change.

But surely, we might counter, baseball, that great American pastime, will never be perceived as anything other than quintessentially American. The evidence from the ESPN telecast introduced earlier suggests otherwise. The ESPN telecast was not an "American event" beamed wholesale into Asia-Pacific living rooms. Rather, Asia was made to be a part of the event. This was made apparent when one of the announcers said, "It's Friday night here in Cleveland, Saturday morning for those of you in the East." This and many other comments were directed toward viewers in Asia. After one announcer produced a series of complicated statistics, the other said, "translate that into Mandarin," which, while perhaps poking fun at a language they did not understand, did at least reveal their awareness that the work of announcers in Asian languages was corresponding with their own commentary. One of these Asian announcers became the topic of conversation when the ESPN announcers publicized an upcoming series of telecasts from Taiwan. The announcers talked about getting to hear from their "good friend" Doug Yuen, whom they called "the voice of baseball in Taiwan." Another series of games, the Japan Tour, played between American major leaguers and Japanese teams, was also publicized.

It could be argued that the inclusion of Asia in the ESPN telecast is actually an indicator of Cable-TV marketing trends, or more sinisterly, American cultural hegemony, than it is of the changing status of baseball as the American game. However, the organization of a Japan Tour by American baseball clubs in cooperation with Japanese clubs suggests a growing global quality in baseball itself. Back when Hank cheered for the Yankees, the idea of American major leaguers playing against Japanese teams would have been inconceivable to many Americans. But today there is an increasing integration of American baseball with Japanese, Taiwanese, and Korean baseball. This is indicated in a 1994 article in *Transpacific* magazine profiling South Korean Chan Ho Park and Japan's Makoto Suzuki, who signed contracts amounting to $1.2 million and $750,000 respectively with American major league clubs:

> For years American baseball players either past their prime or on the fringe have packed their equipment bags and taken their waning skills to Japan. . . . With few exceptions—the most notable being Masonori Murakami, who pitched for the San Francisco Giants in 1964 and 65—the migration of professional ballplayers has been exclusively West to East. That trend is on the verge of collapse, however. (32)

Just a look at recent Major League playoffs in the last several years supports the point that the movement of players from West to East is reversing. The playoffs have featured outstanding performances by Hideki Matsui of the Yankees and So Taguchi of the Cardinals, both outfielders and clutch hitters, and Chien Ming Wang as one of the Yankees starting pitchers.

According to 2004 statistics, compiled by *Sports Illustrated* for a four-part series on the globalization of American sports, American major league baseball broadcasts outside North America have their highest rates in Japan, Latin America, and the Netherlands (3,301–5,700 hours per year), second highest rates in Taiwan, Korea, Australia, the Middle East, and northern Africa (1,001–3,300 hours per year), and the third highest rates in China, South Asia, Southeast Asia, Africa, and South America (526–1,000 hours per year; Wertheim 75). To further promote the game in their country, China has been airing more baseball on national television, and they have hired former Los Angeles Dodgers infielder Jim Lefebvre as their national team manager. Lefebvre spent four years playing in the Japanese leagues (Wertheim 80). *Sports Illustrated* reports, "driven by a desire to catch up with the growth of baseball in other Asian countries and a fear of getting embarrassed on the diamond at the 2008 Beijing Olympics—the host country gets an automatic bid—Chinese sports ministers have declared *bangqiu* an athletic priority" (80).

The fact of baseball's increasingly global image was driven home to me somewhere around the fourth or fifth inning of the game on ESPN in 1998. The Yankees' pitcher gave up a few more home runs, and, as any baseball fan could guess, the next image on the screen was the activity in the bullpen. What was surprising, at least to this viewer, was to see that the pitcher (a man of six feet, four inches and two hundred and forty pounds) in the Yankee uniform getting ready to assume the mound was Hideki Irabu, a player acquired by the Yankees from Chiba, Japan.

Today, thanks to the growing success of Asian players in the Major Leagues, the image of an Asian pitcher warming up in the Yankees bullpen is no surprise. (Hank, back in the 1980s, would have fallen off his sofa.) There will come a day, I believe, when the American World Series will be a global World Series and the way we perceive baseball, America, Asian Americans, and Asian American literature will be significantly altered.

6 Change and the Playful Reader

READING SHAWN WONG'S *AMERICAN KNEES*

> The presentation of a world in a work of art, and in general in a work of discourse, is a playful presentation. Worlds are proposed in the mode of play. . . . In entering [play] we hand ourselves over, we abandon ourselves to the space of meaning which holds sway over the reader.
>
> —PAUL RICOEUR, *Hermeneutics & the Human Sciences*

THE INFLUENCE OF THE TEXT

The reception of Chinese American literature is influenced by the reader's preconceptions of the author's ethnicity, and, as chapter 5 sought to establish through an analysis of the signifier *baseball* and its fast-waning status as an emblem of America and whiteness, the reader's expectations are bound to change as the meaning of the signifier *Chinese American* evolves in society. In examining the reception of Chinese American literature, we should not assume that Chinese American texts are inert and impotent objects that are acted upon by omnipotent readers and are helpless against the evolution of culture. As I described it in chapter 1, reception is a dynamic interplay of reader, author, and text, not a unilateral transmission of information on one hand or a tyranny of interpretation on the other. Chinese American texts can influence the ways readers perceive Chinese Americans. In fact, I believe that the experience of reading texts that challenge readers' racial preconceptions is a powerful factor in changing negative attitudes toward Chinese Americans. For this reason, I shift my focus in the present chapter to the influence of the text—in this case Shawn Wong's novel *American Knees*—upon the reader.

I chose Wong's novel because of its direct engagement with racism and racial stereotyping and, thus, the novel's insistence on challenging the reader's racialized thinking. *American Knees* unabashedly confronts racialization through Asian American characters who not only maneuver against their racialization by white society, but who also wrestle with interethnic and internalized racial stereotypes. These characters are, to borrow Anne Anlin Cheng's words, wrestling with "the complex question of how raced subjects participate in melancholic racialization" (106). According to Cheng,

> To propose that the minority may have been profoundly affected by racial fantasies is not to lock him/her back into the stereotypes but to perform the more important task of unraveling the deeper identificatory operations—and seductions—produced by those projections. The "truth" of "Asian Americanness" or "African Americanness" has always been and will continue to be a site of contestation for both those raced subjects as well as for whites. To remain complacent with the assumption that racial fantasies are hegemonic impositions on minorities denies complexity on the part of the latter's subjective landscapes. (106)

As Cheng argues, sweeping the issue of race under the rug (by ignoring it, or by muting it with terms such as ethnicity and culture when what we really mean is race) is a disingenuous approach to the pervasiveness of racialized thinking in the U.S. today. As we will see below, Shawn Wong's novel confronts these issues head on, and, when we consider Paul Ricoeur's reading phenomenology, invites his reader into the racially charged world of his characters.

"IT'S AN ASIAN THING"—OR SO WE'RE TOLD

In the fifth chapter of *American Knees*, Raymond Ding and Aurora Crane try to come to terms with the reason for their separation. They had fallen in love after meeting at a party in Washington, D.C., where Aurora worked as a photographer for the *Washington Post* and Raymond was visiting on business from California. Eventually Aurora moved to California and Raymond moved in with her. But now, after experiencing what seemed in every respect to be a sound relationship, they are breaking up. They wonder whether it is the difference in their age. No, they decide, "it's not the age thing" (64). Is it the difference in their experience? No, "it's not the experience thing" (64). In the end, they realize that the reason they cannot stay together is that Aurora cannot be the kind of Asian American woman Raymond wants her to be (71). Raymond leaves her apartment:

> Down on the sidewalk, in front of Aurora's apartment, an Asian woman passed him. She was wearing a T-shirt that read, *"It's an Asian thing. You wouldn't understand."* She caught him reading the slogan across her chest and smiled as if he understood. A pain settled on him, a simple despair invaded the air around him. (72, emphasis added)

The "pain" and "despair" that Raymond feels, a clear instance of what Cheng calls "the melancholy of race," are no doubt caused by the realization that the woman's T-shirt answers the question about him and Aurora: their break-up is an "Asian thing." While other couples break up because of infidelity, fear of settling down, unfulfilling sex, growing apart (reasons they have rejected [71]), Raymond and Aurora are breaking up because Aurora could not be Asian enough.

The T-shirt slogan, besides identifying *being Asian* with a problematic specific to Asian identity and culture, also serves to brush off and exclude outsiders. To put it another way, it serves to ghettoize Asian life into a kind of Chinatown. The claim, essentially, is that non-Asians cannot understand the complexities of Asian life; that what is "inside" is unknowable to those on the "outside." This brings to light a question about the novel itself: does *American Knees* wear this slogan as well? That is, while the novel, like the T-shirt, presents Raymond and Aurora's separation as an "Asian thing," does it also, like the T-shirt, make the claim that outsiders (i.e., readers, and more specifically, non-Asian readers) are unable to understand? Does it, in other words, participate in the production and preservation of literary Chinatown? Obviously, the fact that this "Asian thing" is presented in a novel suggests a rudimentary answer to the question: readers *are* meant to observe it, engage with it, and understand it. But what is it that readers will understand? Does the novel open up ways for us to experience an Asian perspective, or does it reveal that the "Asian thing" is just too complicated to understand, too *mysterious* and *inscrutable*? And does it let the white reader off the hook by ignoring the fact that the "Asian thing" in America is a racialized construction built on and by a white hegemonic order?

In my view, reading the novel does not simply present the complexities of Asian American identity, but brings the reader into that identity *experientially*. It is not that readers simply "identify with" Raymond and/or Aurora or imagine themselves in the position of these characters. This phenome-nological experience of *catharsis*, as Plato called it, is supplemented by a process of *transformation*, as Paul Ricoeur explains: "when a reader applies a text to himself, in the case of literature, he recognizes himself in certain possibilities of existence—according to the model offered by a hero, or a character—but, at the same time, he is transformed; the becoming other in the act of read-ing is as important as is the recognition of self" (*Reflection & Imagination* 492–93). In my reading of *American Knees*, I wish to trace the phenomeno-logical interaction of reader with text in order to discover the meaning pro-duced, as Ricoeur puts it, *in front of the text*—a meaning that is akin to the experience of the characters. The *experience* of reading *American Knees* is an intricate meeting of two "worlds" that pushes and pulls the reader in much the same way that being Asian American is experienced by the characters.

ASIAN AMERICAN GROWING UP

As explained above, I chose *American Knees* for this study because it engages with notions of Asian American life and identity in ways that openly con-front the literary Chinatown. The novel reflects Shawn Wong's experience as an Asian American *and* an Asian Americanist. Wong's influence in the aca-demic and literary debates which have sought to define Asian American iden-tity is formidable: as a writer (his first novel, *Homebase* [1979] is a significant text in the Asian American canon), as an editor (he edited *Asian American Literature: A Brief Introduction and Anthology,* co-edited the *Yardbird,* and is per-haps best known for co-editing the groundbreaking *Aiiieeeee!* and *The Big Aiiieeeee!* anthologies), as an Asian American scholar (he and his colleagues Frank Chin, Jeff Chan, Lawson Inada, and others are responsible for recov-ering numerous important Asian American works from obscurity), and as a teacher (he is a professor in the Department of English at the University of Washington, Seattle). *American Knees,* his second novel, comes sixteen years after *Homebase* and represents a kind of "growing up" in both his own work and in Chinese American literature.

By "growing up," I'm not suggesting that early works like *Homebase,* Louis Chu's *Eat a Bowl of Tea* (1961), Kingston's *The Woman Warrior* (1976), and others are not artistically accomplished and thematically mature or that *American Knees* is somehow better and more advanced literature. What I mean is that *American Knees* rests upon a background of established Asian American themes—coming to America, assimilation versus nativism, growing up Asian American, intergenerational conflict, racist exclusion—and it continues from there. In other words, rather than returning to the familiar ground of "becoming" Asian American, *American Knees* wrestles with one man's struggle to "be" Asian American. Patricia P. Chu sees Wong's novel in a similar light. In the coda to her book, *Assimilating Asians: Gendered Strategies of Authorship in Asian America*, Chu cites *American Knees* as an example of how Asian American literature is broadening: "Shawn Wong's casting of Asian Americans as cultural mentors to each other and to whites in *American Knees* [signals] the prospect of Asian American subects' true interpellation into the nation and a corresponding broadening of the subjects about which one may write" (189).

The novel begins with Raymond Ding's divorce from Darleen, a Chinese American woman whose father owns "two upscale Chinese restaurants that cater to a white clientele" (6). Raymond's motivation for marrying Darleen was, like a filial Chinese son, to please his parents. Not only was Darleen Chinese, but her family, with the patriarchal hierarchy and the successful restaurant business, was one-hundred-percent Chinese. Divorcing Darleen, on the other hand, marks for Raymond the severing of his Chinese ethnicity: "What good was a good Chinese son without a Chinese family in which to practice his legendary Chinese filial duty? What would Raymond do—go around telling people, 'Hi, my name is Raymond Ding. I used to be Chinese, but my wife got custody of my ethnicity'? (3) Ethnicity, for Raymond, has meant following the traditions and meeting the expectations of his parents. Now that he has become "the first in his thin branch of the family tree . . . to divorce" (15), Raymond's definition of ethnicity is thrown into question. In a sense, meeting his parents' expectations of being Chinese was an easy way to comprehend his ethnicity. His identity was framed by the external markers of Chineseness—the Chinese wife, the Chinese business, the family connections, the filial piety—and thus did not need to be questioned or consciously defined. But now that his life is unframed and decontextualized, he feels that he has no ethnicity. Thus, the novel begins with divorce: divorce from Darleen, but more significantly, divorce from the context of his identity. The rest of the novel interrogates the ethnic identity of a man set adrift from his identity markers.

When he meets Aurora, Raymond enters the world of adult relationships minus the pressures of filial duty. Yet in choosing a woman who is part Asian and part Caucasian (Aurora's mother is Japanese American and her father is white), he wonders which part he chose her for. Aurora faces a similar question: does Raymond's Asianness in some way "complete" her Asian side, making her more Asian American? Or, she wonders, is he more interested in *what* she is rather than *who* she is? (72). Indeed, Aurora's hybridity is central to the novel because it brings to light the constructedness of Asian American identity. As I will argue below, the reader participates in the constructing of this identity as Raymond and Aurora's experience of self-conscious interplay between "inside" and "outside" becomes an experience that is not only performed *for* the reader, but *by* the reader.

PAUL RICOEUR AND THE PLAYFUL READER

My phenomenological reading is focused on two chapters of *American Knees*: "Eye Contact," in which Raymond and Aurora meet for the first time, and "Chinese Girls," in which Raymond discusses their breakup with Aurora's best friend Brenda. My intention is to read these chapters "in play" (that is, allowing myself to enter the world of the text—to abandon myself to the space of meaning opened by the text [187] as though I am taking part in that world) in order to discover the meaning projected *in front of the text*. These terms are central to Paul Ricoeur's description of the phenomenology of reading and will be the basis of my approach. As explained in the introduction to this book, Ricoeur's concern with the transformation of self through the experience of literature is based on a philosophy of hermeneutics that privileges the self-reflexive potential of experience. Ricoeur illustrates this self-reflexivity by explaining the production of meaning as a dialectical phenomenon of one world (the world of the self) meeting another world (the proposed world of the text) that takes place in front of both text and self (rather than beneath the layers of the text, in the intentions of the author, or in the projections of the reader).

In Ricoeur's view, readers come to a text in and through distance; they then appropriate the textual horizon by reading "playfully"; and ultimately they reflect on their own being from the position of players in a proposed world. Distanciation, appropriation, and self-reflection are therefore central to the transformation of the playful reader and will thus provide the basis of my approach to *American Knees*.[1] In the following, I will examine three elements of playfully reading *American Knees*: (1) the formal features of the text which serve to "alienate" the reader, which is discussed in the following section; and (2) the fusion of horizons which is figured as appropriation, which I will discuss together with the third element; namely, (3) the potential transformation of the reader through self-reflection.

FORMAL FEATURES: "THIS ASIAN THING BETWEEN THEM"

The narrative of "Eye Contact" is preoccupied mainly with the mental sizing-up between Raymond Ding and Aurora Crane as they meet for the first time at a party in Washington, D.C. Distance appears in the first sentence of the chapter: "When Raymond stepped through the front door, Aurora Crane wondered when he would notice they were the only two Asians at the party" (25). The distance introduced here and sustained throughout the chapter can be described as I/he (or I/she) and us/them. I, the playful reader, "know" Raymond from the first two chapters and thus his "otherness" is being replaced by familiarity. At the opening of the third chapter, this process is interrupted. Raymond enters a room full of strangers. The one with whom I am familiar becomes "he" again and I am forced to view him again as a stranger. This opens up a new distance between me and him.

In this first sentence, I am introduced simultaneously to a new subjectivity and a new cultural distance. The new subjectivity is Aurora Crane, whose thoughts I am suddenly privy to. *She* is a stranger to *me*. The "he" is Raymond, whom *I* know, but *she* does not. *He* is a stranger to *her*. Aurora knows there are no other Asians at the party because she belongs to the party. *She* is one of *them*. *He* is a stranger to *them*. Yet, despite his strangeness to both her and the party, Aurora categorizes both *him* and *her* together as "the only Asians." *She* and *he* are "*they*." Thus, Aurora and Raymond are paired and set at a distance from the rest of the partygoers.

The next three sentences that make up the first paragraph reinforce this paradox of distancing and pairing. "She tried to avoid him. . . . She touched him accidentally. . . . They watched each other furtively from across the room." *She/him, she/him* reestablishes the distance between them, while the accidental touching and the pairing in the pronoun "they" brings them together again. However, the use of "they" in this final sentence is ambivalent because of the physical distance established by the "room" between them. They're paired by the activity of "watching," but they're separated by the physical distance of the room.

Flirtation is at first implicit with the "accidental" touching, but is quickly made overt by the "furtive" watching. Reading "playfully," that is abandoning myself to the play of the text, I begin to appropriate the horizon of the text as I perceive the collapse of distance suggested by this flirtation. However, this appropriation is thwarted momentarily by Aurora's musing about her boss and the other members of the party, whom I now know are "*her* friends, *her* office mates" (25, italics in original): "With dread, Aurora realized that her boss would make a special point of introducing him to her, and that one by one her loyal friends would betray her and pair her with their Asian guest. . . . It would make sense to them" (25). The complication of the possible pairing of Raymond and Aurora with what is later called "this Asian thing between them" (32) distances them from me. As with the T-shirt slogan, I am situated "outside" a specific cultural milieu. Yet, in my awareness of the erotic possibilities presented by the text, I begin to enter the proposed romance between these two "Asians." As I join the game of the text, reading playfully, I see the absurdity presented by Aurora's train of thought. Why should she be paired with Raymond just because they are the only two Asians at the party? Why should race or ethnicity determine who is attracted to whom? Why should skin color or ethnic background be the basis of a relationship? I, the playful reader, identify with Aurora and Raymond. However, in identifying with the only two Asians at the party, I recognize in the reference to the ignorant assumptions of the boss and office mates that, in terms of the text, I (the non-Asian reader) am not grouped with Aurora and Raymond, but with the non-Asian office mates. Thus, I identify with the two Asians, but I recognize myself too as an observer on the outside, where the boss and office mates are situated. In this, my self is distanced from my self, or as Ricoeur writes, my subjectivity is "placed in suspense, unrealised, potentialised" and a "distanciation in the relation of self to itself" emerges (*Hermeneutics* 144). The expression "It was all very complex in her mind, but simple in theirs" (*American Knees* 25–26), becomes for me a dual space that I occupy simultaneously. I begin to see the complexity from the inside, as part of the proposed world of the Asian characters; but I also see how "their" (i.e., the non-Asians') assumptions of simplicity or naturalness are also (or were also) "my" assumptions.

The *to and fro* action of my self in relation to both the text and my self is paralleled in the text by the two Asian characters. As discussed above, the chapter opens with a distancing/pairing, pairing/distancing movement between Aurora and Raymond and the non-Asian partygoers. This action continues throughout the chapter, charging the narrative with an ambivalent sexual and racial/ethnic energy. Eye contact is made and a kind of "war" (27) ensues. The first "battle" or "competition" is the eye contact that self-consciously dismisses shared ethnicity. This is described through Aurora's imagined scenario about the Asian man and Asian woman crossing a street. Unlike Aurora's black friends who explicitly acknowledge other black people even though they are strangers, Aurora recognizes that Asians resist such acknowledgments. While this battle may place distance between Aurora and Raymond as strangers, it also ironically serves to bring them together. That is, the "battle" or game that they play is one of distancing, but the fact that they are the only two participants actually unites them. Furthermore, the suggestion that the "eye contact" battle may be the result of ethnic differences among Asians (e.g., "distrust" or "historical animosity" [28]) implies the non-Asians' ignorance of Asian heterogeneity (no one seems to be aware, for instance, that Aurora and Raymond do not share the same ethnicity)—and thus, Aurora and Raymond are paired once again by virtue of their "insider" status and "difference" from the other guests.

The next stage of the battle is Aurora's defensive attempt to culturally distance herself from Raymond. She surveys him for any sign of Chineseness, "cheap haircut . . . gold-rimmed glasses . . . baggy-butt polyester pants, a shirt tucked in way too tight" (28). Raymond displays none of these signs, but he is carrying a gift for the host in a plastic bag, which Aurora derogatorily labels "Chinese Samsonite." The callousness of her appraisal, she quickly recognizes, is a distancing mechanism. She is subconsciously searching for points of difference to circumvent any attempt by her office mates to bring them together. However, when her boss finally introduces Raymond (not to her, to her surprise, but to the whole party), the irony of Aurora's "chinaman" (29) evaluation is revealed. Raymond is not a "fresh-off-the-boat chinaman" but "the assistant director of Minority Affairs at Jack London College in Oakland" (29). Suddenly the stylish clothes and non-Asian trappings, which Aurora deduced to be Raymond's pathetic attempts to distance himself from a "chinaman" image, take on an authentic aura. "Maybe he thought he was too good for her," Aurora thinks (29). The defensive distance induced by her "cruel" (28) assessment of Raymond is now reversed; rather than the superior observer, Aurora is now the inferior observed. As the object of her thoughts, he was pathetic; now in imagining herself the object of his thoughts, *she* is pathetic. The view is upended, but distance is maintained.

On the piano bench, the *to/fro* of the text reaches a climax of sexual ambivalence. The two are together, but after an unsuccessful attempt at conversation, they are seated "back-to-back." Again, the image of distance and pairing is performed, only the space between them is no longer "the room," but a small space on the bench dubbed "the demilitarized zone" (31). Yet the war continues. Distanced by the turning of face, Aurora and Raymond are nevertheless brought together by the occasional "leaning back," "touching," and most erotically, "grazing" (31). Their conversations are directed outward and away, but their attention and thoughts are directed inward and toward.

The playful reader, drawn into the world of the text by this ambivalent, erotic performance, is, however, immediately distanced by the entrance of a new language—the Asian rhetoric of geomancy. The explanation begins with what seems to be a drawing in of the reader: "The 'six breaths of nature' moved between them: wind, rain, darkness, light, *yin*, and *yang*" (32). Here I am given insight into "Asian spirituality" and what "mysterious" and "exotic" forces may be at play in this scene. Given this insider information, I begin to see the deeper connotations of "this Asian thing between them." However, the geomantic discourse is rudely shattered with the sentence, "but that was just so much Orientalism under the rug" (32). Wong, either through the authorial voice or the indirect discourse of the characters, invites the reader into "this Asian thing between them" only to reject and trivialize the rhetoric. Rather than identifying fully with the world of the Asian characters, I am (as with the T-shirt slogan) dumped firmly again into the outsider position. Distanciation is bridged by appropriation and frustrated by further distanciation. The Orientalist discourse thus serves to purposely disrupt the reader's horizon of expectations for "poetic" effect. According to Hans Robert Jauss, "the ideal cases of the objective capability of . . . literary-historical frames of reference are works that evoke the reader's horizon of expectations, formed by a convention of genre, style, or form, only in order to destroy it step by step—which by no means serves a critical purpose only, but can itself once again produce poetic effects" (*Towards an Aesthetic of Reception* 24).

Aurora and Raymond eventually do get together. They speak face to face. Aurora pulls him toward her to avoid collisions with plate-carrying guests; Raymond steps back again. *To and fro*. On the steps of the Lincoln Memorial, she pulls him to her again and this time he does not retreat. They kiss in a public display of affection Aurora identifies as "a rare sight" for "Asians" (35).[2] The non-Asians at the party were right that Aurora and Raymond would find each other (right, that is, if Aurora is right about their assumptions). Only to them it is "simple" and "natural," but to Aurora and Raymond, and now the reader, it is fraught with complexity.[3]

The chapter, however, does not end with their coming together at the Lincoln Memorial. The final sentence reads, "Two years later, in San Francisco, they were packing their separate things and parting" (35). The distanciation of the opening line is regained and the *to and fro* of the chapter remains unresolved—suggesting, perhaps, that the "naturalness" of their relationship based on their Asianness is more complex than an outsider might presume.

APPROPRIATION AND SELF-REFLECTION

"Reading is, first and foremost, a struggle with the text," said Paul Ricoeur in a 1987 interview (*Reflection & Imagination* 494). By this, Ricoeur calls our attention to the "textual constraints" (495) which prevent both arbitrary readings and "fallacious recapitulation and identification" with a text (494). What is described in the above section is indeed a struggle. The formal features of the text, the inside/outside and *to/fro* movement inherent in the pairing and distancing of various subjectivities, provide the constraints of our experience with the text, or, what is called the horizon of the text. As the characters act out their erotic and ethnic war of *to and fro*, the playful reader is pulled in and pushed away with equal vigor. As I, the playful reader, begin to come alongside the Asian American characters, I am reminded of my own outsider status. Thus, the horizon of the text is something like a field on which the play of the text is performed.

Yet to say that I identify with the Asian American couple and learn to despise my former assumptions and stereotyping is to oversimplify the struggle with the text. The text is not something I confront and overcome; rather, it is a playful presentation of a world that invites me into the game. The formal features define the world of the text through which play is experienced. Considering Hans-Georg Gadamer's meditation on the work of art, Ricoeur explains play in this way:

> Whoever plays is also played: the rules of the game impose themselves upon the player, prescribing the to and fro and delimiting the field where everything "is played". Hence play shatters the seriousness of a utilitarian preoccupation where the self-presence of the subject is too secure. In play, subjectivity forgets itself; in seriousness, subjectivity is regained. (*Hermeneutics* 186)

However, to say that subjectivity is "regained" through seriousness should not imply that there is not a "serious side" to play. This serious side of play is essential to Ricoeur's phenomenology:

> In play, nothing is serious, but something is presented, produced, given in representation. There is thus an interesting relation between play and the presentation of a world. This relation is, moreover, absolutely reciprocal; on the one hand, the presentation of the world in a poem is a heuristic fiction and in this sense "playful"; but on the other hand, all play reveals something true, precisely because it is play. To play, says Gadamer, is to play at something. In entering a game we hand ourselves over, we abandon ourselves to the space of meaning which holds sway over the reader. (186–87)

This revelation of "something true" through play is akin to the masquerading of a child as a pretend figure. The child's "disguise" is an expression of "his profoundest truth" (187). "In play there occurs what Gadamer calls a 'metamorphosis' (*Verwandlung*), that is, both an imaginary transposition marked by the reign of 'figures' (*Gebilde*), *and* the transformation of everything into its true being" (187). Therefore, in this sense, truth is not found in the text's formal features, nor is it found in the reader's performance as interpreter and critic. Rather, the truth in reading fiction is projected "in front of the text" through the act of play. "The player is metamorphosed 'in the true'; in playful representation, 'what is emerges'" (187).

The constant *to and fro* that I have identified in the reading of the party scene in "Eye Contact" only *appears* to thwart my appropriation of the text. It may seem that what is projected in front of the text is a world in which I participate in the hesitancies, preoccupations, and eventual union of two Asian American individuals. It may seem that I am invited to step into that world and look back on my own prejudices and racism with distaste. But this is not the entire effect. The text does invite me to "see with" the Asian American characters and I do experience that critical self-reflection; however, the text continually returns me to my old self. Yet this is not really my "old self," my reality. Rather, it is a playful part that I play—a part that is just as playful as the one that allows me to go inside the experience of the Asian American couple. The *to and fro* that I experience in reading the text is not a *to and fro* between the fictional world and my own world, but a *to and fro* between two playful positions *in* the proposed world of the text. In other words, the truth of the text does not lie in my identification with the Asian American characters, but in the frustration of my desire to identify with them.

The imaginary me in the poetic universe of Wong's text vacillates between inside and outside, understanding and misunderstanding, knowing and not knowing. What I experience as the playful reader is the frustration of shuttling between two identities, the frustration of shuttling *to and fro*. If the phenomenological experience of the text essentially pulls me into the lives of these Asian Americans *only to* dump me back into my own way of seeing, that is, to reject me and exempt me from understanding, then the text is wearing the T-shirt slogan discussed earlier. However, the phenomenological experience described above is the experience of the Asian American characters themselves—the frustration they experience as Asian Americans in a predominantly white-oriented society. Thus, the "pain" and "despair" Raymond feels may not be caused simply by his realization that the T-shirt slogan explains why he and Aurora are breaking up. Rather, it is the frustration of the inside/outside dichotomy—the fundamental reason that the "Asian thing" exists between him and Aurora—that causes the "pain" and "despair," the "melancholy of race."

The reader of *American Knees* inhabits more than the two playful positions described above. This is apparent when we go beyond the "Eye Contact" chapter to consider other episodes in the novel. Like "Eye Contact," "Chinese Girls" (chapter 8) is a *to and fro* contest between two characters that is sexually and ethnically charged. Raymond and Brenda Nishitani are alone in Aurora's apartment. They are distanced from each other by their relationships with Aurora, one as her ex-lover and the other as her best friend. Brenda further distances Raymond by her continued reference to his age and what she sees as his pathetic midlife crisis. Despite the distance between them, Raymond fantasizes about sex with Brenda:

> Raymond looked at how the contrasting colors of her unitard accentuated her lovely butt. He imagined walking up behind her and pulling her hands down from her hair, pushing his fingers through the braid and loosening it, resting the palms of his warm hands on her shoulders, *then her eyes would tell him to pull the unitard off her shoulders and down, freeing her sumptuous breasts.* (131, italics in original)

While Raymond has mental sex with Brenda, the conversation between them reveals the essential cause of the distance between them:

> "All I know is that Ro and I used to have a lot more fun before you put all those ideas in her head about identity. Ro is Ro. You made her start talking all that nonsense about being an Asian American woman" [said Brenda].
> "She *is* an Asian American woman" [said Raymond].
> "You were trying to make her into a politically correct Asian American robot."
> "I wasn't making her into a robot. It's a racist world; she needs to know how to defend herself."
> "Defend herself!" Brenda turned to face him. "I suppose she's defending herself when she calls my boyfriend a racist." (134–35)

In this exchange, it is clear that Brenda resents Raymond for changing Aurora. However, in considering the centrality of Asian American issues to the novel, it is clear that the distance between Raymond and Brenda is not wrapped up entirely in this resentment, but more fundamentally in their opposing views of ethnicity and what it means to be Asian American. Raymond believes Asian American identity is something to protect and project; whereas Brenda finds all the talk about ethnic identity to be unnecessarily serious and stifling. Raymond, because of his moral and professional position, should be put off by Brenda's lack of concern—yet he finds himself romanticizing Brenda and fantasizing about a sexual relationship with her.

At issue here are, of course, two views of Asian American identity for Asian Americans: one that sees Asian American identity as central and the other that does not. However, with the element of erotic tension infused in this encounter comes much more than a dialogic encounter between two ideologies. For the playful reader, the sexual tension elicited by Raymond's fantasy remains a steady undercurrent throughout the exchange. The angry words denote distance, but the fantasy of sex, the flirting, the facing each other, the moving closer physically, suggest a slow and subtle collapse of distance. I acknowledge the issues between them, but I sense the erotic possibilities. Thus, the meaning that projects in front of the text is not an answer to who is right. Rather, the reader gains a strong sense of Raymond's predicament. Toward the end of their conversation, Brenda says, "the difference between you and me is that I'm willing to admit that I harbor some contradictions and even some double standards. What do you want—to be politically correct or to get Aurora back?" (137–38). Brenda detects from his look that he would sacrifice his ideological stance to reconcile with Aurora. However, the experience of the text suggests that he would also sacrifice ideology and possibly his chances with Aurora to sleep with Brenda. For one, there is the sexual tension between them. In addition, he suggests to his friend Jimmy Chan that he is "hoping" to sleep with Brenda (143) and he even buys a fancy sports car immediately after receiving a gift and message from Brenda (144, 146). There are plenty of contradictions and double standards in Raymond.

The text's vacillation between ideological distanciation and sexual fantasy gives the playful reader the experience of Raymond's contradictions and double standards. This meaning projected in front of the text through the experiencing of the world of the text does not depend on the ethnicity of the reader. The gray area and paradoxes of Raymond's being and

Asian American identity are the experience of anyone who reads this text playfully.

Ricoeur writes, "The metamorphosis of the world in play is also the playful metamorphosis of the ego" (*Hermeneutics* 144). As the reader playfully steps onto the playful stage of the fictional text, the alien horizon of the text is appropriated for the reader by the fusion of his/her horizon with the text's horizon. This opens up new ways of imagining the world to the reader, as the referent of the world is not an existing reality, but a combination of potentialities produced (not reproduced) in front of the text (not inside it, under its layers). This is the metamorphosis of the world in play. Precisely by acting as a player in that proposed world, the reader, "by the long detour of the signs of humanity deposited in [the text]" (143), in a potential and self-reflexive moment, comes to an altered self-understanding. This is the metamorphosis of the ego.

"It is not a question of imposing upon the text our finite capacity of understanding," says Ricoeur, "but of exposing ourselves to the text and receiving from it an enlarged self, which would be the proposed existence corresponding in the most suitable way to the world proposed" (143). In my analyses of these two chapters, I hope to have demonstrated that the experience of reading *American Knees* has the potential to change (or "enlarge") a person in the way described by Ricoeur. However, in establishing that the experience of reading *American Knees* playfully "enlarges" the reader, we have automatically placed a positive label on the experience. To speak of horizons expanding and consciousness enlarging seems to assume that the changes described are desirable and good.

The possibility of a playful reading of a text having a negative effect on the reader by reinforcing rather than expanding that reader's horizons is suggested in the following passage from *American Knees*. In it, Raymond is having lunch with a white university administrator named Dr. Lothrop "Red" Taylor who is interviewing Raymond for a job:

> "Have you read this new novel *Lucknow Nights Without Joy in Chinatown?*" [asked Red.]
> Raymond had tried but could not get past the first chapter. Red continued without waiting for an answer. "Man, what a tearjerker

when Mei-mei and her mother triumph over the vicious cycle of
Chinese misogyny and despair."

"Hmmmmmm." Raymond kept his attention on his hash browns. (211)

In this brief exchange between Red and Raymond, we see the literary
Chinatown clearly at work. To Red, the novel is an exciting and emotional
book (a "tearjerker") that shows the "triumph" of two women over the
Chinese patriarchal system—which he calls "the vicious cycle of Chinese
misogyny and despair" (211). (Is he quoting from the publisher's description
of the book?) Red's response to the novel is one of extreme pathos toward
what he sees as a distinctly Chinese (even a Chinatown) problem. Yet to
Raymond, the novel is so repulsive he "could not get past the first chapter"
(211). Raymond seems to see the novel in a way that Red cannot or will not.

The depiction of the literary Chinatown in this passage is not simply based
on Wong's notion of a fictitious novel and a fictitious reception. The title
Lucknow Nights Without Joy in Chinatown makes a veiled reference to Amy
Tan's *The Joy Luck Club*: not only does the title contain the words "Joy" and
"Luck," but it also satirizes the awkward phrasing of "Joyluck" with the more
ridiculous "Lucknow" and thereby pokes fun at Tan's manipulation of
English to create a sense of ethnic authenticity. Yet even this subtle critique
of a real novel is aimed more at its reception than its representation. That is,
it is not the novel alone that produces the effect, otherwise Raymond would
have responded in the way that Red responded; rather, it is Red's Euro-
American expectations and the way the novel meets those expectations that
accounts for the different responses.

Red unquestioningly accepts the novel's world because it conforms to his
Euro-American expectations, while Raymond remains aloof because he sees
through the novel's attempt to pander to white tastes. Raymond's aloofness
would necessarily prevent him from reading playfully, giving himself over
to the intentions of the text, because he sees in the text a proposed world
that he detests and therefore resists. In contrast, Red "hands" himself "over"
and "abandons himself" to the textual world (*Hermeneutics* 186)—but what
is produced through this process is a reinforcement of what might be considered negative and false stereotypes of Chinese American ethnicity. If this
is the case, then we must recognize that the literary Chinatown is not erad-
icated by a certain mode of reading—what I have been calling, after Ricoeur,
a playful mode of reading. Indeed, I wish to stress here that it is not reading
playfully that will change the literary Chinatown, but playfully reading texts
that, like those by Shawn Wong, David Wong Louie, Gish Jen, Shirley Geok-

lin Lim, and Li-Young Lee, challenge and displace the Euro-American horizon of expectations regarding Chinese Americans and Chinese American literature.[4]

In this final section, I wish to address more fully the issue of the proposed
world produced by *American Knees*. What kind of novel is *American Knees*?
Can we say that the experience gained from reading this novel playfully is a
positive and desirable experience? In what follows, I will try to establish what
kind of picture *American Knees* paints of Chinese Americans in relation to
both Euro-American discourse about Asians and Asian American literary and
academic discourse.

1. Euro-American Discourse

One of the most significant ways that *American Knees* confronts the typical
Euro-American depiction of the Chinese is in its representation of Chinese
sexuality. *American Knees*'s sexual vision deconstructs Euro-American stereotypes and fantasies about Asian American sexuality. This is especially apparent in the stereotype of the subservient Asian female—the fantasy of the
sex slave. As James S. Moy claims in his book, *Marginal Sights*, "Asian women
in America have come to be perceived as possessing special mastery of sexual practices" (136). But the mastery of these sexual practices, as Moy's list
of pornographic advertisements makes clear, is not for the Asian woman's
pleasure, but entirely for the pleasure of the man:

> The [video] box cover for *China deSade* (1987) . . . introduces the star as
> "the embodiment of the Oriental ideal of perfect sensuality—dedication
> to forbidden pleasures, obedience to her sexual masters. . . ." *China Girl*
> (1989) [says] "just sit back and let her desparate [sic] need to please you
> take over." (137)

In these advertisements the Asian woman is objectified as a sex slave whose
only desire is to please "her sexual masters." The Asian woman's sexuality
is characterized thus as subservient and obedient, existing only for the man's
pleasure. Phrases like "forbidden pleasures," "obedience," and "need to please"
do more than mark an erotic experience, they tap into a Euro-American fantasy discourse about Asian sexuality.

In *American Knees*, the notion of the subservient Asian woman is seen to
be not just a Euro-American expectation, but one that is often internalized
by Asians as well. Raymond is self-conscious about this stereotype to the point

of telling Aurora the first time she massaged and scrubbed his back in the bathtub that she did not have to do it. But Aurora tells him, "it's not very politically correct [. . . but] you loved the image as well as the feeling, in spite of yourself" (102). The accuracy of Aurora's assessment, and the extent to which Raymond has bought into the image, is revealed in Raymond's answer to Aurora's question about sex and race—whether there is a difference between sex with a Caucasian woman and sex with an Asian woman. Raymond's reply is that he "was always surprised at how much Asian women enjoy sex" (143). In this confession, we see the stereotype of the all-giving, subservient Asian woman is so pervasive that it is difficult even for Raymond to admit to himself that it is not true.

Ultimately, however, *American Knees* undermines the Euro-American fantasy of the Chinese sex slave. For example, when making love, Aurora asks Raymond to indulge her with stories and fantasies that transport her to another place. When they first make love, Aurora says, "Say something . . . put me somewhere" (74). In other words, the telling of sex stories is *her idea* and the stories are meant to do something *for her*. We are told "the sex stories [Raymond told] Aurora were politely phrased and plotted to indulge her" (41). Thus, it is clear that Aurora's sexuality does not exist to entertain or serve her man. Rather, Raymond willfully performs fantasies for Aurora's enjoyment.

Raymond's conversation with Jimmy about a 1930s book called *Chinese Girls in Bondage*, brings issues regarding Chinese male sexuality to the fore. In the *Bondage* novel, the "Chinamen sold their women into slavery and prostitution, bound their feet, laughed in their faces with yellow, opium-stained teeth, probed their bodies with long, dirty finger-nails" (139). Chinese male sexuality is presented in this book as perverted, twisted, and dirty; the men regard Chinese women as objects of ridicule and commodities for financial gain. Raymond and Jimmy's tongue-in-cheek commentary on the novel serves to frame it for Wong's readers as a white Orientalist fantasy:

> "Why were we selling our women?" [asked Raymond]
> "They were being sold into prostitution." [said Jimmy]
> "Why didn't we just be the pimps? Isn't that more profitable in the
> 　　long run?"
> "We were stupid and evil."
> "And why would we sell Chinese girls? Wouldn't we want to keep
> 　　them? There weren't any Chinese women around then."
> "Ray, Ray, stop being a fucking sociologist. It's pulp fiction from the

thirties. It was written by a white guy. Evil Chinamen are evil Chinamen, plain and simple. We sell women. We live in tunnels in Chinatown." (140)

The sarcasm in this conversation highlights the incredulity of the *Bondage* novel's narrative, but it also explains the narrative's misrepresentations of Chinese male sexuality as a Euro-American construction. For Jimmy and Raymond, the only logic behind the novel is white racism: "It was written by a white guy."

The discussion of *Chinese Girls in Bondage* furthermore serves to promote a Chinese male sexuality that is virile and sexually macho. In the novel, we are told, "poor wayward but Christian Irish girls . . . came for the drugs and, it was hinted, the men" (139). When an Irish policeman enters "the den of perversion and despair" and removes an Irish woman, she cries out "I must have it!" and "her last words before she fainted were 'Chang! Chang!'" (140). For Raymond and Jimmy, this constitutes a "happy" ending for the Chinese male:

> "Shit man," Jimmy said . . . , "it wasn't the opium Meghan was after. It was the dudes."
> "Uh huh, you got that right," Raymond replied. . . . "She wasn't scream-ing for no weed at the end; she wanted Chang." (140)

While this conversation is, as noted above, tongue-in-cheek, it nevertheless seriously rewrites the image of Chinese male sexuality presented by *Chinese Girls in Bondage*. "Isn't it better to be evil and Chinky," says Raymond, "than to be sexless and obsequious?" (140). While explicitly Raymond is saying that the image of perverted sexuality is better than the image of asexuality, the tenor of the conversation presents an entirely different image. Raymond and Jimmy perform through their commentary a version of Chinese machismo. Ideologically, their conversation values male virility and sexual performance as markers of Chinese male sexuality. Getting the girl, especially the white girl, is valorized as the epitome of Chinese manhood.

A second example of *American Knees*'s disruption of Euro-American dis-course and expectations is its emphasis on heterogeneity. As noted in my def-inition of the literary Chinatown in chapter 1, Chinese American literature is often delimited and contained by Euro-American assumptions of a homo-geneous cultural vision among Chinese American writers. These assump-tions, along with the expectations regarding intergenerational conflict, are predicated upon a view of Asians as homogenous and clannish. *American Knees* disrupts these assumptions by constructing numerous links and tensions across Asian ethnic boundaries. This is perhaps most evident in Raymond's three significant relationships represented in the novel: his wife Darleen is Chinese, Aurora is Japanese and Caucasian, and Betty Nguyen is Vietnamese.

What is important here, however, is not just that the novel represents a variety of ethnicities through these characters, but that each relationship brings to light the cultural and experiential heterogeneity of Asian Americans. This heterogeneity, the novel suggests, is not simply racially/ethnically based. For example, we might expect Raymond to have more in common with Betty than he does with Aurora: Aurora is not only much younger than Raymond, but her culturally white upbringing in the upper Midwest contrasts starkly with Raymond's experience growing up in an Asian household in San Francisco. Moreover, Aurora's lack of connectedness to Asian American communities and her indecisive stance on issues of identity clash with Raymond's professional role in Minority Affairs at the college and his personal ideology. Betty, on the other hand, is not only the same age as Raymond, but she is a full-blooded Asian who is personally and professionally involved in minority politics (she works in Raymond's department).

However, the difference between Betty and Raymond that proves more formidable than age, identity, or ideology, is Betty's experience as an immigrant. Raymond's inability, or perhaps unwillingness, to get inside Betty's life rests in this immigrant experience that he cannot know, understand, or share with her. Betty makes this point as the two of them discuss the collapse of their relationship:

> "Maybe you can live in Aurora's world better than mine. I'm an immigrant and my parents are immigrants. She fits into your family better than I do. You belong there."
> It sounded so obvious, but Raymond had never thought of it that way. He had always thought it was Aurora who needed to belong to his world.
> "We don't share the same history, Raymond." (197)

Raymond's belief up to this point that Aurora needed to fit into his world relates to his doubts regarding her identity and ideology: the reason for his separation from Aurora was essentially that she could not be Asian enough for him. Yet Betty brings him to realize that he belongs to Aurora's world more than Betty's. What Betty means by "history" is clearly not relationship history, but her immigrant experience, which stands in contrast to Raymond's American-born experience. Thus, it is the experience of immigration rather than the ontological status of Asianness that proves the deciding factor in their relationship. It is suggested here that Raymond and Aurora's shared Americanness will hold them together.

If a reader is to gain an "enlarged self" via the experience of reading *American Knees*, we can conclude from this discussion just how it would be enlarged: that it would be so in the sense of going beyond, questioning, and undermining common notions held by non-Asian Americans and perpetuated in a Euro-American discourse. However, where *American Knees* stands in relation to this discourse is not our only consideration. Below, I will briefly examine some ways in which the novel interacts with Chinese American literary and critical discourse.

2. Chinese American Discourse

American Knees engages with Chinese American discourse by presenting alternatives to some common fictional representations. This is evident in my earlier point that the novel builds upon narratives of immigration and adolescence that predominate in the Asian American canon. This relation to Asian American literary representation can be seen, for example, in the depiction of the father figure. In much Chinese American fiction, the father figure is severe, distant, sometimes abusive, or simply left in the background.[5] Woodrow Ding, Raymond's father, shows some of the aloofness and unwillingness to openly express feelings that is often associated with this Chinese father figure, but without the severity. This is especially apparent in the episode between Raymond and his father during the period immediately following his mother's death: "They couldn't talk about depression, or sadness, or pain, or grief, or any other unspoken and undefinable emptiness that invaded their lives and occupied the space between father and son, man and boy" (20). But the silence between them was not an inexpressive silence; rather, as Wong puts it, "Silence was a bond, an understanding. Silence was love" (20). This love between father and son, indeed the vulnerability and sensitivity of the two men, is poignantly revealed when Woodrow, two nights after his wife's funeral, tells his son, "I need you to sleep in the bed with me . . . there's too much space there" (20). Rather than an unmanly or pitiful request, however, Wong paints it as courage: "it was the bravest thing his father had ever done" (20).[6]

The importance of the silence between Raymond and his father confronts (or broadens) King-Kok Cheung's feminist thesis regarding silence in works by Hisaye Yamamoto, Kingston, and Joy Kogawa, as presented in her book, *Articulate Silences*. Even in the case of *China Men*, Cheung insists on the feminine orientation of silence: "*China Men*, which portrays the silencing of Chinese American men, at once employs feminist strategies and inverts certain feminist preconceptions" (102). Wong, however, presents silence not only as communication between father and son, but as a male mode of expression: "Raymond's father gave him his place in the family *by not asking, by not saying* what was on his heart. It was *the manly way* of doing things. *This was how Raymond became a man*" (22–23, emphasis added).

This broadening of Asian American representation is seen in other challenges in the novel to the theses of other Asian American scholars. For instance, a further challenge to Asian American feminism can be seen in Aurora's admission after their breakup that she had once *needed* Raymond:

> "When I'm with you I'm safe from blame" [said Aurora].
> "Just because I'm Asian?" [said Raymond]
> "That's part of it, and it's what I wanted. I wanted at least our identity together to influence me, to lead me, to make me feel *like I belonged to you*."
> "Feminists—"
> "Not in a way that'll have every Asian feminist up in arms, pointing her finger at me—."
> "At me the misogynist or, at the very least, the domineering Asian man making a slave of you, the impressionable young girl." (63, emphasis added)

Here, Wong puts the criticism of Asian American feminism in a female mouth and the possible defense of that feminism in a male mouth. Both Raymond and Aurora are aware of this feminist discourse, but their conversation qualifies it by suggesting that Aurora's desire to belong to Raymond is neither unthinking subservience on her part, nor patriarchal domination on his.

Another example of Wong's engagement with Asian American scholarly discourse is found in his characterization of Raymond and Aurora's mothers. Raymond says, "I was raised by a mother who raised me on extravagance and perfection. When my mother arrived from China, she took photography and painting" (53). Furthermore, "Raymond's mother never saved anything, never bought the economy size" (59). Aurora's mother, on the other hand, is a *nisei* who taught Aurora to save things: "useful things like the

Styrofoam trays meat was packaged in, rubber bands, wire ties from plastic bags" (59). In this we see an obvious reversal of Sau-ling Cynthia Wong's necessity/extravagance thesis. Building on ideas in Kingston's *The Woman Warrior*, Wong writes, "something about the immigrant situation, if not immediate memories of privation, then the shock of permanent relocation to a white-dominated society and the daily attritions of adjustment—causes the first generation to value efficient eating unquestionably" (28). Thus, frugality, saving, and eating staple foods (i.e., necessities) (44), according to her, are characteristic of Asian immigrants. Sau-ling Cynthia Wong contrasts this with the "extravagance" which characterizes the "American-born": "candies, snacks, and fancy foods from stores and restaurants . . . going beyond what is needed for survival" (44). Yet in Shawn Wong's portrayal of Raymond and Aurora's parents, the immigrant mother is extravagant and the American-born mother is driven by necessity.

Shawn Wong's position within Asian American scholarship implies that *American Knees's* counterthrust to various notions within the discourse reflects an effort on his part to broaden, disrupt, or contradict certain theses. This element of the novel is important to my study because it shows a significant way in which Chinese American literature is changing by presenting such self-conscious re-visions which broaden the representation of Chinese Americans in fiction and reveal the heterogeneity of experience, convictions, and expression among them. It also highlights the interaction of academic and creative writing and throws into question the sociological relevance of Asian American literature discussed in chapter 2—that is, the view that Asian American literature is valued for its ability to teach us about the "real" lives of Asian Americans. Analyzing the ways that *American Knees* brings us into Asian American life through the phenomenology of reading must be qualified by our recognition that fictional representations of Chinese Americans cannot be seen as authoritative and definitive. In other words, because fictional representations are presented through the individual perspective of an author, we must recognize that what we experience in Chinese American literature is not simply the "truth" about Chinese Americans, but at best a version of the truth. This, I would argue, is something readers tend to accept with "mainstream" literatures, but not with "minor" literatures.

THE TRUTH AND THE TEXT

"Through the work of art," writes Gadamer, "a truth is experienced that we cannot attain in any other way" (xxii–xxiii). This notion of the gaining of "truth" through a text is essential to my phenomenological reading of *American Knees*—yet to understand it we must look at this notion of "truth." First, we must recognize that in terms of phenomenology, truth does not necessarily reside within the text. As Ricoeur explains,

> Through fiction and poetry, new possibilities of being-in-the-world are opened up within everyday reality. Fiction and poetry intend being, not under the modality of being-given, but under the modality of power-to-be. Everyday reality is thereby metamorphised by what could be called the imaginative variations which literature carries out on the real. (*Hermeneutics* 142)

Thus, the knowledge and truth that emerge in the reading of fiction are fuelled by the text, by its "imaginative variations," but are not constituted by the text. The text does not give being; it suggests the power to be.

Yet even these "imaginative variations" are not encapsulated simply in the text. Rather, it is through the interplay of the reader and the text that knowledge and truth emerge. "Ultimately," says Ricoeur, "what I appropriate is a proposed world. The latter is not *behind* the text, as a hidden intention would be, but *in front of* it, as that which the work unfolds, discovers, reveals. Henceforth, to understand is *to understand oneself in front of the text*" (143, italics in original). Ricoeur is talking less about understanding the text than he is about understanding ourselves, or rather, he is talking about understanding ourselves through the experience of reading the text. Thus, in reading a novel like *American Knees*, what knowledge I may gain of Chinese American life is less important to my understanding than the dialectical experience that occurs between my world and the fictional world of the text. What unfolds in front of the text is my own interaction with a proposed world of Chinese American life.

"It must be said," Ricoeur writes, "that we understand ourselves only by the long detour of the signs of humanity deposited in cultural works. What would we know of love and hate, of moral feelings and, in general, of all that we call the *self*, if these had not been brought to language and articulated by literature" (*Hermeneutics* 143). The self-reflexivity that is central to Ricoeur's philosophy is apparent in this statement. He is not saying that authors of literature present the truth about the world and we who read automatically learn from these authors. This is why I emphasize that in *American Knees*, Shawn Wong does not necessarily give "the truth" about the Chinese American experience, but he gives us his version of it. What I have attempted to explore in this chapter is the way that the version of truth in *American Knees* interacts with the reader's version of the truth to create a new understanding of both through the experience of reading.

While the alteration of one's perspective through reading fiction may be familiar to most readers, the phenomenological processes involved may not be. My exploration of Shawn Wong's *American Knees* via the phenomenology of Paul Ricoeur has been an attempt to unfold those processes that allow us to enter the world of a Chinese American text and experience the playful metamorphosis of our ego.

PART IV

Reading New Horizons

American means being whatever you want, and I happened to pick being Jewish.

—MONA CHANG, in Gish Jen, *Mona in the Promised Land*

7 Beyond Multicultural

CULTURAL HYBRIDITY IN THE NOVELS OF GISH JEN

If there is one thing I hope readers come away with, it's to see Asian Americans as "us" rather than "other."

—GISH JEN

CHALLENGING ETHNICITY

The literary Chinatown described in this book is fundamentally a "ghettoizing" phenomenon. The reader's assumption that the ethnic author speaks for the Chinese community forces Chinese American literature into a minor role with a specialized and limited vision. I argued in chapter 6 that the experience of reading a text like *American Knees* can change the perspective of readers by bringing them into the experience of being Asian American. In this chapter, I examine another formidable opponent of the literary Chinatown horizon: namely, the notion of cultural hybridity. Below, I discuss Gish Jen's first two novels, *Typical American* and *Mona in the Promised Land*, in order to discover the ways in which her exploration of cultural hybridity re-fashions ethnicity as a dynamic field of intersections and permeations that serves to dissolve the literary Chinatown's us/them dichotomy. To put this discussion of Jen's work into perspective, a brief discussion of cultural hybridity, including critical objections to the model, is needed in order to highlight Jen's challenge to the literary Chinatown horizon.

CULTURAL HYBRIDITY

"The very concepts of homogenous national cultures," writes Homi Bhabha, "the consensual or contiguous transmission of historical traditions, or 'organic' ethnic communities—*as the ground of cultural comparativism*—are in a profound process of redefinition" (5). Cultural hybridity, as Bhabha and others assert, is a concept at the forefront of this "redefinition." The theory of cultural hybridity is an attempt to conceptualize the identity of a person or a group in terms that recognize the existence of cultural differences as well as the roles of *invention*[1] and *agency* in the articulation of those differences. In Bhabha's view, hybridity is marked by the "in-betweenness," the "inter-stitiality," caused by the continuous negotiation between the foreign and the familiar. In this way the process of identity formation is ongoing. There is no pre-defined whole into which an individual consciousness is growing; indeed, the very concept of culture is re-defined as a fluid, dynamic process of change and creolization, rather than a homogenizing whole. As with the Derridean distinction in the word "différance," in the cultural hybridity model, individuals and communities *differ* (i.e., are marked as different) from one another, while at the same time their own meaning, definition, or identity is *deferred* (i.e., put off, postponed) indefinitely. Even the definitions of self or culture on which individuals and groups may agree are reconstituted by this view as emerging through the social and political moment, rather than as statements of organic quality or essence.[2]

Thus, the theory of cultural hybridity radically transforms the commonly held notion of culture as a "complex whole" (as defined by E. B. Tylor in his influential *Primitive Culture* [1958], qtd. in Wicker 31) by contesting its belief in a tangible, even pre-existent, cultural essence. In the words of Alberto Melucci, "the identity of a self becomes [in the hybridity formulation] more of a field than an essence: not a metaphysical reality but a dynamic system defined by recognizable opportunities and constraints" (64). By freeing the individual from the idea of culture's conforming forces, hybridity theory introduces an element of individual and group choice in the expression of identity. According to Melucci,

> If identity is no longer an essential nucleus or a metaphysical continuity, definition of its borders and maintenance of its continuity are entrusted to our capacity to respond—that is, to our ability to recognize and choose among the opportunities and constraints present in the field of relations that constitute us at any given moment. (65)

This idea that identity can be shaped by the individual's ability to "recognize and choose among . . . opportunities and constraints" liberates the individual from ascribed identity and initiates a democratized process of self-identity.[3]

The theory of cultural hybridity seeks to eradicate hegemonic structure by subverting the general notion of culture as a static, primal, totalizing force and replacing it with a more historically viable model in which all cultures are characterized by "internal variation, diachronicity and transitions" (Wicker 37) and an adjacent process of democratization. This coincides with the position taken by Lisa Lowe in "Heterogeneity, Hybridity, Multiplicity: Marking Asian American Differences." For Lowe, the impression of Asian American literature as fixated upon a nativist/assimilationist dialectic "essentializes Asian American culture, obscuring the particularities and incommensurabilities of class, gender, and national diversities among Asians" (26). Furthermore, Lowe claims that by accepting an essentialist version of "Asian American identity," one remains trapped within the binary logic of hegemonic politics:

> In accepting the binary terms ("white" and "non-white," or "majority" and "minority") that structure institutional policies about ethnicity, we forget that these binary schemas are not neutral descriptions. Binary constructions of difference use a logic that prioritizes the first term and subordinates the second. (31)

Lowe prefers to represent Asian Americans as a heterogenous people, varying "across racial and ethnic, gender, sexuality, and class lines" (31). In terms of cultural texts and their interpretation, Lowe privileges a hybridic view which "refuse[s] static or binary conceptions of ethnicity, replacing notions of identity with multiplicity and shifting the emphasis from ethnic 'essence' to cultural hybridity" (33).

Some Asian American scholars, however, object to the re-definition of Asian American culture as hybrid. For example, in her response to Lowe's argument Sau-ling Cynthia Wong raises a number of salient points that serve to question the unqualified acceptance of the hybridity model in Asian American studies. "Theoretically," she writes, "I could ascribe a great deal of power to interstitiality and subjectivity-shuttling . . . ; in practical political terms, however, I can't see how an interstitial, shuttling exercise of power is done" ("Denationalization" 19). Cultural hybridity may be a more accurate description of actual cultural transformations in a world increasingly typified by globalization, diaspora, and transnational flows of culture and capital, yet culture articulated as hybrid within the everyday reality of the nation-state may render disadvantaged groups politically impotent. Wong's concern is that if Asian American cultural criticism abandons its efforts toward establishing the Asian American voice in American culture and politics for a model of fluidity and interstitiality, then "certain segments of the Asian American population may be left without a viable discursive space" (19).

Other objections to the hybridity model center on its tainted linguistic genealogy, its literal botanic reference to the mixing of two essences, and its euphoric and utopian promise to eradicate essentialism. Anne Anlin Cheng, for instance, asks whether the hybridity model sets up a false dichotomy

> between hybridity and essentialism, as though the former cures the latter, as though differences of class, gender, and nationality eliminate essentialist positions when clearly those different positions are themselves each effecting their own brands of allegiances, each demanding 'an' identity. (26)

Vijay Prashad claims that the problem with the hybridity metaphor is that its literal definition "retains within it ideas of purity and origins (two things melded together)" ("Bruce Lee" 54). Added to this is the problem of hybridity's historic origins in the racial theories of the Victorian era. In *Colonial Desire: Hybridity in Theory, Culture and Race*, Robert J. C. Young cautions against an uninformed acceptance of the language of hybridity in today's Cultural Studies, a language he claims utilizes "the vocabulary of the Victorian extreme right" (10). Hybridity found its earliest and most prominent articulations in the racialized debates of nineteenth-century colonialism. Hybridity, the biological mixing of the races, was portrayed as a threat to the white colonialist's mandate and responsibility as the superior race to rule the world. The dissemination of the white man's seed among the inferior races would lead to the disintegration of civilization, an idea that was most poignantly expressed in the trope of the hybrid's supposed sexual impotency. Young is therefore reticent to attribute an enlightened status to modern hybridity theory. "There is an historical stemma," he says, "between the cultural concepts of our own day and those of the past from which we tend to assume that we have distanced ourselves" (27).

For some Asian American critics, postmodern concepts of identity such as cultural hybridity are useful in opposing essentialized notions of ethnic subjectivity, but they also introduce a problematic for a raced subject. Traise Yamamoto writes, "for subjects marked by race, or by gender and race, fragmentation is very often the condition in which they already find themselves by simple virtue of being situated in a culture that does not grant them subjecthood, or grants them only contingent subjectivity" (75). The problem then, as Yamamoto states it, is that postmodern subjectivity seeks to destabilize that which has never been stable. Cultural hybridity may thus rightly deconstruct Euro-American expectations of an Asian essence, but it may offer little assistance to Asian American individuals who feel they have never attained "wholeness" in U.S. culture. David Palumbo-Liu shows similar caution:

> While appreciating the ways that postmodern and postcolonial criticism can break up outmoded perspectives on literary studies in order to comment upon ethnic literatures, Asian-American literary and cultural criticism must recognize as well the historical and theoretical differences that complicate such literatures if it is to better understand its own location within contemporary cultural politics. ("Ethnic as 'Post-'" 167)[4]

Cultural hybridity therefore has its limitations. On the whole, however, many theorists today argue that cultural hybridity is a positive formulation, a "radical inversion" of racist constructs (Papastergiadis 257). Even Young does not wish to suggest that hybridity is regressive or ineffective as a cultural theory, but he does caution that we not assume an inherent superiority of modern hybridity theory over nineteenth-century dialectical thinking: as he argues, "the interval that we assert between ourselves and the past may be much less than we think" (28).

In her objection to Lisa Lowe's argument for the cultural hybridity model, Sau-ling Cynthia Wong explores the possibility of applying the concept to Asian American identity politics and at the same time overcoming its political impotency by articulating culture as a conscious negotiation between natural flux and intentional stasis: that is, as shifting between modes of change and modes of internally defined essentialism. In a similar move, which I will explicate toward the end of this chapter, Pnina Werbner makes a cogent argument for a crucial distinction between "modes of objectification" and "modes of reification." I will return to these issues later in the chapter, and in the conclusion I will take into consideration Prashad's suggestion that we abandon the term "hybridity" altogether, replacing it with polyculturalism, a word that signifies multiple rather than binary mixing.

One contemporary Chinese American writer who clearly engages with these postmodern articulations of ethnicity is Gish Jen. Her commitment to the cultural hybridity model (although she may not use the precise term) can be seen in her works, but also in what she says about her writing and the impact she hopes it will achieve. For example, in reply to a question about what she hopes readers would learn from *Mona in the Promised Land*, Jen writes,

I hope that they will understand that ethnicity is a very complicated thing, not a stable, unified thing. Right now many people hold the view that if you're a Chinese American, that is far and away the most important fact about you. That is what you were born and will be forever. To try to make yourself something else is being false to your true self. I think that's entirely wrong. I think that all the groups in America have rubbed off on each other, and that no group is pure. There is really no such thing as one who is purely Chinese American or anything else. If you look at what it means to be Chinese American today, for instance, I think you'll find that a lot of our ideas about group identity have been borrowed straight from Jewish and black people. To imagine that being just one thing is the be-all-and-end-all truth about yourself is pretty naïve. (qtd. in Partridge 230)

In her novels, Jen presents a radical and provocative formulation of ethnicity. In terms of the literary Chinatown, I argue that Jen's articulation of cultural hybridity profoundly disrupts the ghettoization of Chinese American literature. I will begin with a discussion of linguistic and cultural hybridity in her first novel, and then present a more lengthy discussion of cultural hybridity in her second, and I will make observations about her third novel in the conclusion.

TYPICAL AMERICAN AND BAKHTINIAN HYBRIDITY

Gish Jen's first novel, as its title suggests, interrogates the notion of what it means to be typically American. For Ralph, Helen, and Theresa Chang, "typical American" is a buzz word they use for the things Americans do:

> "Typical American no-good," Ralph would say; Theresa, "Typical American don't-know-how-to-get-along"; and Helen, wistfully, "typical American just-want-to-be-the-center-of-things." They were sure, of course, that they wouldn't "become wild" here in America, where there was "no one to control them." Yet they were more sure still as they shook their heads over a clerk who short-changed them ("typical American no-morals!"). Over a neighbor who snapped his key in his door lock ("typical American use-brute-force!"). Or what about that other neighbor's kid, who claimed the opposite of a Democrat to be a pelican? ("Peckin?" said Ralph. "A kind of bird," explained Theresa; then he laughed too. "Typical American just-dumb!"). (67)

"Typical American" is thus Ralph, Helen, and Theresa's name for what they consider to be foreign, a designation that distances them from all that they dislike about Americans, as well as all that they do not understand. As this passage indicates, their aggressively xenophobic posture masks their fears of becoming "wild," becoming wild being a version of "going native." In other words, behind the rhetoric here is an anxiety of enculturation.

"Typical American," as a buzzword and as the title of the novel, becomes increasingly ironic as the story of the Changs develops. One irony, of course, is the fact that the deepest fears of Ralph, Helen, and Theresa are slowly materializing: they are increasingly becoming "typical Americans." However, the deeper irony of "typical American" lies in its function as a definition for Americanness, an irony that I would argue is central to the entire novel.

The Americanness of the story is emphasized in the very first line of the novel: "it's an American story" (3). Yet what is first described is young Ralph's journey by ship from China to America. He is obviously not American, but, we are told, this is an American story. In light of the "Americanization" of Ralph, which seems to be the subject of the story, it would appear that the irony here is that Ralph, who was once a typical Chinese, becomes through the process of assimilation a typical American. As such, the title would speak not about *being* typically American, but about *becoming* typically American. Yet by the end of the novel, it is clear that the story is not simply about the assimilation of Ralph and the others. "Becoming American" is a phrase that rests secure in the idea of the signifier "American." That is, the phrase suggests a given knowledge or understanding of what "American" is. This notion of *"American"* is thrown into doubt, most notably by Ralph's epiphany that "America is no America" (296).

Ralph's admission that "America is no America" (296) undermines a reading of *Typical American* as simply a story of integration and assimilation. Ralph's epiphany questions, rather, the whole notion of Americanness. "America is no America" is a sentence that negates America. At first glance, this phrase seems to suggest that the accepted definition of America does not actually or adequately define America, as recognized in a phrase like "he is no gentleman," or "she is no Christian." In these examples, the subject of the sentence is described as not living up to the standards that the speaker expects these terms to describe. But to say "he is not a gentlemen" does not change the meaning of "he is no gentleman" in the same way that "she is not a Christian" changes the meaning of "she is no Christian." The man can be judged according to a definition of "gentleman" whether or not he professes to be one; therefore, replacing "no" with "not" still suggests that the man does not live up to a certain standard. In the latter case, however, replacing "no" with "not" incurs an ontological change. "She is not a Christian" means she does not live up to the standards of Christianity *only if* she professes to be a Christian. Otherwise, the sentence simply means she does not profess to be a Christian. What, then, does it mean to say that America is no America? Is America something other than Ralph believed it to be, or is it something other than it pretends to be? If America is not America, then what is it? Is it nothing? Is it something not yet defined?

My argument is that "typical American" in this novel is, in its most profound sense, a description of people like Ralph, Helen, and Theresa—people who are struggling to define themselves in, and with regard to, America; people who are becoming, changing, and existing in an "in-between space" (as Bhabha calls it). Jen begins through this novel to define "American" as essentially hybridic and interstitial (as defined by deferral, in the Derridean sense mentioned earlier), and this is a definition that culminates in the cultural-hybrid Mona in her second novel. According to David Leiwei Li, Jen "posit[s] a new relation to the dominant culture and . . . create[s] a fiction *beyond* the negative embodiments of race and ethnicity" (*Imagining* 102, emphasis added).

In one sense, by presenting a Chinese American family as typically American, the novel places the Chinese American immigrant experience within the bounds of American identity. This sensibility aligns it with the Asian American project of "claiming America," which I discussed briefly in the introduction and discussed at length in chapter 4. While the Chinese are often regarded as foreign and unassimilable, and therefore un-American, the novel shows that it is not assimilation to the American way that defines Americanness; what makes Chinese Americans *bona fide* Americans, rather, is their experience as immigrants. The hybridized consciousness which results from the experience of immigration is therefore what is typically American.[5]

My approach to the hybridity in the novel centers on the Bakhtinian notion of stylized hybridity in character speech. This will be useful in revealing some of the ways *Typical American* destabilizes assumptions of cultural loss and assimilation. Moreover, it will help to show that the process of hybridity, at least for Ralph, Helen, and Theresa Chang, began long before coming to America.

Hybridity enters the novel in the Bakhtinian double-voiced discourse of the protagonists. According to Bakhtin,

> In the everyday rounds of our consciousness, the internally persuasive word is half-ours and half-someone else's. Its creativity and productiveness con-

sist precisely in the fact that such a word awakens new and independent words, that it organizes masses of our words from within, and does not remain in an isolated and static condition. (345)

In this way, the dispersion of one's consciousness and the formulation of hybrid identities are constructed not as diffusion and loss, but as the very seeds of "creativity and productiveness." Hybridity is reformulated by Bakhtin as accumulation, as gain, as awakening. The negative assumptions of dispersion are thereby replaced with a positive formulation of growth and change; furthermore, as Bakhtin reduces this hybridic construction to the individual consciousness, the concept of hybridity is naturalized as a common, universal human process.

In *Typical American*, Gish Jen represents identity formation in this Bakhtinian manner. The influence of the self-made man Grover Ding on Ralph Chang is one example. The first encounter between them shows Grover Ding's language of self-actualization and positive thinking (or "imagineering") being internalized by Ralph:

"Keep your eyes open," [Grover said].
"Eyes open," [Ralph said].
"Keep your ears open."
"Ears open."
"Know who you're dealing with."
"Know who I'm deal with." (108)

Here we see a bicultural dialogue between Ralph's current way of thinking, produced by his upbringing in China, and the thinking of the capitalist businessman, or, to borrow Li's terms, between the "precapitalist mode of production, in which kinship relations play a major role, and . . . a capitalist mode of production, in which market relations dominate all forms of human exchange" (*Imagining* 104). In his conversation with Grover, Ralph internalizes the cultural logic of the capitalist businessman in a complex pattern typified by Bakhtin's notion of the "internally dialogized hybrid" (361). On the simplest level, Ralph internalizes the foreign by mimicry and repetition. "Eyes open," "Ears open": these phrases repeat the essence of Grover's sentences in Grover's words.

In the sentence, "Know who I'm deal with," however, we witness a deeper form of hybridization. By shifting the personal pronoun from "you" to "I", Ralph transposes the sense of Grover's language onto his own consciousness. The meaning of Grover's words is thereby occupied by Ralph's consciousness and forced to become Ralph's own. Finally, the alterity of Grover's language is marked within Ralph's own speech by its broken English. In a real sense, therefore, it is both his and not his. Bakhtin describes the "internally persuasive" ideological discourse of someone else as being of "decisive significance in the evolution of an individual consciousness: consciousness awakens to independent ideological life precisely in a world of alien discourses surrounding it" (345). It is thus the contact and struggle between these two languages, and their subsequent internal hybridization, which reveal the "evolution" of Ralph's consciousness.

Another example in *Typical American* is Helen's hybridization of real estate jargon and her own language. As the Changs' household income increases, the possibility of buying an American dream-home captures Helen's imagination.[6] Through the help of a Chinese realtor friend named Janice, Helen begins to immerse herself in the house-hunting scene: newspaper ads, open houses, drives through neighborhoods. Jen marks the foreignness of real estate language to Helen's language by italicizing Chinese in her speech and leaving English words in regular font. Here Helen is speaking to her sister-in-law Theresa: *"Today Janice took me to this house with a* winding walkway. *Really darling! However, it was very* overpriced, *they're going to have trouble selling it for anything near what they're asking. And yesterday I saw a* breakfast nook with beautiful built-in benches" (152). As with Ralph's internalization of capitalist business-speak, there are several dimensions to Helen's hybridized language. For one, Helen is adopting not only real estate jargon ("winding walkway," "breakfast nook," "built-in benches") which one would glean from advertisements, but also a language that connotes an attitude toward the property described. She may have adopted the use of "darling" and "beautiful" as descriptors of property from real estate advertisements, but the word "overpriced" must originate from a different source, one that is capable of making such a negative judgment. Most likely, this word belongs to her realtor friend Janice. Thus, both real estate jargon and the opinion of another toward possible purchases are hybridized within Helen's language.

Jen's hybridic stylization of English and Chinese within Helen's speech reveals graphically the coexistence of two seemingly incompatible languages within one language, one that we recognize as Helen's native Chinese and the other as her adopted American English. Bakhtin argues that in "intentional semantic hybrids" such as this, "two points of view are not mixed, but set against each other dialogically" (360). Indeed, in the above segment, Helen's native language is, like Ralph's broken English and business jargon, set against real estate jargon. They are dialogic in the sense that each "unmasks," to use Bakhtin's terminology, the foreignness of the other. The result is parody, an "ironization" of each other, which is a clear source of humor in these segments but is also a vivid "image of a language" (361) in the process of hybridization. In Bakhtin's summary to his discussion on discourse in the novel, he states:

> In a word, the novelistic plot serves to represent speaking persons and their ideological worlds. What is realized in the novel is the process of coming to know one's own language as it is perceived in someone else's language, coming to know one's own belief system in someone else's system. There takes place within the novel an ideological translation of another's language, and an overcoming of its otherness—an otherness that is only contingent, external, illusory. (365)

Since the struggle between ideological structures reveals a process of "translation," of "overcoming . . . otherness," it may be said that the foreignness of business-speak and real estate-speak are unmasked by Helen's Chinese and Ralph's broken English. Clearly, then, the linguistic hybridity of *Typical American* reveals a deeper tension, a conflict that is ideological, moral, and aesthetic. The tension for the Changs is one of in-betweenness, of interstitiality.

The mistake often made in reading this "clash of two cultures" is to assume that living in-between is predicated upon the stasis of the two extremes, that is, that Chinese culture and American culture are fixed and whole, and hybridity describes the melding of the two essences (Prashad, "Bruce Lee" 54). *Typical American* rightly complicates this view of cultural hybridity by revealing that the Changs' process of hybridity began long before they came to America. Growing up wealthy in Shanghai, they were influenced by music, dress, lifestyle, and ideas in their everyday lives and in their education that can be deemed Western. This they sometimes forget as they recollect their past. For example, when Theresa remarks that in buying a car Ralph was becoming Americanized, Ralph responds, *"What's so American? We had a car, growing up. Don't you remember?"* (128, italics in original to denote Chinese speech). This is the problem with which Helen grapples when she considers the possibility of losing Theresa after the car accident: "She had considered the great divide of her self's time to be coming to America. . . . But she was mistaken. That was not the divide at all" (288). It is all too easy, when looking at the life of an immigrant, to assume that there is a great divide between the life in the old country and the life in the new. In fact, the ongoing re-conceptualizing of identity knows no such boundaries.

The Changs' lifestyle in Shanghai reveals another significant disruption of reader expectations. While one might expect culture to be this novel's preoccupation, I would argue that social class is the greatest marker of difference. Sau-ling Cynthia Wong's necessity versus extravagance thesis is again useful. Wong shows that the immigrant is conditioned by experience to be a creature of necessity (eating all types of food and all parts of animals; saving money to the point of miserliness), while the second generation is prone to extravagance (being more particular about food and preferring sweets; spending money on leisure and beauty). But Ralph, Theresa, and Helen all come from well-to-do families. In China, they owned a car, had servants, and enjoyed position in society by virtue of their family history. Helen is the most striking example because she was sickly as a child and was accustomed to being pampered. In America, she is forced to live on a small income and to learn to cook and take care of herself and Ralph (whom she married soon after immigrating). She even learns to fix a broken furnace in the basement of their dilapidated apartment building. The astounding monetary risks Ralph takes are likewise more related to his former and current social class than they are to essential differences in Chinese and American cultures. His determination to make money is less a mindless capitulation to American cultural norms than a desperate attempt to re-gain the social position he lost when fleeing China before the communist takeover. His motivation for making money is the realization that social standing in America depends on money.

Nonetheless, it is tempting to fix *Typical American* in a bicultural formulation, one that pits the Changs' "native Chinese mentality" against "typical American" ways in a nativist/assimilationist dichotomy. This perception seems justified in several aspects of the novel's plot that suggest Ralph, Helen, and Theresa are sliding helplessly into the American way. For example, through the influence of Grover Ding, Ralph gives up his hard-fought-for tenured professorship in engineering to seek his fortune in the fried chicken business, the kind of risk he realizes he never would have considered in his old life. His quintessentially Chinese motto "make sure" slowly changes to "make money." His aspirations of bringing honor to his family soon turn to greed. His aphorisms of virtue that top his list of resolves à la Jimmy Gatz[7] drafted during his journey to America, are eventually supplanted by the "wha-ingg!" of the cash register and aphorisms gleaned from power-and-success books like "A man is only as big as his dream" (220) and "What you can conceive, you can achieve" (198). It appears, therefore, that Ralph is being

"Americanized" in a negative sense—that all the greed and materialism of American capitalism are seducing a pure and innocent Chinese native. Ralph has, in Li's phrase, "embraced possessive individualism in its most materialistic form" (*Imagining* 104).

Ralph's embrace of a materialist American dream, while coming upon him with the force of hypnosis and cultic devotion, is in fact a survivalist response to a new and threatening environment. Ralph comes to the realization that relationships (the important Chinese concept of *guan xi*) and who you are in society are not the pillars of social standing as they were in China; for a non-white in America it is money that determines position. "Money," says the changed Ralph. "In this country, you have money, you can do anything. You have no money, you are nobody. You are Chinaman! Is that simple" (199). Even Theresa, who is critical of her brother's cold capitalism, has to admit that "to be non-white in [American] society was indeed to need education, accomplishment—some source of dignity. A white person was by definition somebody" (200).[8] Thus, Ralph's "assimilation" is complicated by the presence of racism and the desire—the challenge—not simply to survive, but to overcome. As much as Ralph is blinded by his own greed, he is driven by the challenge to his own personhood presented by this new environment.

Similarly, Theresa and Helen seem to be presented in the nativist/assimilationist dialectic as they fall prey to a different sort of seduction. First it comes to light that their fellow immigrant friend Old Chao is cheating on his wife. When Ralph tells Helen this, she exclaims, "impossible . . . Chinese people don't do such things" (168). They learn later that the woman with whom Old Chao is having an affair is their very own Theresa. As if this is not enough to undermine her indignation, Helen herself later falls into a brief, but devastating, fling with Grover Ding. The assertion that "Chinese people don't do such things" may seem to reinforce the notion of the seductive slide from Chinese innocence to American adulteration. Yet this would be so only if we believe Helen's assertion. Not only does our critical suspicion of any definitive, totalizing construction of culture lead us to read the statement, "Chinese people don't do such things," with caution, but the fact that the four people involved in these extramarital affairs are Chinese suggests that the statement is highly ironic. In fact, Helen's statement points to her own ignorance of what Chinese people actually do and serves to mask her own desire to be different than, and hence better than, the "typical American."

The nativist/assimilationist dialectic, into which the seductions of Ralph,

Helen, and Theresa seem to fall, is most clearly frustrated by the novel's conclusion. As the death of Theresa and of their own relationship looms before
them, Ralph and Helen are confronted with the constructedness of their
America: "Was death possible in this bright country? It was, they knew. Of
course. And yet they began to realize that in the fiber of their beings they
had almost believed it a thing they had left behind, like rickshaws" (286). In
a final epiphany, to which I alluded at the beginning of this section, Ralph
comes to see through his self-deception:

> "What escape was possible?" he thinks. It seemed to him at that
> moment . . . that a man was as doomed here as he was in China. *Kan bu*
> *jian. Ting bu jian.* He could not always see, could not always hear. He was
> not what he made up his mind to be. A man was the sum of his limits;
> freedom only made him see how much so. America was no America. (296)

What Ralph discovers in the end is that there is no typical America, nor, for
that matter, is there a typical China. Both are products of imagination. In
this, the irony of the novel's title is exposed. Ultimately, *Typical American* is
not about becoming typical Americans, but realizing that typical America
does not exist. Ralph's epiphany frustrates the expectation of assimilationist thinking: both the loss of one culture and the gain of another are confused by an uncertainty of any bottom-line definition of those cultures.

Typical American is, of course, a novel about Chinese immigrants and their
experience of adjustment to America. To suggest that the novel is not about
Chinese culture and American culture and how a Chinese American makes
sense of the two would be to ignore the basic premise of the book. However,
what I have attempted to show through my reading of *Typical American* is
that Chinese American identity is not, as is often readily assumed, a synthe-
sis of two monolithic cultures, nor is it a total submission to one or another
monolithic culture. Chinese American identity, as suggested in this novel, is
a dynamic process of cultural hybridity that is ongoing and riddled with
remembrance, invention, and imagination. In Jen's second novel the indi-
vidualization of identity formation reaches a fuller articulation, as is discussed
in what follows.

CULTURAL HYBRIDITY IN *MONA IN THE PROMISED LAND*

"Dispersion leads in turn to accumulation." This quote from the *I Ching: The*
Book of Changes, one of four epigraphs on cultural change at the beginning

of Gish Jen's second novel, displaces the connotation of dispersion leading to dissolution or loss and reinvests it with a positive connotation of gain, as signified by the word "accumulation." Applied to global migration and diasporic peoples, this inverted view of dispersion shifts the critical focus from cultural loss and assimilation to a process of supplement. This paradigm shift parallels the critical transformations witnessed in recent years in Asian American cultural scholarship, as well as in the wider field of Cultural Studies, which I discussed in chapter 4. It is here, at what Sau-ling Cynthia Wong has described as "a theoretical crossroads" ("Denationalization"), that *Mona in the Promised Land* is significantly situated not only within the growing body of Chinese American literature, but in American literature.

As the *I Ching* quote suggests, *Mona in the Promised Land* is about the process of transformation. This may not be surprising, since readers generally perceive Chinese American works as primarily concerned with the transformative tensions and conflicts of assimilation. However, the transformations of *Promised Land* depart from these expectations in a variety of ways which challenge and subvert common perceptions of ethnic and American identities, since Jen problematizes the notion of assimilation through a vision of cultural hybridity which valorizes change, choice, and cross-ethnic creolization in the culturally turbulent 1960s.

Mona, whose surname *Chang* is one letter shy of the word *change*, becomes the prototypical subject of hybridity in *Mona in the Promised Land* when she converts to Judaism and becomes known among her temple-friends as "Changowitz." As with the Bakhtinian model established in Jen's first novel, Mona's hybridized consciousness is marked by speech; often Jewish words and Yiddish grammar are allowed to seep into the narrative voice as it closely parallels Mona's consciousness: "A lot she knows already. All about the holidays, for example, and what is a mitzvah—namely a good deed. Also what is rachmones, namely a type of mercy" (35). The reversal of object before subject in the first sentence, "A lot she knows already" rather than "She knows a lot already," as well as the displacement of the idiomatic American grammatical construction "what a mitzvah is" rather than the Yiddish "what is a mitzvah," expose a hybridized discourse: coexistent within Mona's internal monologue is a dialogic encounter between American and Jewish languages or ideologies.[9] The recognition that this dialogic hybridization is taking place in a Chinese American reminds us that three cultural vantage points are intersecting here (Jewish, Chinese, and American), producing what may be described as a *multi*cultural hybridity (or, when we consider that these three are not monolithic cultures in themselves, we might define them as polycultural). This sort of hybridity, as witnessed earlier in our discussion of *Typical American*'s hybridized speech, is the fundamental producer of individual consciousness. According to Bakhtin, the hybridized, "internally persuasive word" in our everyday consciousness is the impetus for the awakening of "new and independent words" (345). Viewed in this way, the dispersion of Mona's consciousness and the formulation of hybrid identities are constructed not as diffusion and loss, but as the springboard of creativity and productiveness. Although the result of hybridity in both novels is similar (the formation of independent consciousness), the differences between their bicultural and polycultural formations are worth exploring.

The bicultural linguistic hybridity of *Typical American* is highly contentious and confrontative. As discussed previously, the languages of Ralph and Helen, characterized by the naïveté of their cultural assumptions, both unmask and ironize the foreign languages they encounter, while they, in turn, are unmasked and ironized by those foreign languages. The confrontation of these languages results in a mutual parodization that is never overcome in the novel. In contrast, the linguistic hybridity of *Promised Land* is polycultural, a term that I will explore more fully in the conclusion. This polycultural hybridity de-centers the expected clash of Chinese and American culture by introducing not just Judaism as an identity-shaper, but myriad influences: religion, philosophy, circumstance, Japan, African Americans, puberty, popularity, and the social and political climate of the 1960s play significant roles in the novel and create an arena of Bakhtinian heteroglossia.[10]

In *Promised Land*, linguistic hybridity is not constructed as antagonistic but as accommodating and inclusive. The most striking example of this is Ralph's phrase in the epilogue, "Some things just be's that way" (301). In the hybridization of the black idiom and grammar with Ralph's language, a phrase which is attributed to his black manager, Moses, Ralph's acceptance of black people as worthy of responsible positions in his restaurant is reinforced. The hybridity of Ralph's statement reflects the genuineness of his attitudinal change. Therefore, as with Mona's acceptance of Jewishness into her own way of thinking, hybrid speech becomes an emblem of inclusion and dialogic cohabitation rather than conflict, parody, and irony.

Within the heteroglossia of *Promised Land*, the myriad transmutations and hybridizations of Chinese Americans and non-Chinese Americans alike serve to displace the primacy of Chinese American identity in the novel, refocusing instead on the subject of American identity. In Mona's case, becoming American means the possibility of becoming Jewish (though, as I will show below, she assumes this position prior to real experience of U.S. racial hierarchies[11]). For her sister Callie, becoming American means the possibility of becoming more Chinese than their parents ever were: she learns standard Mandarin, practices *qi gong*, wears peasant jackets and cloth slippers, cooks "authentic" Chinese dishes in "authentic" ways (unlike their mother Helen who prepares Peking duck by soaking the bird overnight in Pepsi Cola). For Aunt Theresa, who immigrated to America with Mona's parents and put herself through medical school, becoming American means the possibility of becoming a hippie: she lives in California where she "strolls around on the beach with Uncle Henry all day—rumor has it, in a two-piece bathing suit and sometimes less, and without having gotten married, either" (28), and her attire is directly described as "hippie" (242). Mona's boyfriend, Seth, describes himself as an "authentic inauthentic Jew . . . in the process of becoming an inauthentic inauthentic Jew" (112); he lives in a teepee in his backyard, tries to turn black and then Japanese, and eventually marries Mona and turns Chinese. Barbara Gugelstein is a practicing Jew who undergoes a nose job to alter her Jewish looks because her mother wants the family to identify less with other Jews. Alfred, the black cook at the Changs' pancake house, fosters a mistrust of white people and ridicules Jews, but in the end he marries Barbara Gugelstein's cousin Evie and changes from a self-absorbed victim to a dedicated social activist.

What characterizes Americanness in the novel is not what one becomes, but the very act of becoming. In other words, "becoming," the novel suggests, is the hallmark of being American. Each *self* in the heteroglossia of Gish Jen's America is, to borrow Alberto Melucci's description quoted earlier, "more of a field than an essence . . . a dynamic system defined by recognizable opportunities and constraints" (64). However, Jen does not offer this view in a simplistic vacuum, sealed off from the racialized forces of society at large. In her youthful emphasis on the "opportunities" rather than the "constraints," Mona presents this simplistic definition: "American means being whatever you want" (49). But the events of the novel, primarily the breakup of Camp Gugelstein, reveal Mona's hopeful statement about America to be nothing short of naïve. What Mona has not learned at this point, but will later learn through her friendship with Alfred, is how persistent and pervasive racialized categories are in American society.

In their description of the dynamics that allow this continued insistence on race and racial hierarchy in the U.S., Omi and Winant make a distinction between micro-level social relations and macro-level social relations. At the micro-level "race is a matter of individuality, or the formation of *identity*," whereas at the macro-level "race is a matter of *collectivity*, of the formation of social structures: economic, political and cultural/ideological" (66–67). In Omi and Winant's view, "the racial order is organized and enforced by the continuity and reciprocity between these two 'levels' of social relations" (67). Mona's concept that "American means being whatever you want" is naïve because it assumes micro-level social relations trump macro-level social relations. It assumes, in other words, that individual identity formation is self-determined and works independently from the rest of society. Mona's childish philosophy is the "American dream" in its most uncritical and unrealistic manifestation.

However, Mona does learn her lesson. Her attempts to help Alfred, while hiding her actions from adults and neighbors, reveal her budding awareness that promoting color-blind social relations puts one at odds with the rest of society. Her visit to the Rhode Island resort where her sister is working for the summer opens her eyes to her own place as a Chinese American in the social hierarchy of the United States. Most significantly, the break up of the color-blind experiment called "Camp Gugelstein" shakes her world to the core and teaches her that a trite statement like "American means being whatever you want" is no match for the ubiquity of racialized thinking in the United States.[12] The novel does show, however, that while Mona's early formulation of the American dream is unrealistic and impotent, her continued belief in the power of individual choice and the ideal of racial equality allows her in the end to come to a more mature and viable expression of this idea.

Cross-Ethnic Creolization: Camp Gugelstein

Jen most distinctly renders a multi- or poly-cultural hybridity in the "Camp Gugelstein" segment of the novel. Mona and her Jewish American friends Seth Mandel and Barbara Gugelstein decide to promote minority solidarity by inviting Alfred, the African American cook at the Changs' pancake house, to stay in Barbara's home, which she and her cousin Evie occupy alone while Barbara's parents are away for the summer. Afraid that Evie will inform Barbara's parents that she is harboring a black man in their house, Barbara, Mona, and Seth arrange for Alfred to sneak into the house via a tunnel to the basement (dubbed "the underground railway") and to take up a quiet residence in the empty servant's quarters.

The irony of their brand of social action is soon exposed. The three friends are willing to act on behalf of another minority to the point of inconvenience, but not to the point of endangering their own privileged position. Their inability to show Alfred hospitality as an equal exposes a serious impediment to panethnic alliances: while Chinese Americans, Jewish Americans, and African Americans may share a common position as minorities in a hegemonic political and social environment, their minority status is not equally conceived. Alfred even goes to the extent of lumping Mona, Seth, and Barbara together under the signifier "white" (and "Christian," taking into account the reference below to Christmas rather than Hanukkah). He says to them,

> You white folk look at the calendar, and at the end of the year comes Christmastime, and at the beginning of the year comes a whole new year, maybe the year you pack your white ass off to college, maybe the year you go off traveling somewhere nice. Me, I look at that calendar, and at the end of the year there's flapjacks, and at the beginning of the year there's flapjacks, and when I die, man, they're going to cover me with flapjacks, and put the butter and the syrup on top. (154)

Thus, from Alfred's perspective, Jewish and Chinese Americans may be much closer to the white majority position than blacks. Alfred defines their "whiteness" according to their social position and economic empowerment, not merely by the color of their skin. "Whiteness," as Gwendolyn Audrey Foster asserts in her book, *Performing Whiteness*, "does not exist at the biological level. It is a cultural construct" (2). The culturally constructed line drawn between Chinese Americans and Jewish Americans is, from Alfred's perspective, completely erased. This perception is reinforced in the novel by the apparent ease with which Mona is able to identify with Jewish Americans in contrast to her perception that one cannot become black (118).

The point of *Promised Land*—its central joke—is that Mona becomes Jewish. She does not simply identify with Jews or recognize similarities—she switches, converts, turns. In terms of the physical or blood heritage associated with race, Mona's switch would be an impossibility, as Alfred has in mind when he denies Mona's Jewishness on account of her not "growing" a nose (137). In contrast, Mona insists to her parents that she can become Jewish because it is a religion, but she and her family cannot become black because it is a race. This seems to confuse physical and cultural constructs of both Jewishness and blackness: Mona sees Jewishness only as a belief, while blackness is determined by physical features and skin color. One wonders, therefore, whether within Mona's logic is an aesthetic preference for Jewishness over blackness. Perhaps what makes Mona's conversion acceptable, to her and eventually to her parents,[13] is the perception that she is moving forward, from what in the 1960s was not yet considered a "model minority" to what was at least considered a "better" minority, a move which brings her one step closer to whiteness.

This problematic, which is implicit in Mona's characterization, is explicit in the character of Helen, Mona's mother. Helen fears turning black, by which she means being perceived as socially and economically on par with blacks. When an African American social activist asks her to sign a petition on creating a subsidized family-planning clinic, Helen is insulted at the woman's implication that Chinese Americans would be united with African Americans in what the woman calls a "common cause." "We live in Scarshill," says Helen. "You should see our tax bracket" (119). Helen clearly perceives the racial category "black" as a social and economic position and believes her social status to be markedly higher than that of blacks because of her own economic position. "We are not Negroes," she says to Mona. "You hear me? Why should we work so hard—so people can talk to us about birth control for free" (119). In relation to this issue as a barrier to cross-ethnic solidarity, Vijay Prashad asks, "since blackness is reviled in the United States, why would an immigrant, of whatever skin color, want to associate with those who are racially oppressed, particularly when the transit into the United States promises the dream of gold and glory?" Prashad goes on to explain,

> the immigrant seeks a form of vertical assimilation, to climb from the lowest, darkest echelon on the stepladder of tyranny into the bright whiteness. In U.S. history the Irish, Italians, Jews, and—in small steps with some hesitations on the part of white America—Asians and Latinos have all tried to barter their varied cultural worlds for the privileges of whiteness. (*Everybody* x)

Despite sharing with African Americans a politically minor position in society, Mona and her friends—mainly because they do not comprehend Alfred's experience of being "reviled"—are unable to breach the line drawn between them and Alfred.

Instead, the line is breached for them: returning to Barbara Gugelstein's house one day, they find Alfred and his African American friends partying in the living room with Evie sitting on Alfred's lap. This marks the birth of Camp Gugelstein, an experiment in cross-ethnic integration and solidarity. Every evening for the rest of the summer, Luther the Race Man, Big Benson, Ray, Professor Estimator, Alfred and Evie, and Seth, Barbara, and Mona hang out together at the Gugelstein mansion. They smoke dope, drink, talk, dance, practice yoga, sit cross-legged in a circle, and rap heart-to-heart. They listen to Soul Train, dance the funky chicken and play mah-jongg, chess, and Chinese checkers. Camp Gugelstein becomes for each of them a symbol of interracial communication and alliance. In Professor Estimator's opinion, "*Agape*, meaning love of all humanity . . . redemptive love is still alive here, at Camp Gugelstein, but he thinks elsewhere it is on the wane" (201). The culture of agape in Camp Gugelstein allows the participants to engage in a dialogic interplay of various social languages and ideologies: these include Martin Luther King Jr.'s liberation theology, Malcolm X's black power, materialism, humanism and free will, Protestantism, Judaism, integration versus Jim Crow separatism, and transcendental meditation. From this multiplicity is born a rich polycultural hybridity where difference is embraced and the common bond of humanity is extolled. This is represented in Mona's experience while touching hands during yoga: "There are warm palms and cool palms, firm grips, loose; and attached to them such an amazing array of humanity" (202).

Hybridity in this episode is not merely emotional or ideological; Jen's description of the African Americans as ranging in skin color from "gingerbread" and "cream" to "papaya" and "the color of old iron" (197–98) suggests a complex biological hybridization which is altogether ignored in the term "black." "Black" is thus revealed as an inaccurate description of physical difference, and shown, rather, to be a signifier of difference in racialized constructions that refuse hybridity. Alfred says to Mona, "White is white, man. Everything else is black. Half and half is black" (155). In the context of their discussion, Alfred is clearly not expressing solidarity with Chinese Americans; rather, he is articulating the way racist constructions of race tend to homogenize what is actually diverse. Similarly, the "paper-bag" color of another African American character is explained in this way: "if she were a cabinet door or a shade of hair dye, people would have a name for her exact shade. But as she is only a person, she is called black" (170). Again, the description of difference is not a physical reality but an ideological construction, a way of conceptualizing the foreign in a way that marks and retains its alterity. The fact that the various shades of color represented in these characters is the result of biological hybridizations that include white blood is ignored by the generic term "black."

On the other hand, the same label that the majority uses as a distancing mechanism can become the marker of solidarity for the minority group. Stuart Hall makes this observation in relation to the term "black." In the 1960s, says Hall, "black" was divested of its racist connotations when black people, regardless of color shade and national origin, adopted it as a unifying description that defined their community. The term "black" as a signifier of solidarity and community is what connects Alfred and his African American friends despite their various skin colors, class backgrounds, opinions, and education levels. Thus, while on the one hand "black" is an unfair homogenization of a diverse community, it is paradoxically the same term that unifies African Americans and provides the basis for political and social action.[14] In fact, it is in this ethnic and racial unification that multiculturalism came under attack in the 1990s. While racial tension exposed by such events as the O. J. Simpson trial and the Rodney King beating (and more recently by Hurricane Katrina) reveals that there is a great need for increased interracial and interethnic communication in American society today, multiculturalism, its critics assert, seems to be dividing and reifying ethnic groups into privatized, parochial enclaves.[15] The demise of Camp Gugelstein can be seen as reinforcing this criticism, but the moral vision of the novel does not end with the failure of Camp Gugelstein.

Camp Gugelstein, the utopian, "house with no walls" experiment (208), splinters and dissolves as quickly as it had formed. When Barbara finds an expensive flask missing, she, Mona, and Seth question their guests, and the three accusers are then accused of racism. In an expression of black solidarity, all the African Americans, including Alfred, leave in outrage. The lines between ethnic groups, which seemed to have disappeared under the Camp Gugelstein banner, reappear with a vengeance.

The failure of Camp Gugelstein illustrates the precariousness of panethnic efforts and the tenacity of racist attitudes. The assumption behind Mona, Barbara, and Seth's accusation is racist: in the face of a crime, it is the black man who is immediately suspected of committing it. However, while clearly exposing the latent racism beneath Camp Gugelstein's veneer, the novel is strangely silent about the expression of black solidarity and the role it plays in the closure of dialogue. Mona, Seth, and Barbara express an acute sense of angst and guilt over their actions, but they never question whether the black walkout was justifiable. They assume, apparently, that their own expression of racism, unintended as it was, provided a sufficient defense for the black group's reaction. In this, *Promised Land* may be seen as excusing a gross overreaction by the black members of Camp Gugelstein and placing the blame on the three non-black members who were, despite flaws, acting as "allies" in the black struggle for liberation. Black separatism is thus exonerated and white guilt preserved. This patronizing representation of the black man as a simple "victim" widens the gap between the black and non-black characters, thereby reinforcing Alfred's view that Mona, Seth, and Barbara are white in comparison to blacks. To extend this reading, we could argue that Camp Gugelstein, the utopian ideal, may be less a literary experiment in panethnicity, than a fantasy for a market motivated by the dynamics of white guilt.

Nevertheless, viewed from the notion of cultural hybridity, the panethnic vision of Camp Gugelstein is not entirely lost. In fact, we might see it as the impetus for the deeper transformations in the lives of its participants. As discussed previously, Omi and Winant argue that the "racial order is organized and enforced by the continuity and reciprocity between" the micro-level and macro-level social relations. But the micro-level experiments of individual identity formation in Camp Gugelstein eventually work to challenge and subvert the macro-level social relations signified by racial relations in Ralph's restaurant and the underlying social pressures that force Mona, Seth, and Barbara to hide Alfred in the Gugelstein home. Applying Omi and Winant's argument, and using the terminology they borrow from Gramsci, we might consider the Camp Gugelstein gathering a "war of maneuver," which describes "a situation in which subordinate groups seek to preserve and extend a definite territory, to ward off violent assault, and to develop an internal society as an alternative to the repressive social system they confront" (74). The breakup of Camp Gugelstein forces the members of the group who are truly committed to the cause into a direct political struggle with the racialized hierarchies of society, an oppositional program Gramsci calls a "war of position."

The contact between these individuals of different ethnic backgrounds was not, the novel attests, without its impact. For Mona and Seth the breakup of Camp Gugelstein marks a coming of age in their own development, one that ultimately makes them more dedicated to the cause of interracial dialogue and social action (see 207, for example). Moreover, when they visit Alfred to apologize for the flask incident, there is a real sense of solidarity and friendship between them, a feeling of healing and restoration that suggests barriers have indeed been broken down (290–92). This sense of growth and change is confirmed in the reuniting of Alfred and Evie, who eventually marry and have three babies—hybrids in the flesh—and become staunch activists for social change, "Mr. and Mrs. Community Organization" (297).

Cultural Hybridity: Mona's Choice

Camp Gugelstein's panethnic interaction and its resultant cultural hybridity reflect a significant new emphasis in Chinese American literature. The cultural hybridity of *Promised Land* subverts the literary Chinatown by dis-placing notions of ethnic essence and cultural stasis. The novel suggests that Chinese American ethnicity is not forged through the clash of two mono-lithic cultures, but, as Bakhtin theorizes regarding all consciousness, is con-tinually evolving in a heteroglot multiplicity of social voices and their interrelationships. Furthermore, *Promised Land* significantly de-privatizes the Chinese American novel by re-viewing American identity, not just one ethnic group's identity, as an individualized process characterized by the "internal variation" of hybridity (Wicker 37). This, I suggest, moves beyond "claiming America" to an important process of "transforming America."

Gish Jen's goal is, in her words, to push "the limits and expand . . . the notion of America's view of itself . . . to create a new notion of what it means to be American" (qtd. in Snell 58–59). But *Promised Land*'s "new notion" of America, if we are to accept my reading of cultural hybridity's triumph over separatism, does in fact present serious problems for multiculturalists. Although we might see the failure of Camp Gugelstein as the necessary impe-tus for a "war of position," we should also note that the "positions" taken in the post-Camp Gugelstein phase are almost entirely individual positions. The group that comprised Camp Gugelstein never reunites. One difficulty here is that an articulation of cultural identity as amorphous and fluid is a weak foundation for group solidarity. In the political realities of representational government, a system that necessitates a unified articulation of need, hybrid, fluid, and individualized identities seem powerless and pointless. Indeed, the epilogue to *Promised Land*, which describes the radically different identities achieved by various characters, seems doomed to fail in precisely this area. The only characteristic that unites the disparate identities at the end of the novel is the experience of transformation itself. How, one might rightly ask, can economically disadvantaged individuals and oppressed groups make themselves heard as political constituents when all that unites them is an expe-rience of fluidity and change?

The political sterility of the cultural hybridity model inferred in these objections lies in cultural hybridity's inability as a postmodern theory to accommodate cultural objectification. According to some articulations of postmodernism, all forms of essentialization are to be questioned and con-demned. In a kind of twisted logic, as Pnina Werbner explains, "citizenship rights and multiculturalist agendas are as much dependent on collective objec-tification as are racist murders and ethnic cleansing." However, she contin-ues, "it is critical to establish clearly the difference between modes of objectification and modes of reification" (229). "Reification is representation which distorts and silences" in order to manipulate those of another racial or ethnic community. The violence enacted upon that community is situated fundamentally in the power to name, to define, to essentialize from a position outside that group. Thus, the assumption that a black man stole the flask in Camp Gugelstein stems from a racialized, essentialist definition—a reification—of blacks. However, the kind of essentializing Werbner points to, and what E. San Juan Jr. in a similar context calls "a positional articulation of identity and difference" (150), is an "objectification" that is rightfully performed by a person of ethnicity as a means of social and political identification, as, for example, in the term "black" discussed above—and, significantly, in the naming of the short-lived panethnic community "Camp Gugelstein." "In their performative rhetoric," Werbner says, people of ethnicity "essentialise their imagined communities in order to mobilise for action. . . . In this regard, the politics of ethnicity are a positive politics: they serve to construct moral and aesthetic communities imaginatively" (230). The difference here is that the objectification of the ethnic community is established by the power to name itself rather than the powerlessness necessary to being named.[16]

I agree with Werbner's argument, but I would also argue that internal objectification introduces its own difficulties. Indeed, my critique of Camp Gugelstein's breakup implies that a group's freedom in defining itself does not guarantee racial harmony and fairness. The African American group's objectification of itself in the breakup of Camp Gugelstein did not happen in a vacuum but performed a kind of violence on the community which all of them—African American, Jewish American, and Chinese American—were trying to build. Thus, in an adjustment to Werbner's thesis, I would suggest that within the right of an ethnic community to name and define itself is a responsibility to anticipate and preserve alliances with other communities.

In *Promised Land*, it is the panethnic interaction and its resultant cultural hybridity produced through the Camp Gugelstein experience, not Camp Gugelstein itself, that provide a provocative re-visioning of race and ethnicity. The linkages forged between these otherwise distinct cultural groups is an example of what Vijay Prashad calls polyculturalism. As with hybridity theory, polyculturalism questions our culture's insistent belief in primordial, static, and pure cultures, but it furthermore seeks to actively engage oppressed peoples and white "allies" in actively forging antiracist communities. Although it falls short of a true "war of position," Camp Gugelstein's radical and active cultural hybridity—its polycultural experiment—emerges as a "new notion of America," and Mona might be seen as its poster girl. In the final pages of the novel, Mona discusses with Aunt Theresa the possibility of changing her name when she marries Seth Mandel:

> "To Mandel?" says Theresa, surprised. "No more women's lib?"
> "No, no. To Changowitz," says Mona. "I was thinking that Seth would change his name too." (303)

In choosing the name Changowitz, Mona asserts the power to name herself, to define who she is, a name that was established early in the novel as a marker of hybridity. In suggesting that Seth change his name as well, Mona is establishing a community signified by the hybrid name Changowitz. In other words, by the end of the novel, Mona chooses polyculturalism.

Conclusion

THE EMERGENCE OF THE POLYCULTURAL

Polyculturalism is a ferocious engagement with the political world of culture, a painful embrace of the skin and all its contradictions.

——VIJAY PRASHAD, *Everybody Was Kung Fu Fighting*

To acknowledge our polycultural heritage and cultural dynamism is not to give up our black identity or our love and concern for black people. It does mean expanding our definition of blackness, taking our history more seriously, and looking at the rich diversity within us with new eyes.

——ROBIN KELLEY, "People in Me"

The worlds imagined by the writers discussed in the previous chapters are just that—imagined worlds. These imagined worlds are performed in the phenomenological interaction of reader and text. To suggest that the fictional worlds of these Asian American texts transparently reproduce or enact the *real* American and Asian American world would be to fall into the fallacies mapped out in chapters 1 and 2. These Asian American texts do not represent authentic American and ethnic American life because they are, as Kandice Chuh argues, theoretical—that is, "they offer 'theoretical knowledges'" (20). I argued in chapters 1 and 2 that Euro-American readers tend to see Asian American literature as an authentic, authoritative, and representative window into a culture that is Other or exotic to them. I have noted that Li-Young Lee, David Wong Louie, Shirley Geok-lin Lim, Shawn Wong, and Gish Jen challenge the typical and historical expectations of their readers, but I have not argued that the worlds of their texts are therefore more authentic, more authoritative, or more representational. "Weighted by the burden of authenticity," writes Chuh, "Asian American literatures seem to have some immanent, 'real' meaning to them. Invoking the term 'theory' in this sense is a tactic employed to problematize that kind of understanding of them" (20). In other words, a text, inasmuch as it presents a "proposed world" (Ricoeur, *Hermeneutics* 142), offers a theory for the living of real life.

In the conclusion, I would like to describe the kind of world imagined in the contemporary Chinese American texts I have discussed in the preceding chapters. What kind of world do these authors imagine in the aggregate? What common assumptions do they share? What common visions? If we consider the proposed world of these texts to be a "theory" of U.S. society, what is that theory and how can we best describe it? I believe that what we will see as we bring these texts into dialogue with one another is that they all share at least three major concerns: (1) they are all intensely interested in the experience of Asian American life; (2) they are all committed to a view of ethnicity that is heterogeneous, dynamic, and fluid; and (3) they all recognize that racism is a persistent social reality in U.S. society. This discussion will lead me to consider the emergence of a new organizing principle for race and ethnicity in America: the polycultural.

FLUID AND HYBRID IDENTITIES

The literary Chinatown horizon of expectation imagines Chinese Americans as "split" subjects living between two discrete and monolithic cultures (Palumbo-Liu, *Asian/American* 395–416). Chinese American identity is defined by the schizophrenic tension between these two positions. Assimilationists, or those who adhere to the melting pot theory, define a subject's "health" according to how fully he or she adopts an American sensibility, how fully, that is, he or she is "Americanized." The promotional copy for *Monkey King* appeals to this view of the "healthy" American: "How [Sally] pulls together her Chinese and American identities into a cohesive self and rejoins the land of the living is recounted with a wry and refreshing honesty." In this model, the "pathology" described is a "split" identity. Because "health" is described as "joining the land of the living," that is, joining the rest of America, Sally is portrayed as a kind of zombie, one of the Asian American walking dead who have not attained their full identity as Americans. The only way for Sally to attain "health" is by her own efforts to "pull together" these two diametrically opposed identities into a cohesive self (hence the "model minority discourse and the course of healing" problematic defined by Palumbo-Liu, and the "bootstraps model" defined by Omi and Winant).

Pop multiculturalism would also see Sally as a split-self whose health depends upon a successful negotiation between her Chinese and American identities, but with this difference: rather than seeing Sally's "health" as successfully exorcising the ghosts of a Chinese past and attaining an American identity, the pop multiculturalist would define Sally's "health" according to how well she maintains an appreciation of her Chinese heritage. For the pop multiculturalist, that is, "losing" one's "original" culture is the true pathology (hence, nativism). For this reason, The Joy Luck Club, that paragon of pop multiculturalism, ends with June/Jing-Mei's "return" to the China she had always rejected and her "reunion" with the sisters she had never seen.[1] Upon entering China, her makeup melts away and her "artfully styled" hair falls straight, so that she is afraid the border guard will not recognize the image in her American passport (272). Her "disorder" is cured, by the almost literal unmasking of the American façade and the discovery of her Chinese "identity," once she (literally) sets foot on Chinese soil. She is no longer "June"; she is "Jing-Mei."

One way the contemporary writers explored in this book disrupt the reader's anticipation of the pathological ethnic split between two identities is to complicate the reader's understanding of those two "identities." Rather than imagining Asian American subjects trapped between two discrete and monolithic cultures, these writers expose the constructedness, the interconnectedness, the hybridity of all cultures and of all identities. Li-Young Lee imagines the heterogenous and hybrid immigrant community in "The Cleaving," ending his poem with this poetic mixing and blending of race and gender:

> the sorrow of his Shang
> dynasty face,
> African face with slit eyes. He is
> my sister, this
> beautiful Bedouin, this Shulamite,
> keeper of sabbaths, diviner
> of holy texts, this dark
> dancer, this Jew, this Asian, this one
> with the Cambodian face, Vietnamese face, this Chinese
> I daily face,
> this immigrant,
> this man with my own face. (86–87)

In Lee's poem, the immigrant community is marked by the push/pull signified by the divergent impulses of the term "cleave"—much like the term "Asian

American," which, as Kandice Chuh argues, deconstructs itself in its reference to a constant "state of becoming and undoing in the same moment" (8).

Similarly, Suyin in Shirley Geok-lin Lim's *Joss and Gold* is a hybrid child living in Singapore who ends up with two fathers, one American and one Asian, and thus at least two paths she can choose. Lim imagines a diasporic America in her novel, in which America's significance as the land of opportunity for would-be immigrants is displaced by Singapore, an Asian alternative that serves, with its affluence and multicultural society, as a viable, if not preferable, replacement for the United States in this Asian immigrant narrative.

Shawn Wong's *American Knees* proposes a world in which Asian Americans of various ethnic backgrounds and hybrid constructions manifest that deconstructive energy in the term "Asian American," the constant "becoming and undoing at the same moment," that Chuh describes. Raymond and Aurora constantly interpret their actions, and question their motives, based on their understanding of race and the perceptions of larger society. All the relationships in the novel are fraught with tensions between the terms "Asian" and "American." As my discussion of Wong's book suggests, the characters of *American Knees* do not live within static and predetermined ethnic identities, but they shape and mold their self-concepts amid a variety of social forces—and that shaping and molding is never finished.

Stories like "Warming Trends" in David Wong Louie's *Pangs of Love* theorize a world in which ethnicity has very little bearing on the identity of its characters. Hank and his family are never identified as Asian American, and the only hints that they are simply create an ethnic ambiguity in the reading of the text that is ultimately self-referent for the reader. Readers are made to ask, in other words, whether the ethnic identity of the characters matter. Other stories in Louie's collection, such as "Birthday" and "Disturbing the Universe," are centered upon Chinese American identity in a white, blond, and baseball-absorbed society. Ultimately, the worlds proposed in *Pangs of Love* imagine an America, and an Asian America, that is diverse in its construction of, and emphasis upon, racial and ethnic identity; a world that, to borrow Patricia P. Chu's description, moves us into "the next moment in Asian American literature, a moment when American subjects and their stories will be read as 'American,' when the histories now laboriously or didactically asserted will be gracefully integrated into a wider American consciousness" (187).

Chu's optimistic forecast resonates with the world that Gish Jen evokes in her novels. Her first two novels imagine Americans who are governed by cultural hybridity and the individual choices they make in a web of myriad influences. Mona's assertion that "American means being whatever you want" (*Mona* 49) and Ralph's revelation that "America is no America" (*Typical American*, 296) are competing claims that are not fully worked out until the epilogue of *Mona in the Promised Land*. What Mona, Seth, and Barbara learn in the Camp Gugelstein episode is precisely what Ralph learns after wrecking his business and nearly destroying his family in *Typical American*: "America is no America." But the characters in *Mona in the Promised Land*, including Ralph, learn from the realities of racial tension and collective mistrust that destroy the Camp Gugelstein experiment and go on to construct their own various identities that owe a debt to Camp Gugelstein and Mona's innocent (even naïve) assumptions about race in America. Jen theorizes a world in which ethnic groups rub off on one another as they interact in a dynamic logic of multiethnic hybridity. Ethnic identity is a matter of combination, accumulation, and individual choice. People change and develop. As expressed in the quotation from Ovid that Jen chooses as an epigraph for the novel, "all things change" and "the cosmos itself is in flux": these are the only constants in Jen's world.

Gish Jen's third novel, published in 2004, introduces another dimension to Asian American literature's "era of energetic heteroglossia" (Li, *Imagining the Nation* 189): the hybrid family. *The Love Wife* sets up a quadrangle of signification that can be described in an analogy: adoption is to natural child, as immigrant is to natural citizen. Add to the equation a mixed marriage and one-hybrid child, and you have what Jen proposes to be "soup du jour" (see 156, 211, and 279, for example), or "the new face of America" (see 81 and 157, for example). The Wong family consists of a Chinese American father who does not speak Chinese (Carnegie Wong); a white American mother who does speak Chinese and whose whiteness is embedded in her nickname, "Blondie"; one Asian girl adopted in America and another adopted from China; and one "bio" baby who is the "mulatto" (81), "hapa" (94), "mixed" face of "the future" (156). Added to this mix is a Chinese stranger named Lan who comes to live with the Wongs as a nanny through a proviso in Carnegie's mother's will. The question that strikes them—Blondie first, but eventually all in the Wong family old enough to comprehend—is whether Mama Wong intended Lan to be the nanny who would make the children more Chinese through cultural instruction or the "love wife" (a.k.a. concubine) who would make the family look biologically Chinese.

Jen encapsulates her theory of this new America in Blondie's description of sunflowers. Blondie explains that the birdseed in the Wong's backyard birdfeeder was scattered all over the snow by the birds and squirrels.

But the seeds, surprisingly, sprouted in the spring—and wasn't that natural too? I had assumed the seeds sterile. They ought to have been sterile. One day I noticed in the grass, though, a rosetta of sunflower seedlings—each topped with a little leaf bow tie—which were almost immediately no longer seedlings; which were daily, miraculously, larger and larger—until there they loomed, modestly huge-headed, fantastic with a rightness I wanted to call beauty. (5)

The presumably sterile seeds that nonetheless germinate and produce a "natural" plant are analogous to the birth of baby "Bailey," who came naturally after Carnegie and Blondie gave up trying for their own baby and turned to adoption. But the production of something "natural" from something presumed "sterile" also coincides with the Wongs' adoption of Lizzy and Wendy. The concept of "adoption" is usually placed in contrast with "natural childbirth" and the notion of a "natural" family in the same way that immigration, "naturalization," and assimilation of Asians are treated by some people as "unnatural." (One red-neck in the book states, "A [naturalized] citizen thinks this country is about law. But an American knows it is about who is really American" [341].) But Blondie sees a "rightness" and "beauty" in the family born of scattered and "sterile" seed.

While the world of Jen's *The Love Wife* is not a transparent view into the real world, there is much that coincides with current demographic and social trends in the world she constructs. In her discussion of Asian adoption as a phenomenon that springs from "Cold War Orientalism," Christina Klein writes,

> By 2000, more than twenty-four thousand Chinese children had been adopted into American families. During the 1990s, the multiracial, multinational, U.S.-Asian family formed through adoption that had first appeared in the early Cold War became one of the most visible and widely commented-upon signs of America's increasingly close ties to Asia. (270)

"The new face of America," a phrase repeated regularly in Jen's novel, is precisely the "visible and widely commented-upon" racially mixed family that Klein refers to. David Palumbo-Liu discusses a number of media representations of the "changing face" rhetoric in the 1990s in his book *Asian/America*, including the cover of a special issue of *Time* in 1993 that presents a woman's face that was, in the words of the caption, "created by a computer mix of several races." The caption continues, "what you see is a remarkable preview of the New Face of America" (109). Palumbo-Liu argues that this "new face" rhetoric, while problematic as a rhetoric that elides difference, hegemony, and "material history," compromises the "sovereignty of the nation-state . . . by increased transnational interests; the very constitution of its interiority attests to the demographic changes that accompany globalization" (108). The transnationalism and globalization instantiated by the racially hybrid person or family is also a significant means for Americans to participate in these global communities. As Klein suggests, "these families have become one of the ways in which Americans live globalization in their everyday lives" (271).

ACKNOWLEDGING AND RESISTING RACISM

One problem with hybridity theory, as many critics have pointed out,[2] is that it individualizes ethnic identity and thereby seems to occlude collective efforts for minority rights. The quotation from Robin Kelley at the head of this chapter reveals this tension. For some people, Kelley's embrace of "polycultural heritage and cultural dynamism" predicates a rejection of black identity and the political battle for black rights. Thus, when we seek to replace the celebration of discrete cultures that has become the hallmark of pop multiculturalism with the hybridic, heterogeneous free play of identity that is the hallmark of postmodern identity, we seem to be destroying the foundation of the antiracist political struggle. That is, hybridity theory seems to promote an amorphous, color-blind philosophy in a society that continues to be structured on the perception of skin color.

For many in the United States today, the color-blind society stands as the ideal for which we are striving. For some, it stands as the ideal we are supposed to have already attained. When I ask my university students how important race is for them, for instance, I often sense that students anticipate a model answer—namely, that race doesn't matter. They will say things like "I never think about race when I meet people," or, "I don't care what race someone is, I just treat all people as people."[3] When I conducted empirical research at the University of California at Santa Barbara in the late 1990s, I included in a questionnaire several blanks for students to fill in their biodata. One of the categories I asked them to self-identify was "race." Many students left this blank, and some wrote subversive answers such as "human race" or "person." These answers belie a deep-seated suspicion of the whole issue of race. I believe students assume that race is "supposed to be" nonexistent. They believe that the model answer is "race doesn't matter" because we *are supposed to* be living in an enlightened, color-blind society.

I highlight "supposed to be" because if I switch the question in my classes, I get a different answer. When I ask if racism is still a problem, students will invariably answer "yes." Students are not ignoring the fact of racism when they say "race doesn't matter." They know from experience, whether they are white, black, Asian, or Latino/a, that people are judged and stereotyped based on their skin color in our society. But what they assume is that racism is a problem because some people still believe in race. They believe, moreover, that racial prejudice is confined to an unenlightened minority who cling to old-fashioned ideas about race and white supremacy (usually stereotyped as a white, tobacco-chewing auto mechanic in overalls who speaks with a southern accent). What many students have not been taught is that racism is pervasive and systemic, and that racism continues in our society not because some people still believe in race but because most of us have come to believe—against all empirical evidence—that race just doesn't matter. We too often confuse "should race matter" (we all know it shouldn't) with "does race matter" (we all know it does). Based on their study of racial formation in U.S. society, Omi and Winant make the grim prediction that "Race will *always* be at the center of the American experience" (6, italics in original).

As discussed in my analysis of Gish Jen's work in chapter 7, some critics fault postmodern identity theory with political sterility and the promotion of a utopian ideal that occludes the realities of race and racialization in U.S. society. When we define all culture as fluid, dynamic, and interdependent, are we asserting that "race doesn't matter"? We saw in the previous section that the contemporary Chinese American texts in this study imagine a hybrid and fluid sense of identity, but do they also express a concomitant occlusion of race?

I believe my analysis of their work shows that, far from sweeping race and racism under the rug, these authors show a deep engagement with these issues. Besides the plurality of modes of being-in-the-world represented by Mona Chang, Callie Chang, Theresa, Raymond Ding, Aurora Crane, Betty Nguyen, Hank, Wallace Wong, Suyin, Li-An, the Wong family, and others, these works of literature articulate the contradictions inherent in the signifier "Asian American." Lee's poem is fraught with the "painful embrace of the skin" that Prashad describes in the epigraph, where the speaker cleaves tenaciously to the racist other who cleaves him in two—and he, in turn, eats that racist other as he would a steamed fish. Wallace Wong in Louie's story marks his life with non-Chinese symbols (food, baseball, white woman, white child) in an attempt to erase his ethnic and hence racialized minority status. Raymond Ding and the other characters that animate the world of *American*

Knees live lives of self-fulfilling racial stereotypes—where the desire to talk to the person across the room is overpowered by a fear of doing the stereo-typical racial/ethnic thing. Suyin, in Shirley Geok-lin Lim's novel, is conceived during the race riots between Chinese and Malays in Kuala Lumpur, and she endures the racist epithets of her classmates in Singapore. The New York segment of the novel furthermore highlights attitudes toward Asia, and in particular, India, that reveal a deep racist mistrust among Americans (e.g., that Indians can't be trusted in high tech jobs, but whites ["Europeans"] can be). Mona lives a privileged life in comparison to Alfred, but when she enters the white world of the Rhode Island country club, she is immediately aware that she is marked as the racial Other. The failure of Camp Gugelstein instantiates the persistence of race *even in* well-intentioned efforts to erase racism.

The expression of postmodern concepts of fluidity and hybridity are not, in my opinion, attempts to sweep race under the rug of history. To claim that no cultures are pure and that we are all products of multiple heritages is not to suggest that race is no longer a factor in U.S. society or that racism is some kind of illusion. To embrace postmodern identity theory is not to naïvely assume that we can explain race away with fancy theories. I believe we need to find a way to retain the collective, political energy of multiculturalism without setting up rigid and unrealistic (not to mention unhistorical) boundaries between "discrete" cultures defined by a primordial essence. Can we revitalize multiculturalism, wresting it from the control of pop and commercial culture on the one hand and neoconservative backlash on the other? Perhaps we could do so by adding yet another adjective to the term "multiculturalism" (a seemingly endless exercise in redefinition, as Timothy B. Powell notes). We could call it "neo-multiculturalism" or "postmodern multiculturalism" or "hybrid multiculturalism" or "antiracist multiculturalism." Or we might, as I suggest, embrace a new term that has emerged recently to describe the "mulatto" construction of all identity and to motivate resistance to racism. Based on my reading of Vijay Prashad's work, I would like to suggest that polyculturalism is distinct enough from multiculturalism, and even from hybridity theory, to offer a new paradigm of social organization.

POLYCULTURE

Polyculturalism is a term that has been used in the world music scene to describe the hybrid, polyrhythmic character of world music, where various musical forms from around the world combine to create new sounds, new rhythms, new expressions of culture. In the 1990s, polyculture became a term to describe identity in ways that are distinctly postmodern and fiercely opposed to rigid classification. Historian and cultural critic Robin Kelley's 1999 article, "People in Me," from which Vijay Prashad drew inspiration for his theorization of polyculturalism in *Everybody Was Kung Fu Fighting*, signifies a distinct break from multiculuralism. True to a postmodern, hybridic view, Kelley calls on the reader to recognize that all culture is interconnected, whether by the literal bloodlines of people or by historic cultural cross-fertilization. Kelley writes, "All of us, and I mean ALL of us, are the inheritors of European, African, Native American, and even Asian pasts, even if we can't exactly trace our blood lines to all of these continents." At the same time, Kelley argues for the continued solidarity and antiracist community building that once characterized the multicultural movement. He argues that taking our polycultural history as fact does not negate the possibility of, and need for, "black identity" and "concern for black people" (7). Vijay Prashad saw in Kelley's brief autobiographical piece the seeds of a provocative new vocabulary for combating racism. As I will elaborate below, Prashad has taken the polycultural idea and developed it into a viable theory that combines postmodern identity with collective, multicultural allegiances against racism.

Prashad distinguishes polyculturalism from multiculturalism in several important ways. Where multiculturalism seeks to raise the value of minority cultures in America, polyculturalism, he claims, recognizes the inherent contradictions in embracing minority status. Where multiculturalism emphasizes the need to promote, protect, and perpetuate distinct cultures in our pluralist society, polyculturalism emphasizes the hybrid quality of cultures and individuals. As Prashad writes, polyculturalism "assumes that people live coherent lives that are made up of a host of lineages" (xii). By lineages, Prashad is not referring to genetics and bloodlines; rather, he stresses—as do many of the postcolonial and postmodern critics I discussed in chapter 7, and as does Gish Jen—that people living in a pluralist society rub off on each other (65). Polyculturalism moreover critiques our society's tendency to use multiculturalism as a guise for racial containment and the assuaging of white guilt. "The problem with U.S. multiculturalism as it stands," writes Prashad in *The Karma of Brown Folk*, "is that it pretends to be the solution to chauvinism rather than the means for a struggle against white supremacy" (111). Polyculturalism is, in Prashad's conception, a break from and critique of multiculturalism. According to Prashad,

A close engagement with the concept of multiculturalism allows us to cultivate the category of the polycultural, one that not only encourages the inherent complexity of cultures, but that also stakes its claim to political, and delimited, claims rather than the pretense of universal, and nonembodied, values. (40)

Prashad is clearly critical of the multicultural program: he sees it as a "pretense . . . a principle for the regulation of social life from above" (40). While I appreciate that Prashad is speaking from the painful experience of racism that I, a white man, have never experienced, I would like to suggest that a distinction between polyculturalism and multiculturalism need not rest on a rigid rejection of multiculturalism as though it were a tool for the furtherance of white domination. Multiculturalism may be co-opted by liberal whites to assuage white guilt, and may be paid lip service by conservative whites for the service of status quo policies, but I do not believe these hegemonic phenomena require the condemnation of multiculturalism as a program or philosophy. Multiculturalism, I believe, has served an important purpose in American society that has benefited people of color in significant and tangible ways. In literary studies alone the changes have been great: a look at just about any high school or university curriculum reveals that we have expanded the canon significantly to include not just broad categories of ethnic culture, but also diverse subcategories. Where Asian American literature, for example, was initially understood as Chinese and Japanese American, today Asian American literature is understood as comprising Chinese, Japanese, Korean, Vietnamese, Indian, Malaysian, Filipino, Pakistani, Pacific Islander, and other ethnicities.

Yet, it is precisely in this categorizing of discrete cultures that polyculturalism makes its distinct break with the assumptions of multiculturalism. It is time for the program of multiculturalism to give birth to a new philosophy, one that will carry forward multiculturalism's antiracist aims without reifying culture and prescribing ethnic identity. We can conceive of polyculturalism as a term that rejects the notion of discrete and contained cultures. Prashad explains, "even though people from what appear to be relatively discrete groups (South Asians, African Americans, Latino Americans), most of us live with the knowledge that the boundaries of our communities are fairly porous and that we do not think of all those within our 'group' as of a cohesive piece" (66). This may sound like hybridity by another name, and in some respects it is. Polyculturalism, as a term, evades the British Imperial connotations of "hybridity" and what Cyrus Patell calls hybridity's "philological baggage" (qtd. in Prashad 173). But I would argue for a more significant distinction: that hybridity connotes a passive reception of multiple cultural lineages, whereas polyculturalism connotes an active and strategic accumulation of lineages. According to Prashad, polyculturalism "draws from the idea of polyrhythms—many different rhythms operating together to produce a whole song, rather than different drummers doing their thing" (66). The image of "different drummers doing their thing" represents multiculturalism's emphasis on discrete cultures, which has more popularly been represented by the mosaic or salad bowl. Where the melting pot analogy envisioned a monocultural America, and the salad bowl a multicultural America, we might conceive of polyculturalism as a pluralistic society made up of pluralistic people—people who are continually in the process of (often intentionally) combining the rhythms in an ongoing and ever-changing song. Prashad quotes "community scholar" and hip-hop MC Q-Unique as an example of the type of linkages and combining that are characteristic of polyculturalism: "You study everybody's techniques and you strip away what you don't find necessary and use what is necessary and modify it" (148). This marks a difference between hybridity theory and Prashad's polyculturalism—the former emphasizes the development of the individual as the result of various cultural linkages and is more-or-less passive, whereas the latter emphasizes the individual's active construction of identity, the choosing and rejecting of lineages. In other words, hybridity is received, while polyculturalism is achieved. Mona "Changowitz" is a supreme fictional example of the polycultural idea.

Here, too, I believe polyculturalism sidesteps the postmodern view of race as a disappearing marker, or as a socially constructed marker that, if we could just successfully deconstruct, we would understand "that we are all one" (Palumbo-Liu 393). Polyculturalism's "painful embrace of the skin and all its contradictions" (Prashad xii) recognizes that race will not "cease to be a negative and destructive element of identification" (Palumbo-Liu 393) by simply our choosing to see ourselves as hybrid. Polyculturalism is based on hybridity's theory that our identities are constructed out of a matrix of cultural influences, but it retains a pragmatic comprehension of the realities of racial inequality in today's society. Multiculturalism served as a "defensive tactic" that has allowed people of color to embrace their lineage and regain pride in the face of racism, but polyculturalism offers a "strategy for freedom" that wrenches the good intentions of multiculturalism from the grasp of racists and hegemonic order (Prashad, *Everybody* 147–48). In my discussion of the growth of Chinese American literature, I have argued that the surge of interest in Chinese American writers in the 1980s and '90s was what Said calls a sign of liberation that should not be mistaken for true liberation ("Knowledge" 149). How quickly those signs of freedom for the oppressed become signs of tolerance for the oppressors! The textual worlds I have explored at length in this book begin to push us beyond a self-congratulatory sense of arrival and onto the hard path toward freedom. Arrival is elusive, perhaps because such teleological projections are not the goals of true artists. As Sau-ling Cynthia Wong says, "It would be simplistic to see the development of Chinese American literature in terms of a unidirectional 'improvement' away from the distortions of Orientalism into the sunshine of ethnic pride and historically accurate representations" ("Chinese American Literature" 48). Rather, historically accurate representations and ethnic pride are vehicles to the next phase in the program. Polyculturalism may be the name of that next phase, but it, too, is not arrival. Perhaps it is only, as Rosebud Elijah suggests, "a temporary position to expose the glaring gaps and flaws of the model of multiculturalism" (59). Arrival is elusive because our cultural development is an ongoing project.

I suggest that the worlds imagined by the authors in this book, their "theories" of American race and ethnicity described in the previous sections, are best defined as polycultural. Multicultural seems an inadequate descriptor for the aggregate picture of America imagined by these authors. As I have shown, the characters of these novels, and the persona of Lee's poem, exist in a matrix of forces that extend far beyond the nativist/assimilationist dichotomy (a multiculturalist preoccupation), which previously dominated Asian American narratives and Euro-American reading strategies. Multiculturalism is inadequate as an encompassing descriptor here because the "cultures" that invest these characters are not simply historic traditions to be remembered and recovered and brought to bear on their American lives (which is "nativism" or "primordialism"). Rather, the "cultures" of these characters emerge from a matrix of influences—they are complex, multifarious, and contingent. These "cultures" are ever in the process of becoming. In my exploration of the dynamic interplay of reader, author, and text in recent Chinese American literature, I hope to have shown the seeds and possibilities of change: changing receptions, changing perceptions, and changing horizons. The multiple possibilities enacted in the books in this study collide head on with the ghettoizing and limiting impulse of the literary Chinatown horizon. Readers engaged in these worlds, these "theories," these modes of "being-in-the-world," experience the diverse ways of construing and constructing ethnicity in America. Just as cultures and people rub off on each other in real life, so reading provides ways for individuals to internalize the worlds of others. The possibility for transformation through reading—not toward some static end, but in the continuing evolution of the individual and of society—lies in the nexus of reader, author, text.

Maxine Hong Kingston's prophecy that a wider body of Chinese American literature will allow readers to "see the variety of ways for Chinese Americans to be" has, I believe, come true. One cannot read Chinese American literature today and conclude that there is one monolithic Chinese American culture. The works of authors such as Gish Jen, David Wong Louie, Shawn Wong, Li-Young Lee, and Shirley Geok-lin Lim propose a Chinese American world that is diverse and dynamic. Once limited by the nativist/assimilationist assumptions of the literary Chinatown, the Chinese American reading horizon now appears boundless.

Notes

PREFACE

1. As I make clear below, I am borrowing the concept of polyculturalism and its theoretical underpinnings from Vijay Prashad, whose excellent book, *Everybody Was Kung Fu Fighting: Afro-Asian Connections and the Myth of Cultural Purity*, opened up for me the possibilities of new horizons in ethnic literary studies. Prashad credits Robin Kelley with the original concept of polyculture.

2. Besides Fish, Gubar, and Žižek (cited in the next endnote), other critiques of multiculturalism can be found in E. San Juan Jr.'s *Racism and Cultural Studies: Critiques of Multiculturalist Ideology and the Politics of Difference*; in *Foundational Perspectives in Multicultural Education*, Eduardo Manuel Duarte and Stacy Smith, eds.; in Walter Benn Michaels's *Our America*; and elsewhere.

3. See Fish, "Boutique Multiculturalism or Why Liberals Are Incapable of Thinking About Hate Speech"; Gubar, "What Ails Feminist Criticism?"; and Žižek, "A Leftist Plea for 'Eurocentrism.'"

4. Primordialism is a term used by Prashad and others to denote a view of culture as monolithic and discrete, emanating from a native essence.

5. "Instead of valorizing ethnicity and cultural difference per se," writes San Juan Jr., "we need to concentrate on what Robert Miles calls the 'racialization' process, its ideological and institutional articulations" (98).

INTRODUCTION

1. Interview conducted May 30, 2004, in San Francisco, by John Whalen-Bridge, Jeffrey Partridge, and Amy Clark.

2. Jinqi Ling argues in *Narrating Nationalisms* that Kingston has more than a Euro-American readership in mind. "It is my contention that *China Men* directly and indirectly reflects, first, Kingston's recognition of the need for post-disruption reassessment of her autobiography's [i.e., *The Woman Warrior*'s] impact and, second, her attempt to respond to existing and newly arisen cross-cultural polemics exposed by the controversy. Such an effort obviously involved the author's renewed dialogue with Asian American feminists, Asian American men, and a mainstream literary establishment that tended to interpret works by ethnic writers stereotypically. But the key element of Kingston's undertaking was to tackle the continued power imbalance between Chinese American men and women through a narrative form that could embody both the formal and the ideological complexity of the enunciative position from which she carried out her renegotiating project" (118).

3. For *Book of My Nights*, Lee's biographical information ends with this sentence: "He lives with his wife and two sons in Chicago, where he works in a warehouse."

4. The virtuality of the reading experience and the desire to "escape" or "explore" without leaving one's chair is not confined to the reading of Chinese American texts. In a sense, all reading involves leaving "our world" and entering "another world" in a virtual way. What I mean to emphasize here is not that the advertisement presents a unique purpose for reading, but rather that it presents a fetishized, exoticized image of that "other world." The description does more than report on the contents of the book; it promotes a particular view of Chinese Americans.

5. I use the term Euro-American rather than Anglo-American in reference to a view of the nation-state of America as a product and reflection of European heritage or Western Civilization. It is therefore not necessary for a person to be ethnically Anglo-American to maintain a Euro-American outlook. One of Euro-American lineage could as easily reject this view as anyone else, including a Chinese American, could embrace it.

6. "Incestuous" may seem like a loaded description, but the novel in question, *Monkey King*, is in fact about a woman who was raped repeatedly by her father when she was a young girl.

7. This concept of "claiming America" will be explored in more detail in chapter 4.

8. Noteworthy examples from Chinese American fiction are Maxine Hong Kingston's *China Men*, Shawn Wong's *Homebase*, Gish Jen's *Typical American*, and Frank Chin's *Donald Duk*. Examples of noteworthy critical works include Elaine Kim's *Asian American Literature* and Ronald Takaki's *Strangers from a Different Shore*.

9. The assumption that an Asian American is not originally from the United States is often played for comic effect in literature. For example, in Gish Jen's second novel when Mrs. Ingle asks Mona Chang where she is from, Mona's response,

"the same town as you," is not sufficient for her. She wants to know where she is "from, from" (*Mona* 181). Mona explains that she was born and raised in the United States just as they were, but the Ingles still want to know if she misses China and whether she has ever been "back" (182). This type of experience is also recorded in sociological studies. The authors of *Longtime Californ': A Documentary Study of an American Chinatown* quote one Chinese American as saying, "Just a human being in this culture, in this society, is a white man, he can disappear. I couldn't disappear, no matter how enlightened I was, no matter how straight my English was. Someone, just because they saw my skin color, would detect an accent" (qtd. in Yin 257).

10. I discuss these ideas regarding Kinkead's book at greater length in chapter 1.

11. Jinqi Ling illustrates through his insightful re-readings of Asian American texts from 1957–80 in *Narrating Nationalisms* that Asian American critics often unfairly privilege contemporary Asian American texts as more enlightened and politically engaged than texts of the past. Although limited by the prejudices of their times, these writers show far more resistance than critics usually acknowledge. See also Dominika Ferens's study of Sui Sin Far and Onoto Watanna in *Edith and Winnifred Eaton* and Christopher Douglas's reading of Jade Snow Wong in "Reading Ethnography."

12. In discussing reading communities, I do not mean to suggest that all individuals conform to a specific community. An individual may shift from one community of readers to another as his or her perspectives change through life; some readers may respond relatively independently from any community; moreover, an individual may belong simultaneously to several interpretive communities, and these combinations may produce unique effects in the way a person responds to a text.

13. For example, David Leiwei Li claims that Lin "attempts to redeem Chinese American humanity by playing the role of a messenger from a superior civilization and a mediator of Chinese and American culture" (330).

14. For a definition and discussion of ethnopoetics, see Shirley Geok-lin Lim, "Reconstructing Asian-American Poetry: A Case for Ethnopoetics."

15. For example, Elaine H. Kim's *Asian American Literature*, especially the first two chapters; James S. Moy's *Marginal Sights: Staging the Chinese in America*; the essays, including Moy's "Death of Asia on the American Field of Representation," in Part IV of Shirley Geok-lin Lim and Amy Ling, eds., *Reading the Literatures of Asian America;* the controversial introductions to *Aiiieeeee!* and *The Big Aiiieeeee!* by Jeffery Paul Chan, Frank Chin, Lawson Fusao Inada, and Shawn Wong; and, of course, Frank Chin's "Come All Ye Asian American Writers of the Real and the Fake" in *The Big Aiiieeeee!*

16. As I believe my discussion makes clear, my interest in the intentions of Chinese American authors does not relate to William K. Wimsatt Jr. and Monroe E. Beardsley's well known "intentional fallacy," in which readers equate interpre-

tation with the discovery of the author's intentions. Kingston's insertion of historical data in *China Men* and Amy Tan's use of Chinese phrases and their translations are examples of the ways texts can reveal the author's anticipation of reader expectations.

1 LITERARY CHINATOWN: DYNAMICS OF RACE AND READING

1. In my experience teaching Asian American literature at the National University of Singapore, Central Connecticut State University, and the University of Connecticut, I often find that students of diverse ethnic backgrounds—and even students of diverse Asian ethnicities—are capable of making surprisingly Eurocentric statements about Asian American literature.

2. The representation of Chinatown as dangerous and mysterious explored above is a function of the promotional copy, the text that sells the book. In the book itself, Kinkead historicizes the formation of the Chinese community by referring to the racist attitudes and laws Chinese immigrants have faced (an element of the book that the description mentions almost in passing: "Chinatown is also a provocative reflection on assimilation and racism in this country"). Kinkead even quotes from Ronald Takaki and other Asian American historians. Yet, her text, like the promotional copy, tends to dramatize her own efforts and thus produces a story about the brave white adventurer rather than the community itself. As extracts of the book appeared in the *New Yorker* prior to its publication, we might locate the discourse within a white, upper-middle-class curiosity about culture rather than, say, a historical or sociological study within academia.

3. "Dangerous and mysterious" is not the only characterization of Chinatown and the Chinese that has been produced. The Chinese community is also presented as the "model minority," that is, as a community that proves the viability of minority success in America (often seen in contrast to other minority groups). In the age of multiculturalism, Chinatowns have also been made to represent the diversity of America, where lion dances and Chinese New Year festivals emphasize the colorfulness and openness of America. These images are discussed later in this chapter.

4. One might argue, of course, that the exotic image of Chinatown is an important commodity in its economy, that it is in fact the "bread and butter" of Chinatown's inhabitants. No doubt it is the dramatization of Chinese cultural difference that attracts the "white horde" of tourists to Chinatown's shops, stalls, and restaurants. However, critics within the Chinese American community have argued that justifying the commodification of this stereotype condones cultural prostitution. Sau-ling Cynthia Wong describes it as "reifying perceived cultural differences and

exaggerating one's otherness in order to gain a foothold in a white-dominated social system" (*Reading Asian American Literature* 55). Such practices are like prostitution in that they "wrench cultural practices out of their context and display them for gain to the curious gaze of 'outsiders'" (56).

5. Omi and Winant describe the antiracist basis of the formation of Chinatowns as a "racial *war of maneuver*" (Gramsci's term, italics in original). As they explain, "'War of maneuver' describes a situation in which subordinate groups seek to preserve and extend a definite territory, to ward off violent assault, and to develop an internal society as an alternative to the repressive social system they confront" (74).

6. Naipaul took the title of his 1987 novel from a painting by Giorgio de Chirico (1912).

7. That this "difference" implies "un-Americanness"—even "un-American activities" like sedition—has remained ingrained in the Euro-American consciousness even long after the abolition of the Exclusion Acts. The controversy in 1999, for example, over Chinese American scientist Lee Wen-ho's alleged espionage is an example of the persistence of Euro-American assumptions of Chinese cultural retentiveness, clannishness, and sneakiness. Lee was accused of leaking top secret information regarding the design of one of the United States's most advanced nuclear warheads, the miniaturized W-88. In an interview with the *Washington Post*, Robert Vrooman, the former chief of counterintelligence at Los Alamos National Laboratory and member of the investigative team that brought the case against Lee, charged that Lee "was identified by the Department of Energy . . . as the prime suspect based on a, at best, cursory investigation at only two facilities, Los Alamos and Lawrence Livermore National Laboratory." Vrooman was reported as saying that Lee's visits to a Chinese physics institute in 1986 and 1988 had been considered strong evidence against him. However, he said, "Caucasians at Los Alamos who went to the same institute and visited the same people—I counted 13 of them—were left out of the investigation." The *Post* concludes, "while some Chinese-American rights organizations have previously charged that Dr. Lee was targeted unfairly, Mr. Vrooman is the first high-ranking participant in the investigation to state that his ethnicity was 'a major factor' in his identification as the government's prime suspect" ("N-scientist" 10).

8. For an incisive and detailed discussion of the model minority myth and its influence on readers, see "Model Minority Discourse and the Course of Healing," the appendix of David Palumbo-Liu's *Asian/American*. See also E. San Juan Jr.'s chapter "Allegories of Asian American Experience" in *Racism and Cultural Studies* (95–131).

9. According to Said, "What invariably happens at the level of knowledge is that signs and symbols of freedom and status are taken for the reality: you want

to be named and considered for the sake of being named and considered. In effect this really means that just to be an independent postcolonial Arab, or black, or Indonesian is not a program, nor a process, nor a vision. It is no more than a convenient starting point from which the real work, the hard work, might begin. As for that work, it is nothing less than the reintegration of all those people and cultures, once confined and reduced to peripheral status, with the rest of the human race" ("Knowledge" 149).

10. San Juan Jr. writes incisively about the role multicultural literature plays in this disempowerment: "For the dominant consensus, literature occupies a transcendent space free from prior moral or ideological commitments; hence readers can enjoy Amy Tan and Maxine Hong Kingston on the same level as they would Gertrude Stein or Katherine Anne Porter. Since the sixties, however, the consensus has allowed for the reconfiguration of 'minority' writing in the new category of multicultural literature of the United States, assigning them 'equal and separate' positions. This gesture of tolerance is both compromising and complicitous" (106).

11. "If more prosaic" is a difficult phrase to interpret. Is "prosaic" a positive corrective to the mythologizing and spritualizing of books like *The Woman Warrior*, or does it connote dryness and lifelessness? If the former, one would expect the author of the review to develop an argument against exoticization because the latter meaning coincides with the more common use of the word. Thus I interpret "prosaic" as a negative judgment softened by the phrase "if more." And this raises the question, would the same stories by a John Updike or Robert Stone be termed prosaic, or is it the expectation of "Oriental mysticism" that produces this evaluation?

12. For a discussion of the Asian American *Bildungsroman*, see Patricia P. Chu, *Assimilating Asians: Gendered Strategies of Authorship in Asian America*.

13. Brian Niiya notes that the Euro-American audience's preference for Asian works that are both autobiographical and authored by females became prominent in the 1960s. He writes, "assuming that publishers reflect public taste, it seems safe to say that this phenomenon reflected the American public's preference for autobiographies by Asian women over those by Asian men. This preference may be a foretaste of the public's embrace of Asian American women novelists, like Kingston and Tan" (431). Niiya notes that this American audience was perhaps attracted (in, I might add, a self-congratulatory way) to feminine critiques of Asian patriarchy and were intrigued by what it stereotypically perceived as the author's mystique as an "exotic and deferential Oriental beauty" (432). See also Sau-ling Cynthia Wong's discussion of "feminist/matrilineal discourse" in Chinese American literature in "'Sugar Sisterhood': Situating the Amy Tan Phenomenon."

14. My argument that *Pangs of Love* presents a "dynamic vision of America" is developed in chapter 5. Martha J. Cutter offers a similar reading in her article "An

Impossible Necessity: Translation and the Recreation of Linguistic and Cultural Identities in Chinese American Literature"; in her view, Louie's stories "point towards the healthy context-sharing and interpretation of cultures that the notion of translation in its broadest sense evokes" (584).

15. Possibly reflecting the attitude of editors who rejected Louie's early work, the radio show producer in the story "Birthday" informs the protagonist Wallace that his story is "too complex" and advises him to "simplify it": "He advised me that if I wanted the listeners' sympathy I should consider dropping the 'Chinese stuff'" (9).

16. Some critics, e.g., Vijay Prashad, use the term "primordialist" to describe what Lowe calls a nativist: i.e., one who believes that a primordial cultural or ethnic essence is the foundation of self.

17. It should be noted that arguments against this binary existed well before Lowe's 1991 article, e.g., in the critiques against Orientalism in *Aiiieeeee!*

18. While my analysis of the reception of Chinese American literature is strongly influenced by Fish's notion of interpretive communities, my readings of literary texts in Parts Two through Four of this book are aligned with the reception theory of Hans Robert Jauss and the phenomenological hermeneutics of Paul Ricoeur. Following the theory to its logical conclusion, Fish posits the total instability of the text. The only certitude available in the experience of reading is found in the comfort of interpretive communities; the only stabilizing factor is the fact that we share our interpretive strategies with others. Theories that emphasize reading or literary conventions, for example Jonathan Culler's "literary conventions" and Steven Mailloux's "interpretive conventions," similarly ground the location of meaning in the reader's interpretive community. In these models, reading is constructed as a "socially constituted . . . conventions-governed" (Mailloux 107) process in which the reader interprets the text according to the grammar or rules of literary conventions. Thus, the text remains a stable platform for discussion, but only by virtue of accepted forms of literary communication. Fish also recognizes the existence of such conventions, but in his view they are further evidence of the strength of interpretive communities to constitute texts. Fish argues that his theory of interpretation "does not . . . commit [him] to subjectivity because the means by which [meanings] are made are social and conventional" (*Is There a Text in This Class?* 331). Jauss, on the other hand, sees the text as the historical horizon of the author's intention. As James L. Machor and Philip Goldstein explain, Jauss "takes the author's intention to ground the text's historical 'other' and to preserve its capacity to critique social life and transform readers" (1). Likewise, Ricoeur's phenomenological hermeneutics reasserts, in his words, "the importance of textual constraints" (*Reflection* 495). Reading, for Ricoeur, is not the projection of ourselves upon the text, but engagement with the proposed world of the text. By its very nature

as written discourse, the text is cut off from the author's intent and is opened to a variety of interpretations, but in its ability to propose a world, the text is not open to just any meaning. There is variability, but there is also constraint.

2 WHAT IS AN ETHNIC AUTHOR?

1. As Christine So observed in 1996, "much of literature recently written by Asian Americans does not focus on Asian American communities, but instead deals with the alienation of growing up and living outside those traditional community borders" (141).

2. The reader's expectation that a non-white author writes "collectively" (that is, as a representative of that group) explains why readers tend to view books by authors of color as political statements. In his discussion of Toni Morrison's *Sula*, John Whalen-Bridge suggests that there is a sense in which "any novel by a nonwhite author could be regarded as political—whatever its contents" (133). Whalen-Bridge notes, however, that minority authors often object to this political expectation—or the notion that the political exists in spite of the author. He quotes Ralph Ellison as defending the political impulses of *Invisible Man*, "The protest is there, not because I was helpless before my racial condition, but because I put it there" (134).

3. Furthermore, the discussion of the film version of *The Joy Luck Club* in *The Straits Times*'s "Forum" section was characterized by heated opinions about the authenticity of the way China was represented in the film. One reader criticized the film for misrepresenting China as a backward nation of self-mutilators and infant killers.

4. Ling argues that Edith Eaton's adoption of a pseudonym to enhance her solidarity with the Chinese people living in North America was a heroic act. Thus, passing as ethnic, or enhancing one's ethnicity should not be seen simply and categorically as an ill-intentioned or capitalist-motivated act of deception. Dominika Ferens, in her book on the Eaton sisters, has challenged the view of Edith Eaton as somehow above the racial thinking of her day, and David Shih makes the point that much of Edith's philosophy relied on her ability to pass as white, "for all the potential in [Sui Sin Far's] message 'Individuality is more than nationality,' it is one not easily adopted by others of Chinese ancestry" (65). I wish to note here that even if Sui Sin Far were shown to be a legal or given name, my thesis would not be affected. My argument centers on the ways the use of names, whether legitimate or fictive, enhance ethnic authenticity.

5. See Ferens's book for a detailed discussion of Edith and Winnifred Eaton's ethnographic sources.

6. This idea of ethnic authenticity is crucial to a discussion of the reception of Chinese American literature because it lies at the heart of defining it as a literature, a task that proves extremely problematic. "Placed under interrogation," writes Shirley Geok-lin Lim, "are the nature and boundaries of this body of materials, its categorization and composition, and the interpretations and evaluations brought to bear on it" ("Assaying the Gold" 149). Do we define Chinese American literature as literature about Chinese Americans? Perhaps, but this definition would necessarily include literature written by those who are not ethnically Chinese American. It does not seem acceptable to classify as Chinese American the work of, for instance, a white, or black, or Japanese American writer simply because the work is about Chinese Americans. For example, *Snow Falling on Cedars*, winner of the PEN/Faulkner Award and the American Booksellers Association Book of the Year Award in 1995, could be categorized as an Asian American novel. The murder trial of Kabuo Miyamoto, which structures the novel's narrative, finds both its impetus and its perpetuation in white racism against the Japanese American community. Kabuo is a suspect simply because the wound on the victim's skull reminds the coroner of the kinds of wounds inflicted by Japanese soldiers in World War II hand-to-hand combat; and it is not so much the evidence as it is the enigmatic, "unreadable" face of the defendant that ultimately convinces all but one of the jury that he is guilty. Moreover, the U.S. government's detention and incarceration of Japanese Americans feature prominently in the novel. The theme of racism and unfair treatment against the Japanese American community is thus central to the novel. However, because the author, David Guterson, is a white American, the novel is not categorized as an Asian American work (nor, for that matter, is it considered Euro-American). Is Chinese American literature, therefore, works that are *about* Chinese Americans and *by* Chinese American authors? This seems more sufficient, yet it does raise the problem of who, precisely, is considered Chinese American: is the term determined racially, ethnically, or culturally? In the case of mixed parentage, what fraction of Chinese blood is required? The problem seems to have no tidy solution.

7. Ferens argues in her book that Ling's portrayal of Edith and Winnifred Eaton has influenced critics to judge the more prolific Winnifred as the "bad sister" and her writing as fake. Ferens's book on the sisters seeks to right the balance, showing that both sisters constructed an inauthentic identity and, moreover, that both produced literature that shows signs of the Orientalist thinking of their day, but also often resists such racialized constructs.

8. According to Gilman, such scandals have occurred in many other countries as well, such as in Germany, the United States, and Great Britain: "Toby Forward, an Anglican vicar, managed to persuade the feminist Virago Press that he was a South Asian woman named Rahila Khan. The white Anglo-Saxon Protestant writer

Daniel Lewis James wrote *Famous All Over Town* (1983), which won the 1984 Rosenthal Award for literary achievement, under the Hispanic pseudonym Danny Santiago. The Hessian author Jakob Arjouni, often compared in Germany with Raymond Chandler, persuaded readers that his creation, the Frankfurt detective Kemal Kayankaya, was giving them authentic insight into Turkish life in Germany" (23). Gilman concludes this list of ethnic charlatanism with the comment: "the construction of a fictional ethnic identity seems to be a cultural commodity in societies searching for authenticity" (23). Whether it is the emphasis of the ethnic in an author's legal name or a fictitious construction, it is clear that the perceived ethnicity of the author is more than a significant element in the reception of ethnic literature— it is a valuable commodity to be maintained and highlighted in today's book market.

9. Regarding Lin Yutang, Kim writes, "removed as he was from the real-life experiences of the Chinese laborers, whether in America or in China, Lin depicts a fortuitous blend of feudal Chinese and American capitalist cultures as bringing success and happiness to the laundryman's family." Here Kim clearly locates the inaccuracy of Lin's depictions in his real-life experience. As explained below, my emphasis is not on the validity of assessing the author's works based on his life, but on the fact that it is an important feature in Kim's approach to his text.

10. For a discussion of author photographs and illustrations in the works of Sui Sin Far, see David Shih's "The Seduction of Origins."

11. For example, the copy on the video cover of Mira Nair's *Mississippi Masala* describes the film as "erotic" and "irreverently sexy." In fact, the film contains one love scene between the main characters in which there is nothing more erotic than what can be shown in a PG-13 movie (the only nudity in the film is a peek at Denzel Washington's bare bottom as he slips on his pants). Clearly the marketing copy is not an accurate description of the film, but an attempt to attract an audience by following the old adage, "sex sells."

3 THE POLITICS OF ETHNIC AUTHORSHIP: LI-YOUNG LEE,
EMERSON, AND WHITMAN AT THE BANQUET TABLE

1. Ian Buruma's phrase; see "The Romance of Exile" for a poignant critique of marginality.

2. See pp. 42–43.

3. Deleuze and Guattari are not the only theorists in the poststructuralist, postmodernist, and postcolonial era to theorize the strength of marginality. Even a cur-

sory sweep of contemporary literary and cultural criticism reveals that critical theories today embrace the idea of the ethnic author—or at least the idea of the ethnic author's *position*. In the place of the *"mainstream," middle*-class, white author, today's critical and cultural theory exalts the nomad and the minority (Deleuze and Guattari), the interstitial and culturally hybrid (Bhabha), the exile (Said, Rushdie), the homeless (Bhabha), the writer in the margins (Deleuze and Guattari)— all that is contingent rather than fixed, fluid rather than static, mixed rather than pure; all that is different and always deferring a concrete definition (Derrida).

4. In her book *Reading Asian American Literature: From Necessity to Extravagance*, Sau-ling Cynthia Wong develops a variety of ways to look at alimentary images in Asian American literature. She isolates three dominant manifestations: (1) " 'big eating' to the point of quasi-cannibalism, typically associated with the immigrant generation"; (2) " 'food prostitution': 'selling' oneself for treats [that is, selling out to mainstream culture; denying one's own ethnicity] in the case of the American-born, for basic food-stuffs in the case of prospective immigrants"; and (3) "food pornography," which refers to the act of highlighting the exotic aspects of one's ethnic foodways in order to make money or gain acceptance (55). Of the three, "big eating" is the only positive function of the alimentary motif. As with sexual prostitution and pornography, a person may gain some agency through the selling of her or his body and the manipulation of another's desire; however, this agency is limited by an exterior and exploitive power. A big eater, as "The Cleaving" attests, turns survival on its head.

5. Although she makes no overt reference to "The Cleaving," Anne Anlin Cheng makes use of the linguistic possibilities of this verb to describe the melancholia of a racialized subject: "Words from the invisible man in the epilogue remain to haunt us: 'you carry part of your sickness with you' " (Ellison 575). You carry the foreigner inside. This malady of doubleness, I argue, is the melancholy of race, a disease of location, a persistent fantasy of identification that *"cleaves and cleaves to the marginalized and the master"* (137, emphasis added).

6. The transparent eyeball is a metaphor for the speaker's transcendent experience, a moment of union with God and Nature realized at a moment in the snowy woods: "I become a transparent eye-ball. I am nothing. I see all. The currents of the Universal Being circulate through me; I am part or particle of God" (*Essential Writings* 6).

7. The Shang Dynasty lasted from 1765 to 1112 B.C.—that is, three to four thousand years ago.

8. We might also trace "devour" to T. S. Eliot's poem "Gerontion," in which the speaker in his advanced years is contemplating his imminent death in much the

way that the speaker in Lee's poem confronts his own mortality in the Hon Kee Grocery. "To be eaten, to be divided, to be drunk" in Eliot's poem is the manner in which we eat Christ at the Eucharist, but "Christ the tiger" likewise consumes us: "Us he devours" (562). In Lee's poem, the relationship is signified in similar terms: "As we eat we're eaten" can be seen as a reference to the Eucharist when we consider the God-like stature of the butcher toward the conclusion of the poem. God, who brings change in the individual, shapes the soul of the speaker in a violent manner: "in the trade of my soul's shaping, / he traffics in hews and hacks" (86). Through the poem, the speaker becomes, like the poet gazing upon the body of his Shulamite lover in Song of Songs, "a diviner of holy texts" (86–87). Devouring his race is thus a cultural act as well as a holy act. Some extratextual evidence for this reading of "devour" in "The Cleaving" can be found in Lee's other published poetry, interviews, and reviews/criticism of his work. Lee quotes the Bible in several of his poems and often explores the image of his own father, who was a Christian minister, as an image of God.

4 CLAIMING DIASPORA IN SHIRLEY GEOK-LIN LIM'S *JOSS AND GOLD*

1. Shirley Geok-lin Lim describes the relationship between recent Asian immigration trends and shifts in Asian American notions of identity as follows: "The 1970s' critique of the conflation of Asian American with Asian and Asian immigrant identity, and the enunciation of a U.S. identity not composed of Asian cultural elements, had severely delimited the terms for cultural belonging for smaller and more recent immigrant groups such as South and Southeast Asians and Filipinos (Penaranda et al. 1974). The historical specificities in the experiences of heterogeneous Asian immigrant groups inevitably call into question and destabilize the construction of a monolithic U.S.-identified Asian American identity" ("Immigration" 303).

2. Lim goes on to say: "The double movement of appropriation is marked in the critical reception of her [Kingston's] work, chiefly praised for making accessible to American readers the strange world of Chinese living in the United States. The accessibility works more in one direction than the other. Americans of Chinese ancestry, or even Chinese living in the United States, do not find that *The Woman Warrior* has made the United States more accessible to them, or that the book helps them to negotiate the dominant culture and to appropriate it for their needs. The book's popular reception in the universities suggests that it is the dominant culture that is incorporating Kingston's version of the Chinese into its transcultural psyche" ("Immigration" 302).

3. For a discussion of related issues, see David Leiwei Li's analysis of Asian American citizenship in the introduction to his book, *Imagining the Nation: Asian American Literature and Cultural Consent*.

4. In personal correspondence regarding these issues, Lim wrote, "I believe that the best patriot is the one who dissents, and that probably makes me a patriotic Malaysian, Singaporean, AND American" (April 24, 2004).

5. See, for example, *Crossing Oceans: Reconfiguring American Literary Studies in the Pacific Rim*, edited by Noelle Brada-Williams and Karen Chow, for discussions on the internationalization of Asian American literary studies.

6. Li An's confrontation with English language and literature parallels Shirley Geok-lin Lim's own experience as a student in Malaysia, one of many such auto-biographical crossovers in the novel. In the preface to her book, *Writing Southeast/Asia in English*, Lim makes reference to her "conversion" experience at the University of Malaya in 1966: "This undergraduate conversion, the belief in the necessity for a literature of one's own, has remained my unshakable creed, even as the identity of 'one'—under the multiple deconstructive interrogations of psychology, anthropology, sociology, global economics, politics, linguistics, revisionist history—has grown progressively more shaky" (xi). Lim's autobiography, *Among the White Moon Faces*, reveals more non-fictional crossovers with the fictional world of the novel.

7. Rojak is a popular dish in Malaysia and Singapore that combines chunks of jicama, fried dough (Chinese *you tiao*), fried bean curd, pineapple, and cucumber with bean sprouts and crushed peanuts in a sweet and spicy black sauce. Like salad, it is served cold and, except for the bean curd and *you tiao*, uncooked.

8. The teasing Suyin endures highlights Asian racism, and therefore marks Singapore *as relatively tolerant* in comparison to the Malaysia and United States constructed by the novel. Intolerance in the U.S. toward immigrants is suggested by several conversations in the New York segment of the novel, for instance when Dan argues that it is dangerous to let Indian immigrants work on U.S. defense systems, whereas European immigrants are acceptable because they are "from our part of the world" (125). Even so, I find it difficult to reconcile the novel's portrayal of intolerance with personal and anecdotal evidence I have gathered on the acceptance of Eurasian children in Singapore schools. Students in my Transnational Literature course at the National University of Singapore expressed surprise at Suyin's mistreatment; they concurred with one another that Eurasian children were not teased, but were actually privileged in their schools by teachers and peers alike. This could be a generational difference (my students went through grade school in the 1990s and the novel is set in the 1970s), but anecdotal evidence from older Singaporeans suggests otherwise.

9. The materialist basis of Suyin's euphoric transnational identity provides the basis of a much different reading of *Joss and Gold*. We should not overlook the fact that diaspora is always bound to the material, and that not all transnational flow is voluntary, beneficial, or empowering to the diasporic subject. In his dialectical-materialist approach, E. San Juan Jr. makes the important point that "diaspora enacts a mimicry of itself, dispersing its members around in a kaleidoscope of simulations and simulacras borne by the flow of goods, money, labor, and so on, in the international commodity chain" (372). However, an analysis of Suyin's privileged status in this "international commodity chain" is beyond the scope of my argument here. My emphasis has been on the ways the novel instantiates the tension between ethnic nationalism and diaspora in Asian American literary discourse.

5 CHANGING SIGNIFIERS AND CHANGING HORIZONS: BASEBALL IN THREE STORIES BY DAVID WONG LOUIE

1. I tested these assumptions in an empirical study conducted in 1998. Students read an excerpt from "Warming Trends" and answered questions designed to elicit information about their assumptions regarding the ethnicity of the characters based on their knowledge of the author's ethnicity. Half the students were provided a biography and photograph of David Wong Louie with the story, and the other half were given a fake biography and a photograph of a white man. Those who believed the author to be ethnically Chinese tended to interpret the characters as Chinese American and the story as more political or racially charged than those who believed the author to be white.

6 CHANGE AND THE PLAYFUL READER: READING SHAWN WONG'S *AMERICAN KNEES*

1. In his book, *Phenomenological Hermeneutics and the Study of Literature*, Mario J. Valdés develops a critical method based on Ricoeur's philosophy. What Valdés calls the "stages of operation for literary criticism" are outlined as follows (66): First is the formal dimension, in which we consider how the text operates on the semiotic and structural level; second is the historical, in which we consider what the text is speaking about by bringing "the dialectic of past significance and present meaning into focus" (66); third is the phenomenological dimension of the reading experience, in which we are concerned with what the text says to us "that is common

to the reading experience of others" (67); fourth is "the hermeneutic level of self knowledge," in which the "reflective assessment" of self occurs (67). While Valdés's assessment and elucidation of Ricoeur are rigorous and his critical method holds faithfully to the details of Ricoeur's philosophy, the four-fold approach may be too cumbersome and prescriptive for practical use. This is evidenced in Valdés's application of the method to two brief passages of literature, one by Jorge Luis Borges and the other by Octavio Paz. These analyses move through the four stages deliberately and methodically, leaving one with the impression that, rather than the theory bringing life to the text, the text exists to emphasize the theory. Moreover, in neglecting to introduce an element of flexibility in the application of the theory, Valdés's analyses come across with a certain prescriptiveness and lifelessness.

I admit that my method may lack the faithfulness to Ricoeur's thinking which Valdés achieves. Developing a critical method from Ricoeur's philosophy of reading that does justice to the many intricacies and concerns of his thinking would require much more space than this book would allow. My intention is to formulate a working methodology from my discussion of the playful reader in order to elucidate Shawn Wong's text from the perspective of a phenomenological reading experience. My aim is not to validate Ricoeur's theory through the example of a text, but rather to use Ricoeur's theory to facilitate a unique understanding of *American Knees* and the reading experience it provides. Valdés expresses a similar concern for the integrity and life of the text; my contention is that in practice his readings do not adequately reflect this view.

2. They are not "Asians," but "Asian Americans," and they are standing in the most American of places—before the throne of Abraham Lincoln.

3. Even their sexual intercourse, we learn in later chapters, is laden with distanciation. Their first sexual encounter is performed over the phone with three thousand miles of America between them. When they make love in person, Raymond arouses Aurora with fantasies set in exotic places or hotel rooms, an act which distanciates them virtually from the moment.

4. While I do not want to reinscribe a "good book/ bad book" critical method, one that judges texts based on whether they "demonstrate complicity with or resistance to hegemonic ideologies of assimilation" (Zhou and Najmi 4), I do believe that, in all honesty, our judgment of a literary text's ability to produce a realistic or even positive view of Asian Americans is often our basis for liking an Asian American novel, recommending it to others, and assigning it in our classes. I agree that a text can do much more than simply resist or conform to racial stereotypes, but I am cognizant that my own appreciation of an Asian American text hinges on this issue.

5. For example, this is apparent in two contemporary novels by Asian American women, *Monkey King*, by Patricia Chao, and *Eating Chinese Food Naked*, by Mei Ng. In *Monkey King*, the father is cold and abusive, even to the extent of raping his daughter. In *Eating Chinese Food Naked*, the father is distant, uncaring, and full of pride. (Strangely, however, though the daughter continues to hold this view of her father, he is, in my opinion, the most sympathetic character in the novel.) These examples, together with other fathers in, for instance, Li-Young Lee's *The Winged Seed* and Aimee E. Liu's *Face*, reveal that such depictions of Chinese fathers in Chinese American literature are plentiful. However, exceptions include the fathers in the work of Pardee Lowe and Lawrence Yep, and, I would argue, in Li-Young Lee's *Rose*.

6. The depiction of Rainsford's father in *Homebase* is similarly compassionate: "When I was a boy, my father whispered to me from his hospital bed, 'Rainsford, I love you more and more.' He cried and I thought he was singing" (6).

7 BEYOND MULTICULTURAL: CULTURAL HYBRIDITY
  IN THE NOVELS OF GISH JEN

Chapter epigraph: Gayle Feldman, "Spring's Five Fictional Encounters of the Chinese American Kind," *Publishers Weekly*, Feb. 8, 1991, 25–27.

1. For an intriguing study of cultural invention, see *The Invention of Tradition* edited by Eric Hobsbawm and Terence Ranger.

2. Joseph Tilden Rhea makes a strong case for the close relationship between racial identity and "the interests of the present" (38) in *Race Pride and the American Identity*. Rhea's thesis is that "concrete sociological differences between [racial] groups are reflected in the sorts of histories they have produced" (38). Rhea shows through specific examples of racial violence (e.g., the murder of Chinese American Vincent Chin in Detroit in 1982, who was mistaken by his attackers for Japanese and therefore responsible for the economic climate in the auto industry [39]) that group identity is most powerfully articulated in the face of opposition. An interesting novelistic treatment of this can be seen in *Mona in the Promised Land* when Helen defines her home as Chinese when faced with the threat of Mona's rebellion (cf. 250). The establishment of household identity is only a vague issue up to this point, but in the midst of a crisis, Helen enforces a Chinese identity to resist the threat of American licentiousness.

3. This notion of identity closely parallels recent conceptions of the individual-as-reader enabled by computer hypertextuality, a comparison that helps to clarify the role of the individual in the formation of ethnicity. According to George P.

Landow, in his work on the convergence of critical theory and information technology (*Hypertext 2.0*), the individual reader in a hypertext system navigates through the text with his or her own interests as the investigative principle. Hypertextuality, applied analogously to the formation of identity, allows us to see the strength of cultural hybridity theory to re-define personhood in today's global environment. The consciousness-formation articulated by hybridity is hypertextual, in the sense that the individual moves through a network of intersecting and conflicting perspectives, cultures, ideologies, worldviews, and languages, with him or herself as the *"de facto* organizing principle (or center) for the investigation" (37). Moreover, by shaking off the "linearity" of the "cultural whole" model, cultural hybridity has, as Landow says of hypertextuality, "the potential to prevent, block, and bypass linearity and binarity, which it replaces with multiplicity, true reader activity and activation, and branching through networks" (24).

4. See also Zhou Xiaojing, "Postmodernism and Subversive Parody."

5. Moreover, my analysis of Jen's later novel, *Mona in the Promised Land*, will show that her conception of Americanness as hybrid does not exclude non-immigrants from the definition of America, but rather it highlights the fluidity of all American identity.

6. For a discussion of "house" as a metaphor in *Typical American*, see David Leiwei Li's *Imagining the Nation*, 102–7.

7. Although *Typical American* alludes to Fitzgerald's "great American novel" in various places, I have not engaged in a discussion of such connections because it seems to me outside the scope of this chapter to do so. I read the allusions to *The Great Gatsby* as part of *Typical American*'s "claiming America" strategy, as stressed in the first sentence of the novel, "It is an American story." (Li's *Imagining the Nation*, 104–5, contains a brief discussion of Fitzgerald and Benjamin Franklin in respect to this novel. See also Partridge, "Mona in the Promised Land.")

8. Li sees a subtle difference in this seeming agreement between Ralph and Theresa, or, as he would have it, between Grover and Theresa, the "rival guardians of Ralph's soul" (*Imagining* 105). Grover, Li writes, "professes the link between money and identity, . . . [and Theresa] between identity and race" (105).

9. This Jewish English is, of course, not indicative of many Jewish American people (for example, Barbara and Seth do not normally speak this way). Rather, it is a stylized version of the English spoken by Jewish immigrants and as such serves as a language of parody for Mona and her friends. However, my emphasis is that by adopting this style of English in her own internal voice, Mona's speech reveals her gravitation toward Judaism.

10. The process of hybridity is, furthermore, not restricted to Chinese American identity. For example, Mona detects changes in her best friend Barbara Gugelstein

that reveal a hybridization of her personality with those of the more popular set. "Mona notices Barbara start to look down, as if putting away some more pressing matter, before turning her head to answer someone; she does this the exact slow way Eloise Ingle does" (56–57). Here it is the mimicry of action that reveals internal variation. The hybridization of Barbara's mannerisms with those of Eloise discloses the influence of one individual upon another.

11. I will argue below that her willingness to remain Jewish even after experiencing the racist limitations of American society suggests that individual choice can, through extreme determination, win out over and possibly transform racial hierarchies.

12. For a fuller treatment of this issue, see Partridge, "Mona in the Promised Land."

13. Mona's parents even go so far as to say, "better to turn Jewish than Asian American" out of their prejudice toward Japanese, Koreans, and South Asians (302).

14. This phenomenon of adopting a formerly derogatory term as a positive identity marker is not unusual. "Queer" as a unifying term for the homosexual community provides a very recent example, as do "Hybridity," discussed above, and "Changowitz," discussed later in this chapter. My discussion of "The Cleaving" in chapter 3 reveals the ways in which the speaker in Li-Young Lee's poem embraces Chinese eating habits that are often the object of racial slurs. Frank Chin employs the term "Chinaman" in a similar fashion.

15. Walter Benn Michaels, for example, potently attacks multiculturalism's pluralist foundation in his claim that the essentialist criterion for identity that pluralism seeks to destroy is actually reinforced in pluralism's insistence on the primacy of the group over the whole. Pluralism's claim to locate identity in performative terms ("what we do") rather than essentialist terms ("who we are") is contradicted, Michaels argues, by the legitimization of the local over and against the universal, in which case "performance" can only be validated by "essence" (14–15). The breakup of Camp Gugelstein underscores this inherent flaw in multiculturalism in its reification of group boundaries, but, as I argue in this chapter, polyculturalism (like Mona's) recognizes a responsibility toward larger alliances.

16. Prashad makes a similar argument about strategic deployments of cultural essence and primordialism. "Minority groups may mobilize around the notion of an origin to make resource claims, to show that despite the denigration of the power elite, the group can lay claim to an aspect of civilization and the cultural currency attached to it. Furthermore, to demarcate oneself from the repressive stereotypes, the oppressed frequently turn to their 'roots' to suggest to their children that they have a lineage that is worthy despite racism's cruelty. These are important social explanations for the way we use both origins and authenticity (to protect our tra-

ditional forms from appropriation by the power elite)" (*Everybody* 147). But he goes on to claim that these are tactics for defense that must eventually be transcended by "a strategy for freedom" (148).

CONCLUSION

1. As a child, June rejected her mother's Chinese past: "I wish I was dead! Like them," referring to "the babies she had lost in China" (142). But the novel reveals that the daughters, like June's Chinese "side," are not dead. They are alive and, again like her Chinese "side," living "in her bones," only needing to be discovered. For a similar reading of *The Joy Luck Club*, see David Leiwei Li's *Imagining the Nation*.

2. See the discussion in chapter 7.

3. In the urban community college where I now teach, the majority of my students are black or Latino/a and the response to this question is much different. To these students, race is a central issue that affects their interactions with others on a daily basis.

Bibliography

American League Championships Game 3. ESPN, 9 Oct. 1998.

Anderson, Benedict R. *Imagined Communities: Reflections on the Origin and Spread of Nationalism*. London: Verso, 1983.

Appleyard, J. A. *Becoming a Reader: The Experience of Fiction from Childhood to Adulthood*. Cambridge: Cambridge University Press, 1990.

Bakhtin, M. M. *The Dialogic Imagination: Four Essays*. 1981. Ed. Michael Holquist. Trans. Caryl Emerson and Michael Holquist. Austin: University of Texas Press, 1982.

———. *Rabelais and His World*. Trans. Helene Iswolsky. Bloomington: Indiana University Press, 1984.

Barthes, Roland. "The Death of the Author." 1968. *Modern Literary Theory*. Ed. Philip Rice and Patricia Waugh. London: Edward Arnold, 1992. 114–21.

Bauman, Zygmunt. "The Making and Unmaking of Strangers." *Debating Cultural Hybridity: Multi-Cultural Identities and the Politics of Anti-Racism*. Ed. Pnina Werbner and Tariq Modood. London: Zed, 1997. 46–57.

Bennett, Andrew, ed. *Readers & Reading*. London: Longman, 1995.

Biriotti, Maurice, and Nicola Miller, eds. *What Is an Author?* Manchester: Manchester University Press, 1993.

Bhabha, Homi K. *The Location of Culture*. London: Routledge, 1994.

Bloom, Harold. *The Anxiety of Influence: A Theory of Poetry*. 2nd ed. Oxford: Oxford University Press, 1997.

———. *Asian-American Women Writers*. Philadelphia: Chelsea House, 1997.

Booth, Wayne C. *The Rhetoric of Fiction*. Chicago: University of Chicago Press, 1961.

Brada-Williams, Noelle, and Karen Chow, eds. *Crossing Oceans: Reconfiguring*

American Literary Studes in the Pacific Rim. Hong Kong: Hong Kong University Press, 2004.

Bulosan, Carlos. *America Is in the Heart.* 1943. Seattle: University of Washington Press, 1973.

Buruma, Ian. "The Romance of Exile." *The New Republic* 224:7 (Feb 12, 2001): 33–38.

Cao, Lan, and Himilee Novas. *Everything You Need To Know About Asian American History.* New York: Plume, 1996.

Chan, Jeffery Paul, Frank Chin, Lawson Fusao Inada, and Shawn Wong, eds. *The Big Aiiieeeee! An Anthology of Chinese American and Japanese American Literature.* New York: Meridian, 1991.

Chang, Lan Samantha. *Hunger.* London: Phoenix House, 1998.

Chao, Patricia. *Monkey King.* New York: HarperFlamingo, 1997.

Cheng, Anne Anlin. *The Melancholy of Race: Psychoanalysis, Assimilation, and Hidden Grief.* New York: Oxford University Press, 2001.

Cheung, King-Kok, ed. *An Interethnic Companion to Asian American Literature.* Cambridge: Cambridge University Press, 1997.

———. *Articulate Silences: Hisaya Yamamoto, Maxine Hong Kingston, Joy Kogawa.* Ithaca: Cornell University Press, 1993.

Childers, Joseph, and Gary Hentzi, eds. *The Columbia Dictionary of Modern Literary and Cultural Criticism.* New York: Columbia University Press, 1995.

Chin, Frank. *Donald Duk.* Minneapolis: Coffee House Press, 1991.

———. *Gunga Din Highway.* Minneapolis: Coffee House Press, 1994.

Chin, Frank, et al. "An Introduction to Chinese and Japanese American Literature." *Aiiieeeee! An Anthology of Asian-American Writers.* Ed. Frank Chin, Jeffery Paul Chan, Lawson Fusao Inada, and Shawn Wong. 1974. New York: Mentor, 1991. 3–38.

———. "Introduction." *The Big Aiiieeeee! An Anthology of Chinese American and Japanese American Fiction.* Ed. Jeffery Paul Chan, Frank Chin, Lawson Fusao Inada, and Shawn Wong. New York: Meridian, 1991. xi–xvi.

Chin, Frank, Jeffery Paul Chan, Lawson Fusao Inada, and Shawn Wong, eds. *Aiiieeeee! An Anthology of Asian-American Writers.* 1974. New York: Mentor, 1991.

Chow, Rey. *Writing Diaspora: Tactics of Intervention in Contemporary Cultural Studies.* Bloomington: Indiana University Press, 1993.

Chu, Louis. *Eat a Bowl of Tea.* 1961. New York: Carol Publishing Group, 1995.

Chu, Patricia P. *Assimilating Asians: Gendered Strategies of Authorship in Asian America.* Durham: Duke University Press, 2000.

Chuh, Kandice. *Imagine Otherwise: On Asian Americanist Critique*. Durham: Duke University Press, 2003.

Clark, S. H. *Paul Ricoeur*. London: Routledge, 1990.

"Cleave." *Webster's Revised Unabridged Dictionary*. 1998 ed.

Culler, Jonathan. *Structualist Poetics: Structuralism, Linguistics, and the Study of Literature*. London: Routledge, 1975.

Cutter, Martha J. "An Impossible Necessity: Translation and the Recreation of Linguistic and Cultural Identities in Chinese American Literature." *Criticism* 39 (1997): 581–612.

Davis, Rocío G., and Sue-Im Lee, eds. *Literary Gestures: The Aesthetic in Asian American Writing*. Philadelphia: Temple University Press, 2006.

Deleuze, Gilles, and Félix Guattari. *A Thousand Plateaus: Capitalism and Schizophrenia*. Trans. Brian Massumi. Minneapolis: University of Minnesota Press, 1986.

———. *Kafka: Toward a Minor Literature*. Minneapolis: University of Minnesota Press, 1986.

Derrida, Jacques. "Structure, Sign and Play in the Discourse of the Human Sciences." *Modern Criticism and Theory: A Reader*. Ed. David Lodge. New York: Longman, 1988. 108–23.

Douglas, Christopher. "Reading Ethnography: The Cold War Social Science of Jade Snow Wong's *Fifth Chinese Daughter* and *Brown V. Board of Education*." *Form and Transformation in Asian American Literature*. Ed. Zhou Xiaojing and Samina Najmi. Seattle: University of Washington Press, 2005. 101–24.

Duarte, Eduardo M., and Stacy Smith, eds. *Foundational Perspectives in Multicultural Education*. New York: Longman, 2000.

Dyer, Richard. *White*. London: Routledge, 1997.

Eco, Umberto. *The Role of the Reader: Explorations in the Semiotics of Texts*. Indiana: Indiana University Press, 1979.

Elijah, Rosebud. Review of *Everybody Was Kung Fu Fighting: Afro-Asian Connections and the Myth of Cultural Purity*, by Vijay Prashad. *Encounter* 16: 2 (2003): 58–60.

Eliot, T. S. "Gerontion." *The Harper Anthology of Poetry*. Ed. John Frederick Nims. New York: Harper & Row, 1981.

———. "Tradition and the Individual Talent." *Selected Essays 1917–1932*. Rev. ed. Rahway, NJ: Harcourt Brace, 1950. 3–11.

Emerson, Ralph Waldo. "The Conservative." *The Oxford Book of Essays*. Ed. John Gross. Oxford: Oxford University Press, 1999. 171–86.

———. *Emerson: Essays and Lectures*. Ed. Joel Porte. New York: Library of America, 1983.

———. *The Essential Writings of Ralph Waldo Emerson*. Ed. Brooks Atkinson. New York: Modern Library, 2000.

———. *The Journal and Miscellaneous Notebooks of Ralph Waldo Emerson*. Vol. II. Ed. William H.Gillman et al. Cambridge, Harvard University Press, 1961.

Eng, David L. *Racial Castration: Managing Masculinity in Asian America*. Durham: Duke University Press, 2001.

Ericson, Edward L. *Emerson on Transcendentalism*. New York: Ungar, 1986.

Feldman, Gayle. "Spring's Five Fictional Encounters of the Chinese American Kind." *Publishers Weekly*, 8 Feb. 1991: 25–27.

Ferens, Dominika. *Edith and Winnifred Eaton: Chinatown Missions and Japanese Romances*. Urbana: University of Illinois Press, 2002.

———. "Winnifred Eaton/ Onoto Watanna: Establishing Ethnographic Authority." *Form and Transformation in Asian American Literature*. Ed. Zhou Xiaojing and Samina Najmi. Seattle: University of Washington Press, 2005. 30–47.

Ferraro, Thomas J. *Ethnic Passages: Literary Immigrants in Twentieth-Century America*. Chicago: University of Chicago Press, 1993.

Fish, Stanley. "Boutique Multiculturalism, or Why Liberals Are Incapable of Thinking about Hate Speech." *Critical Inquiry* 23 (Winter 1997): 878–902.

———. *Is There a Text in This Class? The Authority of Interpretive Communities*. Cambridge: Harvard University Press, 1980.

Foucault, Michel. "What Is an Author?" 1969. *Language, Counter-Memory, Practice: Selected Essays and Interviews by Michel Foucault*. Ed. Donald F. Bouchard. Ithaca: Cornell University Press, 1993. 113–38.

Forster, E. M. *Aspects of the Novel*. London: Edward Arnold, 1927.

Foster, Gwendolyn Audrey. *Performing Whiteness: Postmodern Re/Constructions in the Cinema*. Albany: State University of New York Press, 2003.

Freund, Elizabeth. *The Return of the Reader: Reader-Response Criticism*. London: Methuen, 1987.

Gadamer, Hans-Georg. *Truth and Method*. 2nd rev. ed. Trans. Joel Weinsheimer and Donald G. Marshall. London: Sheed & Ward, 1989.

Gilman, Sander L. "Ethnicity-Ethnicities-Literature-Literatures." *PMLA* 113 (1998): 19–27.

Gubar, Susan. "What Ails Feminist Criticism?" *Critical Inquiry* 24 (Summer 1998): 878–902.

Guterson, David. *Snow Falling on Cedars*. New York: Vintage, 1995.

Hagedorn, Jessica, ed. *Charlie Chan Is Dead: An Anthology of Contemporary Asian American Fiction*. New York: Penguin, 1993.

Hall, Stuart. "Old and New Identities, Old and New Ethnicities." *Culture,*

Globalization and the World System. Ed. Anthony D. King. New York: Macmillan, 1991. 41–68.

Hart, Denise. "Gish Jen." *Poets and Writers Magazine* 21.6 (Nov./Dec. 1993): 20–27.

Hobsbawm, Eric, and Terence Ranger, eds. *The Invention of Tradition*. Cambridge: Cambridge University Press, 1983.

Holub, Robert C. *Reception Theory: A Critical Introduction*. London: Methuen, 1984.

Hong, Maria, ed. *Growing Up Asian American: An Anthology*. New York: Avon, 1993.

Hong, Peter Y. "The Changing Face of Higher Education: Trends: Asian Americans." *Los Angeles Times*, 14 Jul. 1998.

Hongo, Garrett, ed. *The Open Boat: Poems from Asian America*. New York: Anchor, 1993.

Howells, Christina. *Derrida: Deconstruction from Phenomenology to Ethics*. Cambridge: Polity Press, 1998.

Hutcheon, Linda. "Crypto-Ethnicity." *PMLA* 113 (1998): 28–32.

Hutnyk, John. "Adorno at Womad: South Asian Crossovers and the Limits of Hybridity-Talk." *Debating Cultural Hybridity: Multi-Cultural Identities and the Politics of Anti-Racism*. Ed. Pnina Werbner and Tariq Modood. 106–36.

Hwang, David Henry Hwang. *M. Butterfly*. New York: Plume, 1989.

Iser, Wolfgang. *The Implied Reader: Patterns of Communication in Prose Fiction from Bunyan to Beckett*. Baltimore: The Johns Hopkins University Press, 1978.

Jameson, Fredric. *The Political Unconscious: Narrative as a Socially Symbolic Act*. Ithaca: Cornell University Press, 1981.

Jauss, Hans Robert. *Question and Answer: Forms of Dialogic Understanding*. Trans. and ed. Michael Hays. Minneapolis: University of Minnesota Press, 1989.

———. *Toward an Aesthetic of Reception*. Trans. Timothy Bahti. Sussex: Harvester Press, 1982.

Jen, Gish. *The Love Wife*. New York: Knopf, 2004.

———. *Mona in the Promised Land*. New York: Vintage, 1997.

———. *Typical American*. New York: Plume, 1992.

———. *Who's Irish?* New York: Knopf, 1999.

Jin, Ha. *Waiting*. London: Heinemann, 1999.

Jones, Charles L. "Afterword and Glossary." *Reader Response to Literature: The Empirical Dimension*. Ed. Elaine F. Nardocchio. 279–302.

Kelley, Robin. "People in Me: 'So, What Are You?'" *ColorLines* (Winter 1999): 5–7.

Kim, Elaine H. *Asian American Literature: An Introduction to the Writings and Their Social Context.* Philadelphia: Temple University Press, 1982.

———. "Asian Americans: Decorative Gatekeepers?" *MultiAmerica: Essays on Cultural Wars and Cultural Peace.* Ed. Ishmael Reed. New York: Viking, 1997. 205–12.

Kingston, Maxine Hong. *China Men.* 1977. New York: Vintage, 1989.

———. "Cultural Mis-readings by American Reviewers." *Asian and Western Writers in Dialogue: New Cultural Identities.* Ed. Guy Amirthanayagam. London: Macmillan, 1982. 55–65.

———. *The Fifth Book of Peace.* New York: Knopf, 2003.

———. *To Be the Poet.* Cambridge: Harvard University Press, 2002.

———. *Tripmaster Monkey.* 1987. New York: Vintage, 1990.

———. *The Woman Warrior: Memoirs of a Girlhood among Ghosts.* New York: Knopf, 1975.

Kinkead, Gwen. *Chinatown: A Portrait of a Closed Society.* New York: HarperCollins, 1992.

Kitchen, Judith. Review of *The City in Which I Love You,* by Li-Young Lee. *The Georgia Review,* Vol. XLV, No. 1 (Spring 1991): 154–69. Reprint: *Asian American Literature: Reviews and Criticism by American Writers of Asian Descent.* Ed. Lawrence J. Trudeau. Detroit: Gale, 1999.

Klein, Christina. *Cold War Orientalism: Asia in the Middlebrow Imagination, 1945–1961.* Berkeley: University of California Press, 2003.

Kogawa, Joy. *Obasan.* 1981. Toronto: Penguin, 1983.

Koh, Buck Song. Review of *The Hundred Secret Senses,* by Amy Tan. *The Straits Times,* 9 Dec. 1995.

Ku, Robert Ji-Song. "Leda." *Asian American Literature: A Brief Introduction and Anthology.* Ed. Shawn Wong. Berkeley: HarperCollins, 1996.

Lahiri, Jhumpa. *Interpreter of Maladies: Stories.* Boston: Houghton Mifflin, 1999.

Landow, George P. *Hypertext 2.0: The Convergence of Contemporary Critical Theory and Technology.* Baltimore: The Johns Hopkins University Press, 1997.

Lee, A. Robert. *Multicultural American Literature: Comparative Black, Native, Latino/a and Asian American Fictions.* Edinburgh (UK): Edinburgh University Press / Jackson: University Press of Mississippi, 2003.

Lee, Chang-rae. *A Gesture Life.* New York: Riverhead, 1999.

Lee, Gus. *China Boy.* 1991. New York: Plume, 1994.

———. *Honor and Duty.* New York: Ivy Books, 1994.

Lee, Li-Young. *Book of My Nights.* Rochester, NY: BOA Editions, Ltd., 2001.

———. "The Cleaving." *The City in Which I Love You.* Rochester, NY: BOA Editions, Ltd., 1990. 77–87.

———. "Eating Alone." *Rose.* Rochester, NY: BOA Editions, Ltd., 1986. 33.

———. "Eating Together." *Rose.* Rochester, NY: BOA Editions, Ltd., 1986. 49.

———. *The Winged Seed.* New York: Simon & Schuster, 1995.

Lee, Rachel C. *The Americas of Asian American Literature: Gendered Fictions of Nation and Transnation.* Princeton: Princeton University Press, 1999.

Lee, Sky. *Disappearing Moon Café.* Seattle: Seal Press, 1991.

Lee, Sue-Im. "Introduction: The Aesthetic in Asian American Literary Discourse." *Literary Gestures: The Aesthetic in Asian American Writing.* Ed. Rocío G. Davis and Sue-Im Lee. Philadelphia: Temple University Press, 2006. 1–14.

Leonard, George J., ed. *The Asian Pacific American Heritage: A Companion to Literature and Arts.* New York: Garland, 1999.

Leong, Russell Charles. "The Country of Dreams and Dust." *Asian American Literature: A Brief Introduction and Anthology.* Ed. Shawn Wong. New York: HarperCollins, 1996. 323–54.

Li, David Leiwei. *Imagining the Nation: Asian American Literature and Cultural Consent.* Stanford: Stanford University Press, 1998.

———. "The Production of Chinese American Tradition: Displacing American Orientalist Discourse." *Reading the Literatures of Asian America.* Ed. Shirley Geok-lin Lim and Amy Ling. Philadelphia: Temple University Press, 1992. 319–32.

Lim, Shirley Geok-lin. *Among the White Moon Faces: An Asian-American Memoir.* Singapore: Times Books International / New York: The Feminist Press, 1996.

———. "Assaying the Gold: Or, Contesting the Ground of Asian American Literature." *New Literary History* 24 (1993): 147–69.

———. "Immigration and Diaspora." *An Interethnic Companion to Asian American Literature.* Ed. King-Kok Cheung. New York: Cambridge University Press, 1997. 289–311.

———. "Introduction." *The Frontiers of Love,* by Diana Chang. Seattle: University of Washington Press, 1994. v–xxiii.

———. *Joss and Gold.* Singapore: Times Books International / New York: The Feminist Press, 2001.

———. "Reconstructing Asian American Poetry: The Case for Ethnopoetics." *MELUS* 14 (1987): 51–63.

———. "Writing Out of Turn." *Profession 1999.* Ed. Phyllis Franklin. New York: Modern Language Association of America, 1999. 214–24.

———. *Writing Southeast/Asia in English: Against the Grain, Focus on English-language Literature.* London: Skoob Books Publishing, 1994.

Lim, Shirley Geok-lin and Amy Ling, eds. *Reading the Literatures of Asian America*. Philadelphia: Temple University Press, 1992.

Lim, Shirley Geok-lin, Gina Valentino, Stephen Hong Sohn, and John Blair Gamber, eds. "Introduction." *Studies in the Literary Imagination (Cross Wire: Asian American Literary Criticism)* 37:1 (Spring 2004): i–xi.

Lim, Shirley Geok-lin, Larry E. Smith, and Wimal Dissanayake, eds. *Transnational Asia Pacific: Gender, Culture, and the Public Sphere*. Urbana: University of Illinois Press, 1999.

Lim, Shirley Geok-lin, and Cheng Lok Chua, eds. *Tilting the Continent: Southeast Asian American Writing*. Minneapolis: New Rivers Press, 2000.

Ling, Amy. "Creating One's Self: The Eaton Sisters." *Reading the Literatures of Asian America*. Shirley Geok-lin Lim and Amy Ling, eds. Philadelphia: Temple University Press, 1992. 305–18.

Ling, Jinqi. *Narrating Nationalisms: Ideology and Form in Asian American Literature*. New York: Oxford University Press, 1998.

Liu, Aimee E. *Cloud Mountain*. New York: Warner, 1997.

———. *Face*. London: Headline, 1994.

Liu, Catherine. *Oriental Girls Desire Romance*. New York: Kaya, 1997.

Louie, David Wong. *The Barbarians Are Coming: A Novel*. New York: G. P. Putnam's Sons, 2000.

———. *Pangs of Love: Stories*. 1991. New York: Plume, 1992.

Loving, Jerome. "Walt Whitman." *Columbia Literary History of the United States*. Ed. Emory Elliott. New York: Columbia University Press, 1988. 448–62.

Lowe, Lisa. "Heterogeneity, Hybridity, Multiplicity: Marking Asian American Differences." *Diaspora* 1:1 (1991): 24–44.

———. *Immigrant Acts: On Asian American Cultural Politics*. Durham: Duke University Press, 1996.

McCunn, Ruthanne Lum. *A Thousand Pieces of Gold*. 1981. Boston: Beacon Press, 1988.

———. *Wooden Fish Songs*. New York: Plume, 1996.

Ma, Sheng-mei. *Immigrant Subjectivities in Asian American and Asian Diaspora Literatures*. New York: State University of New York Press, 1998.

Machor, James L., and Philip Goldstein, eds. *Reception Study: From Literary Theory to Cultural Studies*. New York: Routledge, 2001.

Mailloux, Steven. *Interpretive Conventions: The Reader in the Study of American Fiction*. Ithaca: Cornell University Press, 1982.

Malcolm, Cheryl Alexander. "Going for the Knockout: Confronting Whiteness in Gus Lee's *China Boy*." *MELUS* 29:3 / 4. (Fall / Winter 2004): 413–26.

Melucci, Alberto. "Identity and Difference in a Globalized World." *Debating Cultural Hybridity: Multi-Cultural Identities and the Politics of Anti-Racism.* Ed. Pnina Werbner and Tariq Modood. London: Zed, 1997. 58–69.

Michaels, Walter Benn. *Our America: Nativism, Modernism, and Pluralism.* Durham: Duke University Press, 1995.

Miller, Perry. "From Edwards to Emerson." 1940. Reprinted in *Ralph Waldo Emerson: A Collection of Critical Essays.* Ed. Lawrence Buell. New Jersey: Prentice Hall, 1993. 13–31.

Miller, Stuart Creighton. *The Unwelcome Immigrant: The American Image of the Chinese, 1785–1882.* Berkeley: University of California Press, 1969.

Miner, Valerie. Review of *Mona in the Promised Land,* by Gish Jen. *The Nation,* 17 Jun. 1996: 35–36.

Morgan, Nina, and Jachison Chan. "In Defense of the Real: Frank Chin in Dialogue." *The Diasporic Imagination: Asian American Writing.* Vol. 1. Ed. Somdatta Mandel. New Deli: Prestige Books, 1999. 41–70.

Moy, James S. *Marginal Sights: Staging the Chinese in America.* Iowa City: University of Iowa Press, 1993.

"N-scientist probed 'because of race.'" *The Straits Times,* 18 Aug. 1999: 10.

Naipaul, V. S. *The Enigma of Arrival.* Middlesex (UK): Viking, 1987.

Nardocchio, Elaine F., ed. *Reader Response to Literature: The Empirical Dimension.* Berlin: Mouton de Gruyter, 1992.

Nee, Victor G. and Brett de Bary Nee. *Longtime Californ': A Documentary Study of an American Chinatown.* New York: Pantheon, 1973.

Ng, Fae Myenne. *Bone.* New York: HarperPerennial, 1993.

Ng, Mei. *Eating Chinese Food Naked.* New York: Scribner, 1998.

NIV Study Bible. Ed. Kenneth Barker. Grand Rapids: Zondervan, 1985.

Niiya, Brian. "Asian American Autobiographical Tradition." *The Asian Pacific American Heritage: A Companion to Literature and Arts.* Ed. George J. Leonard. 427–433.

Okada, John. *No-No Boy.* 1957. Seattle: University of Washington Press, 1995.

Omi, Michael, and Howard Winant. *Racial Formation in the United States: From the 1960s to the 1980s.* New York: Routledge, 1986.

Ong, Aihwa. *Flexible Citizenship: The Cultural Logics of Transnationality.* Durham: Duke University Press, 1999.

Palumbo-Liu, David. *Asian/American: Historical Crossings of a Racial Frontier.* Stanford: Stanford University Press, 1999.

———. "The Ethnic as 'Post-': Reading *Reading Literatures from Asian America.*" *American Literary History* 7:1 (Spring 1995): 161–68.

Papastergiadis, Nikos. "Tracing Hybridity in Theory." *Debating Cultural Hybrid-*

ity: Multi-Cultural Identities and the Politics of Anti-Racism. Ed. Pnina Werbner and Tariq Modood. 257–81.

Partridge, Jeffrey F. L. "Mona in the Promised Land." American Writers Classics Volume II. Ed. Jay Parini. New York: Thomson Gale, 2003. 215–32.

Perry, Bliss. The Heart of Emerson's Journals. London: Constable & Co. Ltd, 1927.

Powell, Timothy B. "All Colors Flow into Rainbows and Nooses: The Struggle to Define Academic Multiculturalism." Cultural Critique 55 (Fall 2003): 153–81.

Prashad, Vijay. "Bruce Lee and the Anti-imperialism of Kung Fu: A Polycultural Adventure." Positions 11:1 (Spring 2003): 52–91.

———. "Community Scholarship." Radical History Review 79 (2001): 116–19.

———. Everybody Was Kung Fu Fighting: Afro-Asian Connections and the Myth of Cultural Purity. Boston: Beacon Press, 2001.

———. The Karma of Brown Folk. Minneapolis: University of Minnesota Press, 2000.

"Preliminaries." MELUS 20 (1995): 1–2.

Radway, Janice A. Reading the Romance: Women, Patriarchy, and Popular Literature. Chapel Hill: University of North Carolina Press, 1984.

Reagan, Charles E. Paul Ricoeur: His Life and His Works. Chicago: University of Chicago Press, 1996.

Rice, Philip, and Patricia Waugh. Modern Literary Theory: A Reader. 2nd ed. London: Edward Arnold, 1994.

Richardson, Robert D., Jr. Emerson: The Mind on Fire. Berkeley: University of California Press, 1995.

Rhea, Joseph Tilden. Race Pride and the American Identity. Cambridge: Harvard University Press, 1997.

Richards, I. A. Practical Criticism: A Study of Literary Judgement. New York: Harcourt Press, 1929.

Ricoeur, Paul. From Text to Action. Trans. Kathleen Blamey and John B. Thompson. Evanston: Northwestern University Press, 1991.

———. Hermeneutics & the Human Sciences. Ed. and trans. John B. Thompson. Cambridge: Cambridge University Press, 1981.

———. Reflection & Imagination: A Ricoeur Reader. Ed. Mario J. Valdés. Toronto: University of Toronto Press, 1991.

Rushdie, Salman. Imaginary Homelands: Essays and Criticism, 1981–1991. New York: Viking, 1991.

Said, Edward W. Culture and Imperialism. New York: Vintage, 1994.

———. Orientalism. New York: Vintage, 1978.

————. "The Politics of Knowledge." *Contemporary Literary Criticism*. Ed. Robert Con Davis and Ronald Schleifer. New York: Longman, 1994. 144–53.

————. *Reflections on Exile and Other Essays*. Boston: Harvard University Press, 2000.

Samarth, Manini. "Affirmations: Speaking the Self into Being." *Parnassus* 17 (1991): 88–101.

San Juan, E., Jr. *Racism and Cultural Studies: Critiques of Multiculturalist Ideology and the Politics of Difference*. Durham: Duke University Press, 2002.

Satz, Martha. "Writing About the Things That Are Dangerous: A Conversation with Gish Jen." *Southwest Review* 78 (1993): 132–40.

Shapiro, Anna. Review of *Mona in the Promised Land*, by Gish Jen. *The New Yorker*, 8 Jul. 1996: 78–79.

Shih, David. "The Seduction of Origins: Sui Sin Far and the Race for Tradition." *Form and Transformation in Asian American Literature*. Ed. Zhou Xiaojing and Samina Najmi. Seattle: University of Washington Press, 2005. 48–76.

Simpson, Janice C. "Fresh Voices Above the Noisy Din." *Time*, 3 Jun. 1991: 66–67.

Skenazy, Paul, and Tera Martin, eds. *Conversations with Maxine Hong Kingston*. Jackson: University Press of Mississippi, 1998.

Snell, Marilyn Berlin. "The Intimate Outsider." *NPQ* (Summer 1991): 56–60.

So, Christine. "Racial Combat as Comedy in Gus Lee's *China Boy*." *MELUS* 21 (1996): 141–55.

Sollors, Werner, ed. *The Invention of Ethnicity*. Oxford: Oxford University Press, 1989.

Storace, Patricia. Review of *Typical American*, by Gish Jen. *The New York Review*, 15 Aug. 1991: 9–12.

Suleiman, Susan R., and Inge Crosman, eds. *The Reader in the Text: Essays on Audience and Interpretation*. Princeton: Princeton University Press, 1980.

Takaki, Ronald. *Strangers from a Different Shore*. New York: Penguin, 1990.

Tan, Amy. *The Bonesetter's Daughter*. London: Flamingo, 2001.

————. *The Joy Luck Club*. New York: G. P. Putnam's Sons, 1989.

————. *The Kitchen God's Wife*. New York: G. P. Putnam's Sons, 1991.

————. *The Hundred Secret Senses*. London: Flamingo, 1995.

Tompkins, Jane P., ed. *Reader-Response Criticism: From Formalism to Post-Structuralism*. Baltimore: The Johns Hopkins University Press, 1980.

Travis, Molly Abel. *Reading Cultures: The Construction of Readers in the Twentieth Century*. Carbondale: Southern Illinois University Press, 1998.

Tuber, Keith, and Jill Barnes. "Flamethrowers from the Far East." *Transpacific*, Jun. 1994: 32–37.

Valdés, Mario J. *Phenomenological Hermeneutics and the Study of Literature.* Toronto: University of Toronto Press, 1987.

Werbner, Pnina, and Tariq Modood, eds. *Debating Cultural Hybridity: Multi-Cultural Identities and the Politics of Anti-Racism.* London: Zed, 1997.

Wertheim, L. Jon. "The Whole World Is Watching." *Sports Illustrated,* 14 June 2004: 72–86.

Whalen-Bridge, John. *Political Fiction and the American Self.* Urbana: University of Illinois Press, 1998.

Whitman, Walt. *Whitman: Poetry and Prose.* Ed. Justine Kaplan. New York: Library of America, 1996.

Wicker, Hans-Rudolf. "From Complex Culture to Cultural Complex." *Debating Cultural Hybridity: Multi-Cultural Identities and the Politics of Anti-Racism.* Ed. Pnina Werbner and Tariq Modood. 29–45.

Wilcoxon, Hardy C. "Chinese American Literature Beyond the Horizon." *New Literary History* 27 (1996): 313–28.

Wilson, Rob. "Goodbye Paradise: Global/Localism in the American Pacific." *Global/Local: Culture Production and the Transnational Imaginary.* Ed. Rob Wilson and Wimal Dissanayake. Durham: Duke University Press, 1996. 312–36.

Wilson, Rob, and Wimal Dissanayake, eds. *Global/Local: Culture Production and the Transnational Imaginary.* Durham: Duke University Press, 1996.

Wong, K. Scott. "Chinatown: Conflicting Images, Contested Terrain." *MELUS* 20 (1995): 3–16.

Wong, Sau-Ling Cynthia. "Chinese American Literature." *An Interethnic Companion to Asian American Literature.* Ed. King-Kok Cheung. Cambridge: Cambridge University Press, 1997. 39–61.

———. "Denationalization Reconsidered: Asian American Cultural Criticism at a Theoretical Crossroads." *Amerasia Journal* 21:1 & 2 (1995): 1–27.

———. *Reading Asian American Literature: From Necessity to Extravagance.* New Jersey: Princeton University Press, 1993.

———. "'Sugar Sisterhood': Situating the Amy Tan Phenomenon." *The Ethnic Canon: Histories, Institutions, and Interventions.* Ed. David Palumbo-Liu. Minneapolis: University of Minnesota Press, 1995.

Wong, Shawn. *American Knees.* 1995. Seattle: University of Washington Press, 2005.

———. *Asian American Literature: A Brief Introduction and Anthology.* New York: HarperCollins, 1996.

———. *Homebase.* 1979. New York: Plume, 1991.

Yamamoto, Traise. *Masking Selves, Making Subjects: Japanese American Women, Identity and the Body*. Berkeley: University of California Press, 1999.

Yang, Belle. *Baba*. San Diego: Harcourt Brace, 1994.

Yang, Jeff, et al., eds. *Eastern Standard Time: A Guide to Asian Influence on American Culture*. New York: Houghton Mifflin, 1997.

Yin, Xiao-huang. *Chinese American Literature Since the 1850s*. Urbana: University of Illinois Press, 2000.

Young, Robert J. C. *Colonial Desire: Hybridity in Theory, Culture and Race*. London: Routledge, 1995.

Zhou, Xiaojing. "Inheritance and Invention in Li-Young Lee's Poetry." *MELUS* 21:1 (Spring 1996): 113–32.

———. "Introduction: Critical Theories and Methodologies in Asian American Literary Studies." *Form and Transformation in Asian American Literature*. Ed. Zhou Xiaojing and Samina Najmi. Seattle: University of Washington Press, 2005. 3–29.

———. "Postmodernism and Subversive Parody: John Yau's 'Genghis Chan: Private Eye' Series." *College Literature* 31:1 (Winter 2004): 73–102.

Zhou, Xiaojing, and Samina Najmi, eds. *Form and Transformation in Asian American Literature*. Seattle: University of Washington Press, 2005.

Žižek, Slavoj. "A Leftist Plea for 'Eurocentrism.'" *Critical Inquiry* 24 (Summer 1998): 988–1009.

Index

consumers. *See* readers

criticism, literary, 77–82, 215n3

critics, 7, 12, 207n11

Crossing Oceans (Brada-Williams and Chow), 217n5

Culler, Jonathan, 211n18

culture, xiii, 166, 175, 176

Cutter, Martha J., 210n14

Deleuze, Gilles, ix, 11, 52, 74, 80–82, 83, 101, 214–15n3

denationalization, 101–2. *See also* nationalism

Derrida, Jacques, 166, 172, 215n3

deterritorialization, 80–82, 83, 88, 99

dialogic, 17, 94, 102, 117; and Mikhail Bakhtin, 96, 174–75, 179; and *Mona in the Promised Land*, 179, 180, 185; and playful readers, 18, 150

The Dialogic Imagination (Bakhtin), 96

diaspora, 6, 32, 36, 99, 113, 167, 179, 194, 218n9; Chinese, 106; claiming, 99–104, 112–13

Disappearing Moon Café (Lee), 70–72

discourse: Asian American, 64–74; of China, 127; Chinese American, 157–59; Euro-American, 153–57

distance, 142, 144–46, 149, 150, 219n3

"Disturbing the Universe" (Louie), 126–30, 194

Donald Duk (Chin), 206n8

Douglas, Christopher, 14, 58, 73, 78, 207n11

Dyer, Richard, 52

dynamic(s): of change, 17, 166; ethnic writing as, 42, 78, 210n14; and interplay of author-text-reader, 7, 25, 81, 137, 203; of reception, 14, 16, 31, 43, 117, 137

Eat a Bowl of Tea (Chu), 14, 59, 140

eating, 82–98, 159; big, 17, 82, 83, 86, 96, 97, 215n4; carnivalesque, 97;

cultural/ethnic eating, 84, 86, 87, 88, 123–24, 132, 176, 222n14; for poetry, 96

Eating Chinese Food Naked (Ng), 220n5

Eaton, Edith Maude (Sui Sin Far), 56–57, 61, 207n11, 212nn4–5, 213n7, 214n10

Eaton, Winnifred (Onoto Watanna), 56–57, 61, 207n11, 212n5, 213n7

Edith and Winnifred Eaton (Ferens), x, 207n11

editors, 7, 43, 211n15. *See also* publishers

Elijah, Rosebud, xiii, 203

Eliot, T. S., 215n8

Emerson, Ralph Waldo, 17, 77, 78, 82, 85–86, 88–94, 97, 98, 215n6

Eng, David L., 40, 123

"enlarged self," 151, 157

Ericson, Edward L., 91

essence/essential: and Chinese American texts, 46, 55; and cultural differences, 32, 167, 168–69, 205n4, 211n16, 222n16; and ethnic identities, xi, 19, 166, 189, 222n15

ethnic author(s), 41, 49–74, 77–82, 215n3; community of, 5; literary studies of, 14, 16, 19, 43, 61, 113, 205n1. *See also* identity; nationalism

ethnic-author function, 19, 49–74, 134; authenticity of, 54–57; commodity of, 59–64, 77; communal, 51–54; socio-cultural value of, 57–59; as tour guide, 64, 69, 72–74, 78

ethnic/ethnicity, xiii, 144, 172, 220–21n3; ambiguity of, 43, 131; in America, ix, x; Asian American, 150, 165; Chinese, 11, 141; Chinese American, 39, 131, 170; perceived, 55–57, 131, 214n8; re-defining, 18, 165. *See also* identity, panethnic

ethnography, 49–50, 58, 61, 72, 73, 212n5

0496